CONTENTS

PART I. THE WRITER WRITES

Chapter 01 You Are a Writer 3

Chapter 02 Writing Plans and Processes 13

Chapter 03 Practice. 29

Chapter 04 Revision. 43

Chapter 05 Reflection 49

PART II. ACTING RHETORICALLY

Chapter 06 Thinking Rhetorically. 59

Chapter 07 Writing Rhetorically—Argument. 77

Chapter 08 Writing Rhetorically—Character. 97

Chapter 09 Writing Rhetorically—Emotion 111

Chapter 10 Writing Rhetorically—Principles of Style 127

Chapter 11 Writing Rhetorically—Anatomy of Style 141

Chapter 12 Reading Rhetorically 167

PART III. THE GENRES OF WRITING

Chapter 13 Opinion Editorial. 193

Chapter 14 Personal Narrative 209

Chapter 15 Rhetorical Analysis 225

Chapter 16 Source-based Argument 239

Mindful
WRITING

Second Edition

Brian Jackson

Brigham Young
University

macmillan learning
curriculum solutions

bedford/st.martin's • hayden-mcneil • w.h. freeman • worth publishers

Printed in the United States of America

10 9 8 7 6 5 4 3 2

ISBN 978-0-7380-8478-7

Macmillan Learning Curriculum Solutions
14903 Pilot Drive
Plymouth, MI 48170
www.macmillanlearning.com

JacksonB 8478-7 F16

Hayden-McNeil Sustainability

Hayden-McNeil's standard paper stock uses a minimum of 30% post-consumer waste. We offer higher % options by request, including a 100% recycled stock. Additionally, Hayden-McNeil Custom Digital provides authors with the opportunity to convert print products to a digital format. Hayden-McNeil is part of a larger sustainability initiative through Macmillan Learning. Visit http://sustainability.macmillan.com to learn more.

Hi there, writing student! My name's Brian. I teach writing. And, heaven help me, I think about teaching writing all the time, even while I'm in the shower. It's a sickness, really, but it's also a professional necessity.

I've been teaching writing, and thinking about teaching writing, for fifteen years now, and I thought I'd sit down and explain what I know and what *we* know as a community of writing teachers. This book synthesizes some of what I think are the best practices for learning to write with power. I'm hoping you're reading this book because you want to write with *real power*—the kind that influences others.

In *Mindful Writing*, I want to persuade you of five principles:

- Successful writing is mindful writing.

- Successful writers are self-directed writers who plan, practice, revise, and reflect.

- Successful writers know how to think, write, read, and act rhetorically.

- Writing and rhetoric are subjects worth studying in their own right, like you'd study chemistry or psychology.

- What you'll learn in this book will help you take on any future writing task, both in your major courses and your career.

In short, I hope this book helps you grow as a writer.

Hey: If you really like what you learn in this class, you might consider studying more of it. At BYU, we have a **Writing and Rhetoric minor** (housed in the English Department) in which you can learn practical writing skills that will help you in any career. You can take classes in writing with style, professional writing, digital culture, visual rhetoric, technical writing, grant and proposal writing, public writing, or legal writing. Or follow/like Team Rhetoric on Facebook (BYU Writing and Rhetoric Minor) or Twitter (@BYUrhetoric).

I'd love to hear what you think about this book—how it's helped you, how it could be better. Drop me a note at mindfulwritingbyu@gmail.com.

One last thought. Because I want this book to sound more like a conversation than a textbook, I chose to write in a more casual, accessible tone. I have all of you, dear students, in my mind as I write.

Many thanks to Brett McInelly, Rebecca Clarke, Delys Snyder, Dawan Coombs, Grant Boswell, Dave Stock, Jon Balzotti, my 610 class (Brittany Bruner, Andrew Doub, Lauren Fine, Hayley Langton, Jean Little, Ian McArthur, Rachel Moberly, Chloe Moller, Scott Porter, Marie-Reine Pugh, Camille Richey, Amanda Shrum, Heather Thomson), my 611R class that started this ball rolling (Elizabeth Brady, Brighton Capua, Brooke Downs, Christa Baxter Drake, Katie Fredrickson, Spencer Hyde, and Ali Porter), Julie Anne Helmandollar, and Julie Anne's writing class for reviewing parts of this book in progress. Thanks to the University Writing team (Jen, Erica, Kristen, and Alisha) and the BYU English Department for their support. Thanks to Jeff McCarthy and Lin Fantino and the Hayden-McNeil team. Thanks, also, to my wife Amy Jackson, who listened patiently to portions of this book as we drove around town. And thanks to Ben, Lydia, Louisa, and Charlotte, my dear kids, who make appearances in the text.

Ready? Let's go.

PART I

The Writer Writes

1

YOU ARE A WRITER

You, my friend, are a writer.

You may not think of yourself that way. You may think of writers as tortured romantic souls who crank out thick novels, or maybe you think of professional bloggers or freelance journalists. In this book I want to convince you that *anyone writing anything for any reason is a writer.* Do you write text messages, emails, lecture notes, letters in the snow or sand, status updates, notes to friends, Post-it notes to yourself, or papers for classes? Then you are a writer. Wherever you are right now, even if people next to you will think you're a bit kooky, I want you to whisper, "*I am a writer.*"

That is the first Great Truth of Writing. (I'm not trying to start a religion here; stay with me.) Are you ready for the second Great Truth?

It's this: *Writers get better at writing by writing.*

It sounds obvious, but it isn't. Some people think writing is like learning to ride a bike: Once I figure it out, I can do it anywhere, any time, for all time. English professor Kristine Hansen tells us that our education system promotes this false assumption about writing when it lets us "get out of" college writing classes by taking courses in high school—as if writing were "a set of low-level skills" you master once and forever and ever, amen (Hansen 2).

Writing isn't like a polio vaccine—a one-and-done deal. It's *iterative,* meaning that it gets better with practice. When you write, your brain cells (called neurons) fire and wire together in what could be called literacy networks. The more you write, and especially the more you write specific types of texts (called genres), the more those neurons fire and wire together and the more proficient you become at that kind of writing.

Your first-year writing class, then, is outfitting you with a new brain—a writer's brain.

Which reminds me of basketball phenom LeBron James, who is also a writer: he tweets @KingJames.

As I write this (because, you know, I'm a writer too), Lebron James, forward for the Cleveland Cavaliers basketball team, is one of the best basketball players to have ever played the game. He's an NBA champion twice over, a four-time MVP (most valuable player), and a perennial All Star. He was also Rookie of the Year. He averages around twenty-seven points per game. At the age of twenty-eight, he was the youngest player to have scored 20,000 points. Oh, and he's also a two-time Olympic gold medalist.

He has mastered the game at such a level that basketball geeks surely would rank him in the top ten players of all time. In recognition of his mastery, the Cleveland franchise pays him twenty million dollars a year. I would be Captain Obvious if I said that LeBron James is an expert at basketball.

I'd also be testing your patience if I told you he got that way by *practicing*—which he still does, even at this elite level. We like to think that elite athletes or chess players or dancers or computer programmers are born with The Goods, and, yes, some people get a cheater's bump by genetics. But experts like LeBron build on their genetic foundation with lots of practice.

We know why LeBron is considered an expert: He scores more points per game than most players, and he can also pass, rebound, and guard opponents better than many other players. He takes his team to championships. He also has some qualities that are hard to put into words: He has *style*, he has *court presence*. His nickname is "King James," for goodness' sake. What, then, is the equivalent of "court presence" or "points per game" for a writer? What are the fundamentals that, like dribbling or rebounding or reading the defense, set apart the skilled writer from the novice?

And why should these questions matter to you? You may not think of yourself as a master-writer-in-training, a LeBron James of prose in the making. However, chances are that no matter what career path you choose, you will end up doing a great deal of writing. I know that's not happy news for some of you, but the world we live in runs on communication, and surely it runs better when communication is *good*. For much of your life, regardless of your profession, you'll write emails, proposals, reports, briefs, blog posts, instructions, newsletters, scripts, bids, descriptions, essays, letters, webpages, and maybe even books. Add to all this writing the writing you'll do when you're not at work—like texts or social media updates—and you start to understand how important writing is to all of us in our personal, professional, and public lives.

Writing is not something we do just in school. It is a vital means of influence, in all facets of life. The more you control it—in other words, the more writing skills you can take out of your toolbox—the more influence you'll have when the situation demands your words. At some point, you'll have to write your way into a job by sending a personal statement or cover letter. We connect with each other through writing, improving relationships and forging new ones. Through writing we collaborate, creating new knowledge and new perspectives. Critical conversations take place in writing, and so do essential instructions. When we read the writing of others, we improve our critical capacities as we learn how to analyze and evaluate. Writing changes attitudes and judgments, leading to higher forms of cooperation. Writing provokes, writing delights, writing moves and changes minds. Writing helps us learn and think. We learn what we really think when we write, and so do our readers. Writing is an extension of ourselves, the words and phrases composing avatars of influence. When we master writing, we master our universe.

Maybe that's laying it on a bit thick, maybe not. You get the point.

And now you know that *writers get better at writing by writing*.

But there's a third and final Great Truth of Writing that adds to the second: *Writers get better when they're **mindful** about getting better.*

In *What the Best College Students Do*, Ken Bain explains that we are mindful when we "think about our own thinking" or when we're "consciously aware" of how we are learning and what we're hoping to get from what we learn (71, 73). Being consciously aware is tricky; we spend a significant amount of our lives on autopilot because mindfulness takes effort. (Try paying close attention to the way you walk or eat. It's irritating.) One time when I was a graduate student at the University of Arizona, I was sitting through a long meeting about student services. As the meeting wore on, I started chatting, quietly I thought, with my good friend David. In other words, I chose to be rude, ignore the presenter, and instead talk to the guy next to me. Halfway through the meeting, a man sitting in front of us turned around and said, through clenched teeth, "You have been talking the *entire meeting*." That's all he said. I find it odd that until that point, I'd been completely unaware of the consequences of my behavior. I was not mindful. I felt so stupid about my rudeness that I apologized to the guy after the meeting.

The Third Great Truth tells us that great writers get better by thinking about what they're doing. Specifically, great writers get better by:

1. **Planning**: by evaluating their writing skills, by making goals about what they need to write and how they'll get the writing done, by analyzing the task and situation.

2. **Practicing**: by learning effective principles and testing them out in writing through drafting, and by learning to give and take constructive feedback (also called *deliberate practice*).

3. **Revising**: by learning how to fail on first drafts, by analyzing feedback and making adjustments, by setting new goals, and by figuring out strategies for making writing better.

4. **Reflecting**: by assessing what they wrote, by explaining the decisions they made as they wrote, by thinking carefully about what they learned and what's left to learn, by constructing a writer's identity, and by anticipating when they'll use this kind of writing in the future.

We will come back to these four points in later chapters. For now, I want you to understand that these principles are based on significant research in neuroscience, learning theory, cognitive theory, and writing studies. This four-part model is based on the work of Susan Ambrose and her research team at Carnegie Mellon (Ambrose).

So writing improvement is mindful. If you're looking for a fancier way to say that, we can call it *metacognition*, or thinking about thinking. Metacognition is central to learning (National Research Council 12).

You improve as a writer when you plan, practice, revise, and reflect— mindfully.

Back to LeBron. The Cleveland Cavs franchise is willing to pay LeBron James the big bucks because he has mastered several skill domains necessary for any MVP. He had to learn to dribble, rebound, pass, guard, shoot the long ball, go up against defenders under the basket, dish the ball to teammates when he's double-teamed, and make free throws. Even after being recognized as the NBA's MVP, he flew down to Houston to meet with Hakeem Olajuwan, a retired NBA hall-of-famer, to learn how to play more aggressive offense closer to the rim, a skill he considered a self-weakness. Now that's deliberate, mindful practice.

Like basketball, writing requires basic mechanical skills (like spelling or typing) that you need to master before you can improve. It also requires mastery of several major knowledge domains (see Figure 1). A "knowledge domain" is an area of expertise or know-how. The six domains in Figure 1 are based on years of research by writing specialists (i.e., writers who also happen to study writing for a living—bless their souls). I have adapted this list from Anne Beaufort's book *College Writing and Beyond* and John Bean's *Engaging Ideas*.

Notice how each of these domains grows out of the three Great Truths of Writing, represented in the center of the figure by the phrase, "Learning to Write (metacognition)."

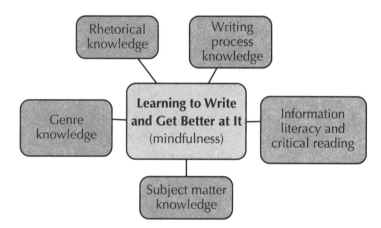

Figure 1. Domains of writing expertise, adapted from Anne Beaufort, *College Writing and Beyond* (2007).

Your instructor will help you understand what these domains mean and how you can improve your abilities in each of them. Here's a primer and a preview:

Rhetorical knowledge—When we write, we write for specific purposes at specific times in specific ways for specific audiences or readers. Writing, then, is *situated*, and effective writers have good judgment about what kind of writing is appropriate for each situation. Rhetoric is the study and practice of how people achieve various purposes through communication. When you write to get someone to feel, think, or do something, you're using rhetoric. Rhetorical thinking is vital to effective communication.

Writing process knowledge—Writing is not just a product but a *process* that involves various methods of planning, thinking, organizing, drafting, getting feedback, revising, replanning, and ultimately delivering it to audiences. Each writer has her own unique process; some processes work better than others.

Genre knowledge—Recurring situations in life require semi-formalized writing responses called genres. A genre is a particular kind of writing for a particular situation. Genres take their shape because readers expect certain moves in writing for certain situations (obituaries, for example, when someone passes away). Genres are rhetorical acts, not just textual conventions.

Information literacy and critical reading—Writing is closely associated with careful reading. Effective writers know how to find, analyze, evaluate, and use the ideas of other writers in their own writing. They read with purpose and mindfulness.

Subject matter knowledge—We're better writers when we write about things we know. Cognitive research tells us that the more "domain-specific expertise" we have (about, say, microbiology or Chinese history), the easier it is for our brains to produce writing (Kellogg 15). Good writers know what they're writing about.

Learning to write and get better at it (mindfulness)—Anyone who writes is a writer. Writers improve the more they write. Writers improve when they're mindful about improving.

I've written this book to help you improve your writing abilities in five of these six domains. Subject matter knowledge is tricky in a writing class; you're going to have to major in something to get specific subject matter knowledge, though your instructor may assign a topic for your college writing class to write about. Research and reading, even if you cram it into a few short weeks, will make you a better writer on a given topic. Furthermore, I want to convince you to treat *writing and rhetoric* themselves as topics worthy of study, since they are, in fact, disciplines, with their own scholarly tradition going back 2500 years to ancient Greece. What you learn about writing and rhetoric will help you take on future writing tasks with confidence and skill.

Here's a breakdown of where and when we'll talk about the domains:

Writing Skills Domain	Chapter in This Book
Rhetorical knowledge	Chapters 6–12
Writing process knowledge	Chapters 1–5
Genre knowledge	Chapters 13–16
Information literacy and critical reading	Chapter 12
Learning to write (metacognition)	All chapters

Though this class will not make you a master writer in the few short weeks of a semester, it will start you on that path by giving you more hours of deliberate practice. By the end of the semester, you'll be a more effective writer than you are now. It will also give you the tools to *think of yourself* as a writer—one who is learning, deliberately and mindfully, how to be better.

You might find the Adventure of Writing Expertise intimidating. I understand the concern. But relax: You're just setting out. Learning to be a good writer is a lifelong process that will challenge you in every new rhetorical situation. I'm still learning how to write, after thirty-five years of doing it and fifteen years of teaching it. The reality is that the kinds of writing you do in first-year writing may not be the kind of writing you learn to do in your major. And when you start a career, you'll need to learn how to write all over again for various audiences in various genres for various situations in the workplace. But the concepts you'll learn in this course will stay with you. You'll master writing much quicker in each new situation if you remember the principles we talk about in this book.

A final word on learning to write. Writing—and I ain't tellin' you anything new here—is *hard*. It's a challenging task. Not only do you need mastery of basic mechanical skills like typing or spelling, you also need to hold in your mind simultaneously your purpose, your audience, and the text you are writing (Kellogg). Experts tell us that you need to clock around 10,000 hours of deliberate practice in something before you master it. Mastery takes years. In other words, don't plan on mastering powerful, persuasive writing in the few years you'll be in college, let alone the few weeks you have in a writing class. As I said, I've been writing and studying writing for a long time, and I still struggle to get my writing where I want it to be. Writing this book was agonizing good fun.

That said, I want to be your cheerleader here as you start your writing class. Though improving your writing will be hard work, it will be rewarding; it might even be fun. And the good news is that *anyone can improve as a writer*. In fact, let's call that the fourth Great Truth of Writing. Anyone, with focused practice and hard work, can improve as a writer. Good writing skills are not innate, like height. When some people tell me "I'm just not good at writing," it's as if they're saying, "I'm just not six feet tall, and I'll never be six feet tall." On the other side of that coin, I've also heard students say, "This class has nothing to teach me about writing because I'm already a good writer—my high school teacher told me so." Carol Dweck, psychologist at Columbia University, calls this kind of thinking the *fixed mindset*: When you believe that "your qualities are carved in stone," you're not as likely to improve (6). The antidote to the fixed mindset is the *growth mindset*: When you believe that "your basic qualities [like writing ability] are things you can cultivate through your efforts" (7).

No matter how good a writer you think you are, it's useful to think of yourself as a novice, with room to power up. Through a massive study of writing at Harvard University, Nancy Sommers discovered that "students who initially accept their status as novices and allow their passions to guide them make the greatest gains in writing development" (Sommers and Saltz 145). We learn from education research that many students think they're better at learning than they really are; and therefore, "we *underestimate* the amount of time and practice it takes to master a new skill" (Hattie and Yates 119). You can—and will—improve as a writer, regardless of your current ability, if you think of yourself as a novice, set some clear writing goals, seek feedback from your instructor and peers, and commit to the hard, rewarding work of writing. Every day.

I've heard it said before that writing is never really perfect, only due. As writers, we work toward perfection without ever actually reaching it. In some ways, writing mastery is like an *asymptote* in algebra. That's the line that a curve approaches but never touches. Daniel Pink, writer of the book *Drive*, explains that mastery is "a source of allure….The joy is in the pursuit more than the realization" (Pink 125).

I hope you will feel some of that joy as you improve your rhetorical powers through writing.

Works Cited

Ambrose, Susan A. *How Learning Works: Seven Research-Based Principles for Smart Teaching*. San Francisco: Jossey-Bass, 2010.

Bain, Ken. *What the Best College Students Do*. Cambridge: Harvard UP, 2012.

Beaufort, Anne. *College Writing and Beyond*. Logan: Utah State UP, 2007.

Bean, John. *Engaging Ideas*. 2nd ed. San Francisco: Jossey-Bass, 2011.

Dweck, Carol. *Mindset*. NY: Ballantine, 2006.

Hansen, Kristine. "The Composition Marketplace: Shopping for Credit versus Learning to Write." *College Credit for Writing in High School*. Ed. Kristine Hansen and Christine R. Farris. Urbana, IL: NCTE, 2010. 1–39.

Hattie, John and Gregory Yates. *Visible Learning and the Science of How We Learn*. London: Routledge, 2014. Print.

Kellogg, Ronald T. "Training Writing Skills: A Cognitive Developmental Perspective." *Journal of Writing Research* 1.1 (2008): 1–26.

National Research Council. *How People Learn*. Exp. Ed. Washington, D.C.: National Academic P, 2000. Print.

Pink, Daniel. *Drive*. NY: Riverhead, 2009. Print.

Sommers, Nancy and Laura Saltz. "The Novice as Expert: Writing the Freshman Year." *College Composition and Communication* 56.1 (2004): 124–149.

WRITING PLANS AND PROCESSES

A writer in the act is a thinker on full-time cognitive overload.
—Linda Flower and John Hayes

In this chapter, I want to help you understand how to think about the writing process in a sophisticated way so you can use it to your advantage as a writer.

You sit down at a computer, you think stuff, and suddenly your fingers tap the keys and words appear on the page in front of you. Quite a magic trick. How the heck does that happen?

I don't know. Frankly, I'm as baffled as maybe you are at the mysteries of how our brains produce language. I know that writing is *not* like speaking; if you were raised in a house with other people, you did not need to be taught how to speak (if you were raised by wolves, however…). Language is an "instinct," says Steven Pinker, the famous Harvard psychologist, and we "know how to talk in more or less the sense that spiders know how to spin webs" (5). Children just somehow start talking, and they put their subjects before their verbs and verbs before objects and they pluralize nouns, when they need to, and they past-tensify actions with brilliant internal logic, even when making what we perhaps mistakenly call errors ("I *holded* the doll").

Writing, however, is not an instinct—not by a long shot. Pinker tells us, further, that "Children must be taught to read and write in laborious lessons" (186). A toddler's first instinct when given a book is to eat it. I'm sure you have early memories, as I do, of large colorful letters on blocks and toys and posters and games and books, all suggesting to our three-year-old brains that these squiggles not only sound something but *mean* something when they stand around in groups. Words appear gradually as we synthesize sound, shape, and meaning. We struggle to read out loud with a parent, and then, like magic, we're reading chapter books like *Junie B. Jones* and *Magic Tree House* on our own. And at the same time, we're struggling to write our own words, on paper with green lines like little roads running across them—first letters, then words, then sentences, then paragraphs, then stories. Being a writer is a miraculous and inspiring thing.

It's also incredibly taxing on our brains. For little children, the first big hurdle, after grasping the letter-sound relationship, is mastering the mechanics of producing letters. Writing, we must remember, is a mechanical skill, and children struggle to get their ideas on paper when they haven't quite mastered the physical process of writing (called *transcription* in the research; see McCutchen). To get a sense of what it's like to struggle to write when transcription is a problem, sit down at a keyboard and cross your arms at the wrist and type with your hands in reverse order. Children under the age of 10 or children with literacy or motor disabilities feel that way all the time when asked to write. We become more fluent writers when we master how to make words appear. You've likely seen this in your own life as you've mastered thumb-texting on a cell phone. Writers get better by writing.

Transcription (i.e., creating words with tools) is just one of several tasks that cognitive scientists tell us our brains must handle when writing. There are other processes going on at once (like monitoring what you've written), and there's one manager that oversees the entire process. It's important for you to know this as a writer, so stay with me.

Cognitive scientists call this overseer the *central executive*. (A cognitive scientist studies how we think; cognition is the action of thinking, understanding, or perceiving.) Let's use an analogy to describe the role of this cognitive function. Imagine you are invited into the control booth for a major television event like the Super Bowl or the Grammy Awards. The booth is full of computer banks where people with headsets press buttons and turn dials and monitor flashing lights. You notice that one person in the booth, sitting higher than everyone else at the back of the room, is telling everyone else what to do. If you're observing a football game directed by Bob Fishman, legendary director for CBS Sports, you see him scanning 100 TV monitors, each showing a different angle on the football game; he's looking for the next live shot, and then the next one, and the next one. ("Ready camera three. Take three!") In a thirty-second interval, Bob Fishman—called "Fish" by his broadcasting team—might shift live shots every three seconds (Bowden). For three straight hours.

Your central executive does that for your brain when you write. Generally speaking, the "Fish" of your mind has three major tasks: *planning* to write, *producing* the writing, and *reviewing* or *revising* what's been written. Each of these tasks requires knowledge, skills, and habits that all help the central executive do its job. For example, deep in long-term

14

memory—that's the place that stores information you may need some time in the future—you have a bank of possible words to use, some grammatical understanding, knowledge about your topic or audience, strategies for writing that worked in the past, and a cache of potential "text structures" we call genres (McCutchen, Teske, and Bankston 460). These tasks are also influenced by your own disposition as a learner emotionally engaged (or not) in the creative work of writing. The central executive draws from these resources to make your writing work (see Kellogg 2–3).

If the central executive gets stressed, well, it's harder to write. We already talked about what happens if you struggle physically to write or type words. There are other ways to burden your central executive. If you know absolutely squat about your topic, then the central executive is going to stress out trying to get the writing done. If you don't set goals or plan your writing effectively, if you're writing in an unfamiliar genre, if you can't predict how a reader might respond, if you don't have a tried-and-true writing process, if you're not interested at all in what you're writing about, if you try to write something while your cell phone pings with incoming text messages—you make writing harder for yourself because your central executive is getting slammed with other tasks.

And of course in the background of all these issues is the *why* of writing, and the *to whom*—what's called the "task environment" of writing (Hayes "New Directions"). We'll talk more about that in chapter six when we talk about rhetoric.

While I do want you to understand the cognitive challenges related to writing, in this chapter I'm more interested in helping you learn to use *writing plans and processes* as a way to aid your central executive while you write. At this point, I hope you have some sense of why it's important to develop a writing process so that planning, producing, and revising your work will be rewarding for you, even as it challenges you. I told you all this stuff about writing and cognition because I want you to be a mindful writer; remember from chapter one, you're a writer who thinks about how to improve as a writer. It's going to take time and practice, of course, but that's why you took this class. (Nice move!)

A Model for Writing Tasks

Before we go further, I want you to take a moment and think about how you've produced writing in the past. What is your standard writing process? ("Standard" is a misleading word, I guess, because we go through different processes for different situations and purposes.) If someone made a gripping Netflix Original Series about your writing process, what would we see you (the hero!) doing as you get the writing done? Where would you be writing? And how? What would you do first, second, third? And which celebrity would you want playing the role of distracting love interest?

Based on what I used to do in high school when assigned a writing task, I know what my television drama would look like:

> Scene, home office. Camera zooms in on our hero, slouching in a chair in front of an eight-inch green-screen Compaq-brand computer the day before the paper is due. He rubs his temples. He hasn't given Thought One to this paper that needs to appear magically in the next few hours. He cracks his knuckles. He says, "Okay, let's do this!" He plays a few rounds of *Bushido: The Way of the Warrior*, just to get warmed up. Then, he writes. Fast-cutting montage of our hero typing each sentence, putting one word in front of the other, checking each phrase and clause for glaring errors, until the small screen is filled with words in 14-point font. A close-up of our hero-writer, sweat on his brow, a look of satisfaction as he takes fifteen seconds to look over what he's written, making sure his commas are where he thinks they should be. He adds a comma in one sentence because he's been told to add commas where you take breaths. Camera pulls back as hero prints out paper on a dot matrix printer and then slides the finished product into a plastic sleeve that reeks of clueless desperation. A hard-rock power jam from the 80s plays as he crams his paper into his backpack, a smug look of triumph crossing his face.

What can I say? It got the job done—sort of. Okay, not really.

Does my writing process sound familiar to you? Of course not, because you care more about your work than I did. Or maybe some of it does resonate. Maybe you, too, have cranked out a paper in an energy-drink-induced sleepless fury the night before it was due. Extensive research on the writing processes of novice writers has revealed that the way I used to write papers is by no means uncommon. We know from research that novice writers "show little concern for conceptual planning," "fail to plan adequately for their readers," and focus mostly on "surface features" like punctuation when revising (McCutchen, Teske, Bankston 454–5). Skilled writers spend much more time than novices planning their writing, setting goals, finding the right genre, thinking about their audience, and working to discover the meaning of what they want to say (Torrance). Like novices, they revise for surface-level issues (gotta get your commas to behave!), but they also revise "holistically," meaning that they take in what they've written "as a *whole*" to make sure they've got it right (Sommers 386). The skilled writer sees the whole project as a *whole*, from beginning to end, and there's power in that.

We want you to have this kind of power when you write. So, I want to teach you a new process for managing writing tasks. Think of this process as your own hero's journey through a creative struggle, from the moment you're assigned to write (the "call" to writing) to the moment you see the results of what you wrote and—like Bilbo Baggins after returning to the Shire from his encounter with the dragon Smaug—start writing the memoir of your quest.

The following chart represents your quest through the writing task:

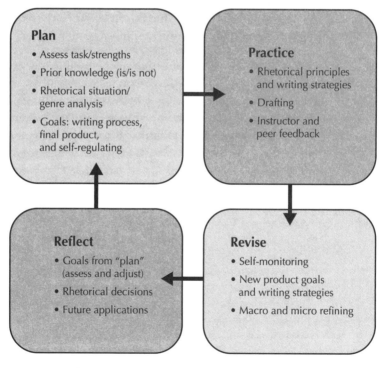

Plan
- Assess task/strengths
- Prior knowledge (is/is not)
- Rhetorical situation/ genre analysis
- Goals: writing process, final product, and self-regulating

Practice
- Rhetorical principles and writing strategies
- Drafting
- Instructor and peer feedback

Reflect
- Goals from "plan" (assess and adjust)
- Rhetorical decisions
- Future applications

Revise
- Self-monitoring
- New product goals and writing strategies
- Macro and micro refining

Figure 2. Adapted from Susan Ambrose et al., *How Learning Works* (2010), p. 193.

You'll recognize these four steps from chapter one when we talked about mindfulness in writing. In *How Learning Works*, professor Susan Ambrose and her research team explain that the most effective students go through a metacognitive process of "self-directed learning" when confronted with an intellectual challenge, like a writing assignment (Ambrose et al. 193). I've adapted this process for writing tasks from this remarkable research. Study this chart carefully. Tattoo it onto your brain. It's one of the things you learn in this class that should go with you to future writing challenges.

In this textbook, we'll cover each of the four steps of the writing process. In this chapter, we'll talk about *planning*, something that novice writers don't do enough of.

Plan

Every writer will adopt a different strategy for writing—a different writing process that best suits his or her particular needs and talents. I was taught a fairly linear prewriting-writing-revising method, but in practice you may do all these things over and over during a complicated writing task.

This is a crucial point: There is no *single* writing process that suits everyone. You'll have to figure out what's best for you as you write your way, mindfully, to glory. And yet there is a more or less better way to think about how to manage writing tasks from the start. Skilled writers, for example, take considerably more time planning their writing than developing writers.

In the *planning* stage, a writer

1. assesses the task and

2. sets goals.

What do we mean by these activities?

Last fall my wife asked me to build a shed-like shelter in the backyard so we could store the lawn mower, a rusty wheelbarrow, and other implements of torture. I'd never built such a thing, so I did what I always do when assigned to do something outside my comfort zone: I stared blankly at the problem. I went out to the potential construction site, on the left side of the house next to the fence, and I stared at the site and tried to imagine what a structure like that might look like. At first I imagined building a full-scale shed with walls and sliding doors, and then when I realized how long that might take me, considering my sub-par acumen with power tools, I imagined a wall-less structure with four wooden posts and a pitched roof. I'd built similar structures when I was a carpenter's apprentice after high school. Maybe I could do that. And if I couldn't, I could ask my friends to come help me with the hard stuff. I decided I'd spend the next whole Saturday working on it, and then every night for a couple of hours after dinner. I needed to be done before it snowed.

I had a hard time at first imagining how the posts would go into the ground and how the roof would go into the posts. So I took my phone around the neighborhood and took pictures of other sheds and lean-tos, paying particular attention to the way the roofs were constructed. I also watched videos on YouTube for how to make lean-to-like shelters. (Are there such videos? Only 171,000 of them.) At work, when I should have been thinking of other things, I daydreamed about what materials I'd use, how much it would all cost, how it all might come together, whether my neighbors would sue me because it blocked their view of the Wasatch mountains. I'd borrow my friend Cam's cement mixer. My neighbor Paul, who built something like this in his backyard, could talk me through the first steps. I'd see if Billy would work with me on the shingles for the roof—he owed me because I helped him paint his house. My wife, of course, would let me know as I drew up some plans whether I was on the right track.

By the time I went out in the yard with a post-hole shovel and all the lumber, I had given the project considerable thought. I had a global sense—a "big picture" sense—of what I was going to do, even if the specific *how* wasn't quite set in mind.

You already know where I'm going with this, so let's go there. Starting a writing project is like what I've just described. An event in your life triggers a *writing task*—a teacher or a future employer will give you a writing assignment, and before you start writing you'll plan your approach. Not always, of course. You don't plan, necessarily, to write a text message or a Post-it note to roommates to stop stealing your milk. But what I'm about to describe is an ideal process for important writing tasks—the kind that get you good grades or scholarships or promotions.

Assess the Task

Here are a few steps you might take while you assess the task (and we'll talk more about these steps in chapter five):

1. **Read the assignment carefully**, making sure you understand what's being asked of you. Before building, I talked over with my wife what she wanted me to do. For writing assignments, you make sure you understand what your instructor wants you to do. Ask yourself: Do I get this assignment? Do I understand what key terms (like "critical thinking") mean? Check due dates. When am I asked to submit outlines, bibliographies, or previous drafts? What is the purpose or outcome? How will I be assessed?

2. **Assess the rhetorical situation.** Who is the audience for this assignment? What do I know about them? What do they want from me? What is my role as writer? What do I want my audience to feel, think, or do as a result of reading my stuff? What strategies will I use to achieve those goals? My shelter would serve my immediate family's purposes, but it would also be seen by neighbors and visitors. What would they think of me when they saw it? (We'll talk more about rhetorical situation in chapter six.)

3. **Analyze the genre in which you're supposed to write** (see p. 66 and 192). Shelters serve various purposes for various people in various situations. Before I built the shelter, I looked at how other people built their shelters to achieve similar or at least related purposes. Genres, according to Carolyn Miller, are "typified rhetorical actions based in recurrent situations" (159). A genre isn't necessarily a convention or a form we follow; it's a rhetorical act we do because the situation (i.e., audience and purpose) calls for it. When someone dies, a relative usually writes an obituary. An obituary is a genre. It's a rhetorical act that follows a familiar pattern and uses semi-typical strategies (like providing life details) that are appropriate for the moment. Rarely do you see an obituary describing the immoral or criminal activity of the deceased—which is unfortunate, because obituaries would be a lot more entertaining if they included that stuff. But that would be *inappropriate*, in a rhetorical sense. Genres take certain shapes because we need them to do certain things for us.

   When you write, you write genres (letters to the editor, proposals, lab reports, grant proposals, analyses, personal statements, etc.), and some of them are more clearly defined than others. For example, at some point you probably wrote a "research paper." What are the genre conventions of a research paper? It depends on who you ask. If you ask scientists, they'll say that a research paper has a section, usually titled "methods," describing how the scientist set up the experiment. Historians will tell you that research papers must have copious footnotes or endnotes listing primary sources the writer consulted for historical analysis. If you'd asked me when I was a junior in high school, I would have told you, "It's this thing you write when you look up some stuff in the Kearns (my hometown) library and write down a few cool quotes and then vomit it all up in a paper with a works cited page and an awesome plastic sleeve." Regardless of the occasional fuzziness surrounding genres, it's important to your success that you write a genre appropriate to the situation. How do you get it right?

Scholars of genre have described a useful method for analyzing the genre most suited to your writing situation (Devitt, Reiff, and Bawarshi). First, you get your hands on samples of the genre. You collect examples from as many different sources as you can. (Maybe your instructor has copies of previous student work you can borrow.) Second, you identify the rhetorical situation for which that genre would be suitable. You ask yourself: Where does this genre show up? Whose purpose does it serve? Who writes these genres and who reads them and why? Third, you analyze the patterns you see in the genre, asking yourself questions like: How is this genre structured? What rhetorical strategies do the writers use? What kind of style or argument or document design or language do I detect across examples?

Analyzing genre in this way will help you understand what's typical in the rhetorical situation you find yourself in before you write a single word.

4. **Review how your prior knowledge or experience might apply.** We know from research that what we already know can either "help or hinder" what we're trying to do now (Ambrose et al. 13). Before I started the shelter, I kind of knew what I knew how to do and what I didn't know how to do. My prior experience helped me understand my limitations and strengths. Before you start a writing task, you should think about what you know about the topic you're supposed to write about and whether you've written that kind of genre or something similar to it before. (How is this rhetorical analysis like

the literary analysis I wrote in high school? How is it *not* like that?) Sometimes prior knowledge can hurt us in new writing tasks. I've had college writing students who had mastered the five-paragraph essay in high school and could not write themselves out of it in my writing class. I'd get five beastly paragraphs stretched out to eight pages, and I'd think, "Gee, their prior knowledge isn't helping them!" You should also think about what prior writing processes have helped you or hurt you before.

5. **Assess your ability to perform the task.** You may also want to spend a few moments thinking about your own abilities as a writer. How confident are you with this kind of assignment? In some ways, it doesn't matter whether or not you think you're a "good writer" in some generic sense: How do I feel about *this* assignment? We know from research that self-perceptions will influence whether student writers work hard, "persevere" when the going gets tough, and bounce back after failure (Pajares and Valiante 159). Remind yourself: I can do this if I work hard each day and get good feedback. *Writers get better at writing by writing.*

6. **Decide what you want to get out of the assignment.** Ask yourself: What's in it for me? What do I want to learn from this writing task? What will writing this genre help me do in the future? How will I make personal connections to this writing task so that I won't be bored or discouraged? As with all the other steps for assessing the task, you should write down answers to these questions to refer to as you work.

Set Goals

The second part of planning after assessing the task is *setting goals*.

I know. The phrase "setting goals" might evoke mixed feelings. You might be thinking about those times when someone—likely a well-meaning adult with power over you—made you set goals you had no intention to keep. January is a busy month for membership gyms because of fleeting New Year's resolutions. I get this.

But think about it this way: Most of our actions are goal-oriented. When I stand up from my desk to walk down the hall to get a drink of water, I've set a goal for myself. It's an easy goal to achieve, as long as I don't go into cardiac arrest in the 100 yards it takes to get to the drinking fountain.

Most action is goal-oriented: We want something, we try to get it. What we're talking about, though, is more purposeful, more (yes!) mindful.

For our purposes here, I suggest two kinds of goals you'll want to set for yourself as a writer at the outset of a writing task:

1. **Specific product goals.** Once you've analyzed the genre you're supposed to write, you'll know better what you need to do as a writer. A "product goal" is a statement explaining to yourself what you want your writing to look like when it's done. And genre helps direct these goals. For example, if I'm writing an opinion editorial on a political topic, one of my product goals might be to end my op ed by calling on Congress to act on some piece of legislation—a futile call, surely, but one that satisfies my desire to tell powerful people what to do. Sometimes the assignment you've been given has explicit goals written for you (like "support your thesis with evidence from peer-reviewed scholarship"). Sometimes you'll make your own (like "I'll use transitional language to help the reader go from one part of my argument to the next" or "I'm going to throw a pop culture reference in my intro to attract interest and set the tone"). The point is to make specific product goals that are not too broad ("I will develop my argument effectively") or too restricting ("I will write three sentences after every topic sentence—one to provide an example, one to...").

   Summarizing research on effective writers, English professor Debbie Dean tells us that "product goals are most effective either before drafting or during revision" (57). Debbie implies here that sometimes your specific product goals, like carry-on luggage, will shift midflight. That's okay! The point is that you're paying attention to those goals, letting them serve as your guide as you crank out the good stuff. Your instructor might include an assignment sheet or rubric that will help you make product goals.

2. **Self-regulating goals.** Sometimes we're our own worst enemies. Wanna get up earlier than you normally do? You'll have to convince yourself, and your self wants to sleep. Gonna get that paper written long before it's due? Shoot, they're playing ultimate frisbee out there on the lawn, and it's such a beautiful day.... Writing is hard, and we do all kinds of things to avoid it. Sometimes when I'm staring at a blank screen, I'll find myself either cleaning my desk with obsessive compulsion or playing the video game Pac-man online. (I just played it now!) Skilled writers have strategies to "regulate" themselves to get

their work done. They trust the better angels of their nature, but they also believe those angels need a nudge now and then. Think of self-regulating writing goals like the alarm clock that shreds dollar bills if you don't get up and turn it off. (Yes, there is such a product.)

When you get a writing assignment, you may feel overwhelmed by the task. ("I've never written one of those before…How many pages?…I don't even know where to start!") You'll see a looming deadline and wonder how you will possibly manage to have something ready by then. Self-regulating goals keep the panic at bay by helping you manage the writing task. Don't stew—*do*. Experts on this subject divide potential regulating strategies into different categories (Graham and Harris). Here are a few you might find useful:

a. **Environmental**—Decide where and when you're going to write, and stick to a schedule. Block out time each day to write or even just to think about your writing project. Write every day, and then when you get stuck, you can quit without freaking out that the paper's due tomorrow; you'll let your work percolate subconsciously while you do other things (see Carey's chapter "Quitting Before You're Ahead"). Surprisingly, there is some evidence that varying *where* we write might actually help us make useful mental connections; consider that as you plan (Carey 61).

    When you sit down to write, turn off your cell phone. Multitasking is a delusion strongly contradicted by cognitive science ("Multitasking: Switching Costs"). You're either writing your paper or text messaging your friends—you can't do both, at least not at the same time. Even listening to music while writing, especially music with lyrics, can throw you off your writing groove because of your "selective attention" (Hattie and Yates 191). Just trust Uncle Brian on this one: You'll get more writing done if you're not shifting attention from your words to your phone or an irrelevant webpage, unless, of course, you're using your phone to write, read, or research something related to your task. Set goals for how you'll control your environment for the most effective writing.

b. **Personal**—Set a goal to check your own progress—this is called "self-monitoring." After each day or writing period, reflect on how well you're doing and decide what you need to do next. Set deadlines for yourself, but adjust them if they don't work for you. The most popular self-monitoring strategy: reward yourself. For example, tell yourself "As soon as I write 500 words, I'll check sports scores on ESPN," or "If I write for one hour today, I will go buy myself a mango pineapple smoothie."

c. **Social**—Just as I talked about the shelter project with friends and neighbors, talk about your writing project with other people. Talking about your work out loud can be a powerful writing tool. Your instructor will likely assign you to work with peers to review each other's writing. Set a goal to have more people than your peer group review your work. Take your writing to a tutor (in the Writing Center, for example) or a trusted roommate. Listen carefully to your readers, even though you should always think of yourself as the owner of your own work.

I've spent all this time on the planning stage—thanks for joining me!—for two reasons: (1) skilled writers spend more time planning than novice writers, so you should develop a planning approach that works for you, and (2) learning how to plan effectively will help you tackle future writing tasks in school and beyond. Your instructor might ask you to set down these plans in writing so he or she can help you make the most of them.

Like all good plans, you'll make adjustments and revisions as you start writing and get feedback. I can't tell you how many times I've tried to write portions of this textbook only to have my plans crash-land in a field of failure. You'll get this. Much of the planning process will become intuitive for you, with practice.

Works Cited

Ambrose, Susan A. et al. *How Learning Works: Seven Research-Based Principles for Smart Teaching*. San Francisco: Jossey-Bass, 2010.

Bowden, Mark. "The Hardest Job in Football." *The Atlantic*. Jan/Feb 2009. Web. 8 May 2015.

Carey, Benedict. *How We Learn*. NY: Random House, 2014.

Dean, Deborah. *What Works in Writing Instruction*. Urbana, IL: NCTE, 2010. Print.

Devitt, Amy, Mary Jo Reiff, and Anis Bawarshi. *Scenes of Writing: Strategies for Composing with Genres*. NY: Pearson, 2004.

Graham, Steve and Karen R. Harris. "The Role of Self-Regulation and Transcription Skills in Writing and Writing Development." *Educational Psychologist* 35.1 (2000): 3–12.

Hattie, John and Gregory Yates. *Visible Learning and the Science of How We Learn*. London: Routledge, 2014.

Hayes, John R. "New Directions in Writing Theory." *Handbook of Writing Research*. Ed. Charles A. MacArthur, Steve Graham, and Jill Fitzgerald. NY: Guilford, 2006. 28–40.

Kellogg, Ronald T. "Training Writing Skills: A Cognitive Developmental Perspective." *Journal of Writing Research* 1.1 (2008): 1–26.

McCutchen, Deborah. "Cognitive Factors in the Development of Children's Writing." *Handbook of Writing Research*. Ed. Charles A. MacArthur, Steven Graham, and Jill Fitzgerald. NY: Guilford P, 2006. 115–130.

McCutchen, Deborah, Paul Teske, and Catherine Bankston. "Writing and Cognition: Implications of the Cognitive Architecture for Learning to Write and Writing to Learn." *Handbook of Research on Writing*. Ed. Charles Bazerman. NY: Lawrence Erlbaum, 2008. 452–470.

Miller, Carolyn R. "Genre as Social Action." *Quarterly Journal of Speech* 70 (1984): 151–167.

"Multitasking: Switching Costs." American Psychological Association. 20 March 2006. Web. 4 Nov 2014.

Pajares, Frank and Gio Valiante. "Self-Efficacy Beliefs and Motivation in Writing Development." *Handbook of Writing Research*. Ed. Charles A. MacArthur, Steven Graham, and Jill Fitzgerald. NY: Guilford P, 2006. 158–170.

Pinker, Steven. *The Language Instinct*. NY: HarperPerennial, 1994.

Sommers, Nancy. "Revision Strategies of Student Writers and Experienced Adult Writers." *CCC* 31.4 (1980): 378–388.

Torrance, Mark. "Is Writing Expertise Like Other Kinds of Expertise?" *Theories, Models, and Methodology in Writing Research*. Eds. Gert Rijlaarsdam, Huub van den Bergh, and Michel Couzijn. Amsterdam: Amsterdam UP, 1996. 3–9.

PRACTICE

The second stage of the writing quest is *practice*. When we talk about practice, we're talking about how you'll use writing strategies—methods for getting the writing done once you've assessed the task and set goals.

When we talk about practice, we're talking about the time period after planning when

you start thinking about what to write

to the moment when

you receive feedback on a full draft of your writing from someone (a teacher, a peer, anonymous commenters on your blog, the worker guy at 7-11, your mom).

I've said before that writing processes vary from person to person and project to project, so in some ways this time frame I've laid out is arbitrary. However, I really like the idea of practice as preparation time for, and a separate activity from, performance. When it comes to writing, performance is when you publish your work or turn it in for a grade. Before then, you take time to practice. Even though practice is meant to improve performance, in practice you permit yourself to take risks, look stupid, write awkward and silly things, make tentative claims, test ideas, and fall on your face—all for the glory of writing!

You already know some of the buzzwords we use when we talk about getting the writing done: brainstorming, clustering, outlining, freewriting, drafting, reading, talking to people, writing paragraphs, reading drafts out loud. You also have various rhetorical principles to guide writing, like thinking of your audience, supporting your claim with good reasons, making effective appeals, writing an appropriate genre, organizing your writing effectively, and writing with an effective style. Your instructor will give you time to practice these writing strategies, so I won't go over them in detail here. Many of these strategies are genre-specific, so we'll talk about them in the genre chapters at the end of the book. But I do want to talk about three practice strategies you'll want to consider as you develop a writing process.

Before we get to the three strategies, two brief complications: These strategies may not help you unless you kind of know what you want to write about—i.e., you've landed on a topic, a specific question, or a problem you want to explore. Your instructor will help you think through how to come up with a topic; the assignment will guide you, but so should your own interests. We know that students who are passionate about their topics, even if their instructor assigned them, have more motivation as writers, and they write better. At any rate, let's proceed with these three practice strategies under the assumption that you've settled on at least a provisional topic to write about.

The second complication is that writing research has shown that effective writers don't necessarily use these strategies in a linear way (i.e., "first I do this…then I do that…"). In grade school, you may have learned a model that looks like this:

$$\text{prewriting} \longrightarrow \text{drafting} \longrightarrow \text{revising}$$

While this model is helpful for starting out, it doesn't quite describe what happens when you're on a writing quest. You may find that your writing process is *recursive*, meaning that sometimes you start revising before you get a draft done or sometimes you'll brainstorm even after completing an entire draft because you hit a dead end. The mindful writer studies her own process to see what works best. (I say "her," but I mean "his," too. I usually pluralize my subjects to avoid sexist problems, but sometimes I want to express a single writer, and then, just because we've used *his* for so long, I use *her* to even things out. What do *you* do to solve this rhetorical problem?)

The three stages of practice we'll talk about in this chapter are invention, drafting, and feedback.

Invention

The philosopher Aristotle believed that studying rhetoric meant studying rhetorical *invention*—or finding, as he put it, "the available means of persuasion." Invention is the process we use to come up with stuff to write. (Invention is kind of a big deal in rhetorical studies.) As you already know, coming up with something to write is particularly hard when you have no idea what you're going to write about. For this section, I'm going to assume that you've settled on a question or problem related to a topic you've been assigned in your class. Of course, invention can also help you land on a problem or question, too; it can also help you narrow your topic to make your writing project more manageable.

What methods of invention have you used in the past? How have they worked for you?

I like to think of invention methods as either *structured* or *unstructured*. When you use structured invention, you attack your topic with specific kinds of questions or categories of thought that writers have used for ages. Unstructured invention taps into more intuitive, organic, and surprising stores for creativity. Both are useful.

Structured Methods of Invention

Using a *structured* method can be helpful if you don't know how to start. For example, students of rhetoric in ancient Greece and Rome used a system called *topoi* to invent arguments. The word topoi is the plural form of the Greek word *topos*, which means place. Topoi are starting places for discovering things to say—places you can go to come up with arguments. The Greeks invented these starting places, I think, because they noticed that there are certain patterns we follow when trying to figure out the world, certain categories of thought we find useful over and over, in different settings. For example, one topos is *definition*—how a word or key term or principle has been defined.

It's useful to think of topoi in terms of the questions they provoke. You've probably heard of the journalist's Who-What-When-Where-Why questions; topoi are like that. The following table lists useful topoi and the questions they provoke to help you come up with something to say related to your writing task.

Topos	Related Questions
definition, category, or essence	What is this thing? How is it defined? How is it classified (with other things)? How does this thing work? What is its purpose?
division	How can this topic be divided? What are its parts? How do the parts relate? Which parts are most important?
comparison	What is this thing like? What is it *not* like? What analogies or metaphors could be used to compare this to other things?
cause or consequence	What happens because of this thing? What are the consequences of it? Who or what is influenced by it?
antecedent or origin	Where did this thing come from? Who started it? What is its history? What is it a consequence of?
authority	Who speaks about this? Who are the experts or stakeholders? Who knows the most about this? Who cares about this?
value	Who values this thing? Is it good or bad? How is this thing evaluated? What laws, morals, or practices are influenced by this? What's the consensus on it? The disagreements?
space	Where is this thing? What is its reach, scope? Where is it concentrated? How far does it go?
possibility	What's possible related to this thing? How much can it change? Who has power to change it? What's difficult or impossible about this?

Once you have a potential writing topic, you can blitz it with these questions to see what comes up. Let's say you're writing a research paper about illegal immigration in the United States. You're not sure what to argue, which is a wise and critically sound place to start, but you have your topoi on hand to help you think through the subject systematically. You could make a table like the one above and write questions or issues related to immigration in the right-hand column, like this:

Topos	Related Questions/Issues
definition, category, or essence	What is immigration? What makes immigration *illegal*? What is the scope of the issue? What is it like to cross the Mexican-American border into the U.S.?
division	Various people immigrate for various reasons, from various places *to* various places in the U.S. What do these differences tell us about immigration? What organizations in the U.S. have an interest in this issue (border patrol, local businesses, human rights activists, etc.)?
comparison	How important is immigration compared to other political issues? We could compare various groups or nationalities who immigrate and what becomes of them.
cause or consequence	What are the consequences of illegal immigration? Who benefits? Who gets hurt? What would happen if immigration stopped?
antecedent or origin	What's the history of immigration in the U.S.? Where does the immigrant's journey begin? We could look at how attitudes or policies about immigration have changed across time.
authority	Who knows the most about this topic? Who are the experts, and who are the "experiencers" (those who experience immigration and its consequences)? Which think tanks or organizations understand this issue most clearly?
value	What are the ethical issues related to illegal immigration? Are illegal immigrants criminals or valuable contributors to culture and economy? What laws govern immigration? We should think, too, about how or why we value this topic.
space	Where does immigration take place? Where do immigrants come from? I'd be interested to know where illegal immigrants end up living and working.
possibility	What can or can't be done about illegal immigration? How do we make changes in the system? Who should change it?

Another structured method of invention is *writing an outline*. No, it ain't sexy. I remember being compelled to write outlines for papers in high school: writing the Roman numerals, tabbing over the subcategories, creating a roadmap I was sure to junk once I started writing. But here's the crazy thing: There's research evidence suggesting that outlining can help you map out the relationship between possible ideas you want to represent in your writing, especially when you haven't thought much about the topic you want to write about (Hayes "New Directions"; Kellogg). They can help you plan out your writing and make product goals. They help you separate your writing task into parts and organize those parts into helpful hierarchies.

At their simplest, outlines can help you think through your main point and all the support you hope to gather, like the following outline for a generic essay:

I.   Cool intro
II. My first point
     A. Support for this point (evidence, arguments, details)
     B. More support for this point (etc.)
III. My second point
     A. Support for this point
     B. Etc. etc.!
IV. An amazing conclusion that ties it together and blows the minds of my readers

Since you're the boss of your writing, you can change your outline to suit your needs as you write. A good outline, though, can give you a path through the thicket before you start out. It sets up a working blueprint for your thinking. Outlines, though, should be *genre specific*, meaning that the kind of writing you're doing will dictate the kind of outline you'll write. Science writers often follow a specific outline with the acronym IMRD: introduction, methods, results, discussion. Sometimes simple outlines are helpful only if you're writing an academic essay. If you're writing a resume or creating a digital document, you'll have to think differently about how to arrange your argument.

One final structured method is *clustering*. My guess is you've already been taught how to do this, but just in case you haven't:

To cluster, just write a word you're interested in at the center of a piece of paper. (You'll need to go Old School for this one: pencil and paper, not computer.) It can be a topic or a question related to your topic—like immigration. Draw a circle around that word or phrase. Then think of related topics or words that have some kind of connection to that center word. Write those words and draw lines like wagon-wheel spokes connecting the ideas. Then, do the same for the words you've just created around the original word, getting more specific the further you go from the key word.

I said go pencil and paper on clustering, but I can also imagine some pretty cool clustering happening digitally on a word processor or design program. I've used presentation slides to invent arguments before.

Unstructured Methods of Invention

So much for the structured invention strategies. If you're more interested in freewheeling, hippie-dippie, space-case, unlock-your-consciousness kind of invention strategies, you might want to try more unstructured strategies, like the following:

Freewriting—Just start writing. As fast as you can, as much as you can. Don't think at all about what you're writing; if you can't think of something to say, write "I'm not sure what to say here so I'll keep writing until something comes…" Take American author Jack Kerouac's kooky, almost incoherent advice and just write "'without consciousness' in semitrance… allowing subconscious to admit in own uninhibited interesting necessary…language what conscious art would censor, and write excitedly, swiftly, with writing-or-typing-cramps" (58). You may discover that there are sentences and ideas that just emerge, almost out of nowhere, from your stream of consciousness. Tap into the inner writing genius hiding behind all that fear of making a mistake in writing.

Some writers also use a strategy called *looping* with freewriting. They'll take a kernel of an idea or sentence out of the freewrite and start freewriting about *that*, just to see where it goes.

Journaling—Keep a journal in a notebook, document, or even blog about your quest to finish the writing task. Write whatever you want—questions, concerns, goals, responses, quotes, issues, prewrites, doodles. When I'm journaling, I'll often make "to do" lists with little boxes to check when I get stuff done (like "look up the study on sleep and test performance mentioned in the *New York Times* science section").

Talking to people—Talk about your topic with everyone you know. Tell your roommates, friends, neighbors, hair stylist, and family members what you want to write about. Annoy people about your plans while on the basketball court or in the hot tub. Talk through your concerns. Use Facebook or some other social media to play around with possible directions and ideas. When you think you have a possible argument (called a *thesis* by some), tweet it out there; my colleague Gideon Burton calls this a "tweethis," which sounds like a word a kid would say after his two front teeth fell out.

Drawing—Doodle while you think about your project. Draw a picture, or some kind of chart or graphic that represents some faint shadow of an idea. Draw shapes to represent various approaches or concepts. Express relationships in abstract symbols and diagrams. Nancy Duarte, design guru, encourages us to represent abstract concepts in diagrams that suggest flow, structure, relationships, hierarchies, or processes (45).

Drafting

Invention can be fun, but at some point you have to sit down and open a word processor (like Google Drive or Microsoft Word) and start writing complete sentences. The second stage of practice, then, is drafting. Some students approach drafting as if they're carving into stone the epitaph of a cultural hero. For some developing writers, drafting is a painful, almost letter-at-a-time process. Writing words should not be like passing kidney stones, but it can feel like that if we're too fixated on getting things right from the start. Remember: You're *practicing* at this point. Drafting is essentially thinking in words and sentences and paragraphs. Though it's essential that you keep in mind your audience as you write, Peter Elbow (a wonderful writer about writing) tells us that during drafting time, it makes sense to write with our eyes closed to our audience, so to speak, so that we are uninhibited, so that we can explore and express before we communicate and connect.

You may encounter writer's block during the drafting process. That's natural, even for professional writers. We get writer's block because we have "inflexible plans" for the writing (Rose); we get it because we're tired, or frustrated, or sorta played out for the day. If you're writing every day, writer's block shouldn't be too big of a problem—if you've set reasonable self-regulating goals, then you'll benefit from the writing habit. But quitting is often the best thing you could do for the writing (remember the *percolating* principle from the last chapter). You can always go back to the invention stage or talk over your problem with someone or even talk through the problem out loud to yourself and record it. A word to the wise: "binge writing" has been shown to cause writer's block and even "dysphoria," which means "general dissatisfaction" (Kellogg and Whiteford 257). You don't want dissatisfaction—that's five syllables of sadness.

I'm assuming your instructor will be your guide for approaching the drafting of your paper, but consider these principles:

1. **Keep your audience in mind.** Yes, I know that a moment ago I echoed Peter Elbow's advice about writing with our eyes closed—i.e., writing with our gut and to heck with audience. But keeping an audience in mind can guide your thoughts as you draft, even if your mental concept of audience is vague. (For example, you imagine you're writing to smart people who enjoy a witty pop culture reference but who are skeptical about your main point.) As you think about what would delight or convince that audience, writing flows from that act of empathy. More on this principle in chapter six.

2. **Keep your genre in mind**. If you've studied several examples of the genre you're being asked to write, then you know your options for shaping the writing. How you design your document, organize paragraphs and/or various figures or images, use transitions, make rhetorical moves in your intro or conclusion—all will depend on the kind of document you're producing.

   I can't stress enough this point about genre. If I were writing a standard handbook, I'd tell you specifically, right here and now, how to write an effective introduction, thesis, body paragraph, or conclusion. But different genres call for different shapes of intros, different types of theses, different approaches for conclusions, etc. I hope I'm not shaking your testimony of a well-ordered universe by telling you that some genres don't even have a thesis. I want this advice on drafting to be portable for all kinds of writing. If you have absorbed the mindful approach, you'll be mindful of your particular genre as you write.

3. **Divide the big task into smaller tasks**. Straightforwardly: Maybe you begin by writing a thesis or an intro. Then you take each section at a time, until you've written a working conclusion. As you draft, think of the writing task as a series of steps you need to take on the way to a complete draft. You might even want to think of yourself as a *paragraph* drafter. Paragraphs function as unique, hopefully coherent

segments of information that break up the reading experience and sequence ideas for your reader. The most popular handbooks suggest different types of paragraphs (like description, compare/contrast, cause and effect, example, and so on). It may help you to think of the drafting process at the level of the paragraph.

4. **Think of drafting as *drafting*.** If you're stuck on the idea that your first draft has to be your best, then it'll be hard for you to want to change anything about that draft. Just convince yourself that you're writing to *discover* what you want to say, not to finalize what to say. Think of your draft as "drafty"; prepare to change what you've written as you come to understand your purpose better. Writer Anne Lamott famously wrote that we're entitled to *really bad* first drafts—though she used more colorful, interesting language to describe this entitlement.

5. **Ignore, as much as you can, sentence-level issues. At least at first**. Novice writers fixate on whether each sentence they write is error-free. There will be plenty of time to work out style and error once you're satisfied with the main point you want to make and the evidence you'll use to make that point. You won't be able to do this very well because your central executive will chime in with monitoring feedback, like an annoying backseat driver. So do your best to write as freely as you can. Shush the backseat driver.

Your goal in the drafting stage is to finish a draft of your writing complete enough to show someone so you can get feedback on how well you're accomplishing your rhetorical goals.

Feedback

In the third stage of practice, you prepare to receive feedback. Without feedback, we're dead in the water as writers. My eighth-grade English teacher was a gifted gusher. She thought everything we wrote sang with poetic power. I remember writing a rap—yes, a *rap*—about Edgar Allen Poe's "The Tell-Tale Heart," in which I rhymed heart with…well, with something only a thirteen-year old boy would think of. With tears welling up in her eyes, my teacher praised my rap as a masterpiece. But vague praise, no matter how tearful, gets you only so far, or, actually, not far at all. And vague criticism is even worse. A lone C+ at the bottom of an otherwise blank paper doesn't tell you much as a writer except that you've earned a C+, which, depending on the kind of expectations you have, can be either devastating or exhilarating. We need task-specific, timely feedback on our writing during the practice stage so we can make the kind of changes that matter. If you're not getting that, you're not learning how to write.

Once you have a full draft, you're ready for someone to take a look at the whole thing to give you feedback on your rhetorical goals so far. (Again, you'll likely want feedback all the way through the project, even from the planning stage.)

We're lucky to have other people who are willing to give us feedback. Peers and teachers and tutors can help us think about what it's like to read our work. They *dramatize* the audience experience for us and offer us direction for revision. But only if we help them help us.

Sometimes when people find out I teach writing, they will ask me to look at something they've written. "Tell me what you think," they'll say. That could mean, like, a hundred different things. "What do I think about... what?" I'll ask. "The topic? The intro? The way the writing is organized? The cunning double-spacing? The use of the word 'plethora' on page three?" Much of the time, they're just looking for a proofreader, because they assume that's what writing teachers were invented for. What I'm wanting as an inspector is some kind of direction. And your reviewers will want some, too.

Here are a few principles to consider as you prepare to give a teacher or peer a draft to review.

1. **Tell them what you're trying to accomplish.** Give them answers to questions like: Why am I writing? Who is my audience, as I imagine them? What am I trying to do, and why?

2. **Give them a brief self-assessment of your draft.** You may want to tell them what you think you're doing well ("I feel like my organization is clear and my transitions are effective...") and where you're most unsatisfied with the draft as it stands ("...but my conclusion is weak—I don't suggest any meaningful implications and my wrap-up seems too obvious, too boring"). This exercise will help you learn whether your assessment of your own work agrees with your readers' assessment of it.

3. **Give them specific tasks as readers.** Give the reviewer some directives, like "Please look at page three where I try to do X" or "Please

feel free to cross out any material that you think is redundant," or ask questions like, "How does my organization work for you?" or "Where are you the most confused or bored?" or "Have I sufficiently persuaded my audience of X—why or why not?" or "What's your favorite part of my paper?" Notice how these questions avoid simple yes/no answers. You can also tell them what *not* to pay attention to (e.g., "Ignore the way I've cited the sources; I'm still working on my APA formatting").

When you receive feedback, you'll be tempted to defend your writing decisions if you disagree with the reviewers. It's natural to be defensive about our darling sentences, but it's not really helpful. You don't need to confront your reviewers; it burns goodwill if you look like you can't take criticism of your work. Thank them for their insights, and consider their feedback seriously. We suffer from *myside bias*, which is a condition in which we think we're right about most things because, hey, we're awesome. Just take all the feedback into consideration, knowing that ultimately you are the owner of your own writing and you'll have to depend on your intuition and understanding to get your writing as good as it can be.

One last note on getting feedback: I suggest that you consider planning separate review periods for *rhetorical* issues (relating to audience, purpose, argument, genre, organization—overall effectiveness) and *surface-level* issues (like grammar, usage, punctuation, diction, spelling, mechanics, or document design). Proofreading an unconvincing paper is like painting a car with no engine or wheels. I encourage you to tell your first reviewer(s) to ignore surface-level issues as they read, since you'll likely revise your sentences in the next stage, based on their feedback. Consider asking for feedback in two stages: for macro issues (like genre, argument, support, organization) and then separately for micro issues (like grammar, punctuation, or word choice). Of course sentence-level issues build into the overall effectiveness of the paper; in practice, it's hard to separate the two, and if you have too many errors, your reviewer will have a difficult time providing macro feedback because of all those speed bumps.

Practice: Feeling the Flow

In the practice stage of the writing process, we put our plans into action. We set out to achieve the goals we made for ourselves. My hope is that once you're knee-deep in the drafting process, you'll feel an emotional connection to your work, even if you weren't that excited about it at the start. You'll see the words fill the page and feel a sense of accomplishment, even as you know you'll end up scrapping half of those words. Psychologists talk about how when we're in the "flow" of an activity like writing that's challenging, governed by clear goals, and rich with useful feedback on our performance, we're in an "optimal experience"—the kind that makes time melt away, the kind that brings us joy (Csikszentmihalyi 71). At times, you'll feel this flow as a writer, especially when you write each day, with no other distractions.

Works Cited

Csikszentmihalyi, Mihaly. *Flow: The Psychology of Optimal Experience.* NY: Harper Perennial, 1990.

Duarte, Nancy. *Slide:ology*. Beijing: O'Reilly, 2008. Print.

Elbow, Peter. "Closing My Eyes as I Speak: An Argument for Ignoring Audience." *College English* 49.1 (1987): 50–69.

Hayes, John R. "New Directions in Writing Theory." *Handbook of Writing Research*. Ed. Charles A. MacArthur, Steve Graham, and Jill Fitzgerald. NY: Guilford, 2006. 28–40.

Kellogg, Ronald T. "Training Writing Skills: A Cognitive Developmental Perspective." *Journal of Writing Research* 1.1 (2008): 1–26.

Kellogg, Ronald T. and Alison P. Whiteford. "Training Advanced Writing Skills: The Case for Deliberate Practice." *Educational Psychologist* 44.4 (2009): 250–266.

Kerouac, Jack. "Essentials of Spontaneous Prose." *The Portable Beat Reader*. Ed. Ann Charters. 57–8. Print.

Lamott, Anne. *Bird by Bird*. NY: Anchor, 1995. Print.

Rose, Mike. "Rigid Rules, Inflexible Plans, and the Stifling of Language: A Cognitive Analysis of Writer's Block." *College Composition and Communication* 31.4 (1980): 389–401.

04

REVISION

The third dimension for handling writing tasks (after planning and practice) is *revision*. And it's *painful*.

Well, not necessarily. It's just that because writing is a challenging cognitive task—your central executive working overtime to coordinate planning, finding ideas, forming sentences, monitoring what you've written—we feel like our sweat has been in vain if we have to change what we've put on the page. We become attached to what we've written—so much so that revising feels like we're "murdering our darlings," as nineteenth-century author Arthur Quiller-Couch put it. And yet if we want to improve, we have to be willing to take the wrecking ball to our writing in the service of success. Revision takes courage. Annie Dillard—a writer like you—thinks of writing like a hammer tapping at the walls of a house you're trying to build:

> Some of the walls are bearing walls; they have to stay, or everything will fall down. Other walls can go with impunity; you can hear the difference. Unfortunately, it is often a bearing wall that has to go. It cannot be helped. There is only one solution, which appalls you, but there it is. Knock it out. Duck. (4)

Revision is reseeing. It's also rewriting in the sense that you get a do-over before you publish your work or turn it in or give it to your boss or post it on the Web. As a mindful writer, you'll need effective *task schemata* for revising. A *schema* is a plan or theory about something; *schemata* is the plural. Developing writers have limited task schemata when it comes to revision. After they've written a draft, they focus mostly on "surface features" rather than concepts, making limited changes to "spelling, punctuation, and word choice" (McCutchen, Teske, and Bankston 455). In one study, young adult writers spent most of their revision time proofreading and actually missing many existing errors in the process (Perl). In another study, students understood revision mostly as "a rewording activity" that left the overall shape and meaning of the writing intact (Sommers 381).

Revision, though, should mean more than merely proofreading your paper with a thesaurus in your hand. Skilled writers tend to think beyond the surface: They want to know whether they've been effective rhetorically. Revision is the process by which we evaluate the full force of our writing, top to bottom, as it influences a particular audience. And in that process, sometimes you have to take a sledgehammer to your own work. As Annie Dillard said, "Knock it out. Duck."

Because the writing process is recursive, you'll be revising the second you put a single word on a page, and even before that. You'll brainstorm an idea on scratch paper, and then maybe crumple up that idea and toss it over your shoulder. You'll write a few sentences and then think, "That sounds absolutely idiotic" and erase them. You'll see errors appear in a sentence you're writing, and instead of finishing the sentence you'll stop typing and reach for the mouse and go back and make corrections. You can't help it. While you want to shut off that annoying mental editor in the drafting stage, you also want to remain mindful enough to make adjustments and improvements as you write. When I'm drafting, I'll usually read (sometimes out loud) what I wrote the day before, making changes as I go.

However, in the last chapter I encouraged you to draft as quickly as you can in the practice stage without worrying much about missteps. Let yourself get into a writing groove before your central executive gets too picky, or some of your best ideas might disappear before landing on the page, like a spring snowflake that never makes it to the pavement. In the early stages, let your ideas flow out of you without interruption.

In this chapter, I'm talking about the kinds of changes you make once you've received feedback from instructors, peers, and others.

Approaching Revision

Revision is a second chance—and a third, fourth, fifth—to do your best, most engaging work. Revision, remember, is not really for you; it's for your audience of readers who are ready to engage with your ideas. An audience-centered writer will spend more time revising than a novice writer who may think of revision as nothing more than proofreading. An effective approach to revision will include the following:

1. **Read (or listen to) feedback carefully and respectfully**. Make sure you understand what your reviewers want you to do, and then decide what to pay attention to and what to ignore. Not all the advice you receive will work for your project. Give it all a fair hearing, though—especially the feedback you receive from your instructor. Ignoring instructor feedback tells your teacher, "I know better

than you." Maybe you do, but that's a bold statement to make, and it might damage your *ethos*. (More about *ethos* in chapter eight.) If you receive feedback face to face, repeat the feedback to make sure you understand it, and then jot down notes (preferably on the draft) to remind yourself what needs to change. Some instructors tell writers to say nothing while peer reviewers provide oral feedback; just listen and take notes. Keep yourself open to feedback, always.

2. **Make a *revision plan*.** Now that you've planned and practiced and received feedback, you may find your plans need to change. Your revision plan may include revised product and self-regulating goals based on the feedback you receive. Your instructor might even ask you to write a revision plan and share it.

Revision Strategies

You'll want to respond to the feedback you got from peers and instructors. As you develop a revision routine that works for you, consider the following possible strategies:

1. Use the "**track changes**" option in your word processor, so you can keep track of the revisions you make and review them when you're done.

2. Ask yourself the "**big picture**" **questions** first: How effectively have I achieved my purpose or answered the needs of the assignment? Is my purpose or main point clear to my audience? Have I used the genre effectively, considering the rhetorical situation and purpose? How will an audience experience my writing as a journey through an idea? Do I sound like a reasonable person—the kind of person who has authority, intelligence, balance, and goodwill? How do I keep my readers emotionally engaged with my work? How have I used my introduction to captivate and excite my audience? How does my conclusion answer the question, "So what?" Have I used enough evidence to support my main point? Your answers to these questions will guide revision decisions, from top to bottom.

3. Once you've settled on the big picture, look at **paragraphs**: Do they flow together well enough? Do they each develop one main point? Do they have internal coherence (in other words, do the first and final sentences connect, showing some kind of development)? Do the sentences lead into each other? Could any of the longer paragraphs be

broken apart and developed more effectively? Are they arranged in a way that makes sense, or could I rearrange them? I've found it helpful from time to time to print out what I'm writing and cut up my paper into paragraphs so I can look at them separately; you could also give the separated paragraphs to a friend and ask him or her to put the whole essay together using the first sentence of each paragraph as guides. (I notice many of my students draft with the double-spacing enabled from the beginning, maybe so they can feel like they're filling the page faster. I like to keep everything single-spaced so I can read the paragraphs more effectively as single units.)

4. **Add new material**, if necessary, **or cut.** You may sense that some of your writing is underdeveloped. Maybe you have a particularly weak paragraph or an argument that could use some support. Maybe you need more examples to make your case. Perhaps adding an image or table would be appropriate for the genre you're writing in. On the other hand, maybe you sense that you're boring your audience with too many details. Your sentences might be too long or too choked with clauses. You may find that some of what you've previously written seems irrelevant. Highlight, delete. Duck.

5. Review **sentences for style**. Read each sentence out loud to see how the words play in the open air. Use principles from chapters ten and eleven on style to help you refine your sentences. And, of course, remember that your style will be influenced by your audience and purpose. Ask yourself: Do my sentences come in a variety of lengths? Do I write mostly in active voice, with clear subjects and verbs? Do I avoid starting too many sentences with the same grammatical constructions? Is there an interesting person behind those words—in other words, can my readers *hear* a human voice? Have I been, at times, *bold*? Are my key terms defined well enough?

6. Once you're satisfied with the way your sentences sound, then you can move into **editing and proofreading.** Read each sentence carefully, with a handbook at your elbow in case a rule is unclear. Have someone else look at it, too (like a Writing Center tutor or a trusted friend). Check to see if you've followed the conventions and document design principles your instructor wants you to follow for the assignment. If you didn't receive document design requirements, then make some design decisions that will make your work distinct. At this

point, you're doing the down-in-the-grass detail work because you want to project the best, most convincing self you can in the writing.

If writing is like problem-solving, then the best problem-solvers will try new strategies in their writing if they learn that what they tried first didn't work well. Bad writers—and I include here writers who think they're so amazing they don't need to change anything—will stick with what they're doing, even if it's not working (Ambrose et al. 199). I'm inviting you here to be flexible enough in your writing process to develop some good task schemata for revision—the kind that knock down walls and kill darlings, if necessary.

We've now covered three of the four steps for handling writing tasks—plan, practice, revise. The fourth step—reflect—we'll talk about in the next chapter.

Works Cited

Ambrose, Susan A. et al. *How Learning Works: Seven Research-Based Principles for Smart Teaching*. San Francisco: Jossey-Bass, 2010.

Dillard, Annie. *The Writing Life*. NY: Harper Perenniel, 1989.

McCutchen, Deborah, Paul Teske, and Catherine Bankston. "Writing and Cognition: Implications of the Cognitive Architecture for Learning to Write and Writing to Learn." *Handbook of Research on Writing*. Ed. Charles Bazerman. NY: Lawrence Erlbaum, 2008. 452–470.

Perl, Sondra. "The Composing Processes of Unskilled College Writers." *Research in the Teaching of English* 13.4 (1979): 317–336.

Sommers, Nancy. "Revision Strategies of Student Writers and Experienced Adult Writers." *CCC* 31.4 (1980): 378–388.

REFLECTION

The Stories We Tell Ourselves

When I was in sixth grade, tragedy struck. No, I'm not talking about the one time I defended Tawni Bell's honor and got the tar beaten out of me by Ben Eason. I'm talking about math.

I was never not good at math. That's my double-negative way of saying that I did OK in math but never thought of myself as a "Math Person." But in sixth grade, I started falling behind. Long division and percentages did me in. Mr. Meldrum would toss a worksheet on my desk, and I'd stare at it, my gut sinking to the floor with the weight of woe. My friend Jeremy, who sat next to me, would race through his worksheet with dizzying speed, while I sat there, frozen, my pencil hovering over the numbers, wondering why my brain had stopped working.

Mr. Meldrum noticed my slide and sent me down the hall to Ms. Dawn's fifth-grade class for math. I'd been demoted. When that happened, I injected a little poison into my brain by telling myself, *I'm not good at math.*

It amazes me how utterly convincing that sentence was. It rang so true to me at the time that it took on the power of an identity: Brian Jackson—*not* a Math Person! It did not occur to me to tell myself alternative statements that might have been equally convincing, like *Looks like you'll need to work a little harder,* or *I'm not getting percentages—maybe Jeremy can explain the concept to me,* or *Math is hard for me, but I like trying hard things.*

In other words, I had no metacognitive tools to help me work through my math difficulties. I told myself one thing, believed it, and never questioned the validity of it until many years later, well after high school, when I took an exam—the Graduate Record Examination (GRE)—that included math problems.

The first time I took the GRE, I scored somewhere close to the 25th percentile on the math portion. (That means 75% of test-takers scored higher than me.) My low score didn't surprise me—after all, I was not a Math Person—and since my graduate program in English didn't care how well I did on the math part, I didn't either. However, two years later when I took it again for a new graduate program, I decided to study the math stuff out of pure vanity; I didn't want a low score again, even if the schools I applied to ignored the scores. I studied the math, and when I scored in the 65th percentile (not great, but mathematically above average), I had a new thought jump into my brain, revising the old thought I had in sixth grade, the toxic thought that told me I wasn't good at math: *I can do math if I study.*

It wasn't until later that I discovered the cognitive science behind my struggle with math. It turns out that none of us sees the world as objectively as we think. Rather, we see it through *interpretation*, through the way we perceive events and make sense of them to ourselves. University of Virginia psychologist Timothy Wilson explains this process with the word *narrative*: We tell ourselves stories about ourselves, our abilities, our relationships, our world. These stories become "*core narratives*" that influence our behavior, helping us overcome adversity and find happiness in the challenges of life (Wilson 9). Our core narratives can hurt us, too.

As I've said before, improving your writing is a challenge. It takes motor control, substantial cognitive effort, and our best creativity to connect with people and influence their attitudes, judgment, and behavior. Our ability to take control of the available means of persuasion is influenced by the way we understand ourselves as writers. Our core narratives influence our writing identities, and those identities influence our writing performance.

Luckily, our core narratives can be *revised*, just like a college essay. Dr. Wilson calls this process "*story-editing*," which he describes as "a set of techniques designed to redirect people's narratives about themselves and the social world in a way that leads to lasting changes in behavior" (11). Story-editing happens through reflective writing. In fact—and I was amazed when I read about this—scientific studies prove that reflective writing helps sufferers of post-traumatic stress disorder, personal tragedy, anxiety, depression, racial prejudice, failure in school, struggling marriages, unhealthy pessimism, low self-esteem, and criminal tendencies (see Bolton; Kost-Smith et al.; Pennebaker; Wilson). Writing is, indeed, a powerful source for good in the world.

This chapter is meant to help you shape a core narrative about your identity as a writer. Remember that *reflection* is the fourth stage of our model for taking on writing tasks (see chapter two). Reflection is the process by which we think about what we're doing, why we're doing it, and how we're doing; reflective writing is the process by which we put those thoughts in writing in a personal, informal style (Yancey 6).

Reflective writing is the ultimate act of *mindfulness*. When we write about our goals, processes, successes, and failures, we "open a conversation" with ourselves, as Ken Bain writes in *What the Best College Students Do*. We learn about the "power of our own paradigms"—the mental frames of reference that shape our experience (Bain 67, 71). We can sort of jump outside our bodies and view our own rhetorical situations with a higher degree of awareness.

Reflective writing strengthens your *self-efficacy* as a writer. Reflection builds confidence; confidence strengthens our writing. Self-efficacy is the term writing experts use to describe how we think about our abilities as writers—our competencies, our weaknesses, our willingness to try hard things, our goals, our sense that the writing we do has value (Bandura). The higher the self-efficacy, the higher the writing proficiency. Writing students with high self-efficacy work harder, persist when the going gets tough, and bounce back more quickly when they fail (Pajares and Valiante). They're also more eager to write and rewrite. Reflective writing helps you assess situations, set goals (both product and self-regulating), and practice with the confidence that you'll succeed as a writer if you write consistently and seek help. Reflective writing helps you balance between the confidence you need to write well and the humility you need to learn new skills. (Yes, *overconfidence* is a debilitating core narrative. I've taught many students who think of first-year writing as a remedial class they don't need. Low grades convince them that they do.)

Finally, reflective writing helps you take control of your own learning, becoming a *self-directed learner*. When I started struggling with math in sixth grade, I let the system wash me down the hall to an easier math class. I had no sense that I could take charge of my own fate, that I could, in fact, become a Math Person if I wanted to. Self-directed learners control their own learning (Ambrose 188–216). Self-direction is the engine of our four-part writing task model (plan, practice, revise, reflect). As Timothy Wilson writes, "it helps to view ourselves as strong protagonists who set our own goals and make progress toward them" (51). We become that personal hero through reflective writing.

The Art of Reflection

So: How do we do it? Your instructor will have some guidelines. I have a few suggestions, too. I've found it helpful to think of reflective writing like Kathi Yancey does in *Reflection in the Writing Classroom*: the art of *projecting* on future tasks and *reviewing* what has been accomplished already. I want you to think of reflection not simply as an afterthought to the writing process—a 200-word busywork thing you dash off after finishing your final draft—but as integral to the entire process. You want reflective writing to catch you in the act of thinking, like you'd catch a bird in flight with a really good camera.

Below you'll find questions you might answer with reflective writing to project and review. You'll recognize some of these questions from chapter two on writing plans and processes.

Projecting

1. **Assignment questions**: What does my instructor want me to do? What key words from the assignment sheet do I need to understand to be successful? What due dates do I need to be aware of? What technology will I be required to use as I write? What kind of reading will I need to get done? How will my writing be evaluated?

2. **Rhetorical situation**: Who is my audience? How *specific* is my audience, based on the writing prompt? What do I know about the values, needs, or attitudes of my audience? What is the exigence and *kairos* for writing? What is my purpose for writing? What rhetorical strategies will be most effective in this situation?

3. **Genre**: What is the genre I'm being asked to write? Is it a specific genre familiar to a specific discourse community? How will I collect and analyze examples of this genre? What moves do I need to make? What do readers of this genre expect? How do audiences, readers, or communities use this kind of writing? Which conventions must I follow? What kind of style is appropriate? How much freedom do I have to innovate? How do I need to format or arrange my writing for this genre? What purpose does this genre serve for the audience for which it's intended?

4. **Prior experience**: What kind of writer am I? How is this writing like writing I've done in the past? What can I use from previous writing experiences to help me with this one? How is it *not* like previous writing tasks? How much do I already know about this topic? How familiar am I with this genre? How has my writing process in the past helped or hurt my success?

5. **Ability**: How confident do I feel about tackling *this specific* writing task? What do I need to do to get more confident? What are my

strengths or weaknesses as a writer? Who can help me along the way? If I'm already confident in my abilities, what will I do to prepare to receive feedback that might tell me I've got more to learn?

6. **Personal value**: What do I want to get out of this assignment? What will this writing teach me how to do that will be valuable to me? How will I use this writing task to improve? Why am I interested in this topic? How can I get interested in this topic?

7. **Product goals**: After looking at examples of this genre, what specific rhetorical strategies will I use in my own writing? How will I imitate examples of the genre I've studied? How will I add my own creativity, my own voice? How will I use strategies explicitly stated in the rubric for this assignment?

8. **Self-regulating goals**: Where am I going to write? When will I write, and for how long? How will I minimize distractions when writing in digital spaces? How will I reward myself for getting the writing done? Who will I talk to about my task? Who will I show drafts to? How and when will I use my instructor, peers, or the Writing Center as reviewers of my work?

Reviewing

(For after you've written a draft or completed a writing task.)

1. **Goals**: How did I do with the goals I set as a writer? Why didn't I achieve my goals? Which goals were most useful to me? Which didn't really help?

2. **Rhetorical decisions**: Why did I make the rhetorical decisions I did? What in my writing demonstrates my awareness of audience? To what extent have I achieved my purposes for writing? Why did I pick the rhetorical strategies I did? How did I use genre effectively or ineffectively?

3. **Quality**: Where in the writing do I feel most confident? Where am I weakest? What would I change if I had more time? If I had a rubric for this assignment, how would I rate my writing with the rubric? What am I most proud of? Where in the writing do I feel I'm most engaging, interesting, clever?

4. **Writing processes**: What writing process did I use to write this? How well did it work for me? What needs to change, moving forward? What

invention strategies did I use, and how well did they serve me? How useful to me were my peer reviewers or instructor feedback? How could I better prepare my reviewers in the future? How thoroughly did I revise this work based on the feedback I received? How carefully did I proofread and edit my draft when completed?

5. **What I learned**: What did I learn from this writing task? What was the hardest part? What's something new I'm taking away from it? What part of the process interested me the most? What is my *theory* of writing now? What did my instructor do to help me learn?

6. **How I'll apply what I learned**: How will I apply what I learned from this writing task to future writing tasks (in my major, for example, or in the workplace)? What in my planning, practicing, or revising needs to change next time I write? What new goals will I want to set?

I hope you're convinced now that being an effective writer means much more than just sitting down and writing the first thing that comes to mind the day before the writing is due. Mindful writers plan, practice, revise, and reflect. They relish the process. Reflective writing will help you grow mindful as a writer, develop self-efficacy, and take control of your own learning.

I'm so glad I decided to study the math portion of the GRE the second time around. Studying made me realize that if I put some time into it, I could figure it out enough to at least not embarrass myself. Now that I have kids struggling with math, I've learned how to help them write a different core narrative about themselves—one that depends on what Carol Dweck calls the "growth mindset." I learned that math ability, like writing ability, is not something DNA does or does not hand down to me. Maybe Jeremy was better than me at math, but that didn't mean I couldn't be a Math Person. I hope reflective writing helps you develop that core narrative about your writing identity so that you think of yourself as a *writer*.

Works Cited

Ambrose, Susan A. *How Learning Works: Seven Research-Based Principles for Smart Teaching*. San Francisco: Jossey-Bass, 2010.

Bandura, Albert. "Self-Efficacy: Toward a Unifying Theory of Behavioral Change." *Psychological Review* 84 (1977): 191–215. Print.

Bolton, Gillie, ed. *Writing Cures: An Introductory Handbook of Writing in Counseling and Therapy*. London: Routledge, 2004. Print.

Dweck, Carol. *Mindset*. NY: Ballantine, 2006.

Kost-Smith, Lauren E. et al. "Gender Differences in Physics I: The Impact of Self-Affirmation Intervention." *AIP Proceedings* 197 (2010). Web. 10 March 2015.

Pajares, Frank and Gio Valiante. "Self-Efficacy Beliefs and Motivation in Writing Development." *Handbook of Writing Research*. Ed. Charles A. MacArthur, Steve Graham, and Jill Fitzgerald. NY: Guilford, 2006. 158–170. Print.

Pennebaker, J. W. *Writing to Heal: A Guided Journal for Recovering from Trauma and Emotional Upheaval*. Oakland, CA: New Harbinger Publications, 1997. Print.

Wilson, Timothy D. *Redirect*. NY: Back Bay, 2011. Print.

Yancey, Kathleen Blake. *Reflection in the Writing Classroom*. Logan, UT: Utah State UP, 1998. Print.

PART II

Acting Rhetorically

06

THINKING RHETORICALLY

This chapter is about rhetorical theory, which is another way of saying rhetorical *thinking*. By the end of this chapter, you should understand what it means to be a rhetorical thinker. Rhetorical thinkers know how to handle life.

Rhetorical thinking, you'll remember (or not—but here I am, reminding you), is one of our six domains of writing expertise. Learning to think rhetorically is one of the most important things you'll learn in college.

Don't be intimidated by the word *theory*—or, for that matter, *rhetoric*. You're already crazy about theory. A theory is just a set of assumptions, ideas, or values that help us understand something or do something. When I tell my four year-old daughter Charlotte to hum "Twinkle, Twinkle Little Star" two times while brushing her teeth, I'm expressing a theory about how much time a child should spend brushing her teeth. You probably have theories about text-message etiquette, optimal study habits, why political discourse is so toxic, why we pay attention to celebrities like Miley Cyrus, why new Xbox games are incompatible with the old Xbox, what a third date means, or what life itself means. You're a theory machine.

Since humans are restless pattern-seekers, we use theories to help us deal with the constant stream of life. Think of a theory as a set of goggles you look through—goggles with tinted lenses that paint the world in a certain light. Theories help us explain, appreciate, analyze, classify, predict, interpret, and evaluate. But most importantly, theories help us *practice* life. In the first five chapters, I have been building a theory of how to think about writing as a socially embedded, mindful process. Rhetorical theory can help you explain, appreciate, analyze, classify, predict, interpret, and evaluate writing experiences. In helping you understand this theory, I hope I've given you equipment for better living.

It's important to note, too, that theories are kind of like propositions or arguments. Some are better (i.e., more supported by experience or evidence) than others. When we say *evolution* is a theory, we're not saying it is not true; we're saying that the theory of evolution is a coherent integration of assumptions, ideas, or values that help us understand natural selection and the origin of species. It's a well-established, convincing theory built from thousands of observations, experiments, and conclusions. I'm not saying that theory is the opposite of truth or fact.

Rhetorical theory is important because it can help you understand and respond well to *any* situation that requires you to communicate. Remember in chapter two that we talked about how to make writing more effective by strengthening the central executive—that part of your working brain responsible for demanding tasks like writing. Rhetoric helps us do that by helping us think through the situations in which we write. Rhetorical thinking helps us approach communication with understanding, with purpose, with mindfulness.

So we need to do two things in this chapter: We need to define rhetoric and then set up a theory of rhetoric that will help you write more effectively whenever you need to write.

Rhetoric

Several years ago, a good friend of mine who was studying to be a chaplain in the Army received a letter from the United States military calling him to service in Iraq, where there was still a sizeable U.S. military presence. The timing was unfortunate: He was almost finished with his degree, and deployment would disrupt his progress to graduation and create a burden on his wife and two children. So my friend decided to write a letter asking that his tour of duty be deferred until he could finish his degree.

Imagine you're in his shoes for a moment. What are you going to write? (I'll tell you what happened to him in the next chapter.)

My guess is you've had such moments in your life—moments when your ability to write or speak might change everything for you. (Ever had to write a cover letter for a job or an essay for college admissions—or a declaration of love, or an email to angry family members?) *Rhetoric* is the study of such moments. It's also the study of the thousands of far less grand moments, like the time a few days ago when I drew a smiley-face on a text to my sister so she'd know I was joking.

Skilled writers understand that rhetoric is **the study and art of effective communication,** especially the kind of communication meant to influence others. Notice I said *both* the study *and* the art: Rhetoric refers to the study (i.e., the theories, research projects, or experiences) of effective communication, and its art (i.e., the way people actually use it through purposeful strategies). Communication can be writing, of course, but it can also be other symbolic behavior like body language, artistic composition, even architecture or gardening, if we think of gardening as the means someone uses to create experiences for someone else. Rhetoric is the study and art of any effort by someone to use symbols (like language) to connect with another human being to influence their experience in some way.

The word *rhetoric* comes to us from the Greek word *rhetor*, for "speaker." A *rhetor* was someone who spoke to other assembled citizens in ancient Greece about problems they all shared. Some ancient philosophers—let's call them *rhetoricians*, people who study rhetoric—studied how people spoke and to what effect so the art could be taught as a general theory of communication. They wanted to make money of course—who doesn't?— but they also wanted to give potential speakers real power to promote shared values, to entertain and delight, to change the course of history with words. Aristotle (384–322 BCE), one of the most important philosophers of all time, shares his thinking on this subject in a book titled *On Rhetoric*, in which he gives us a definition: "Let rhetoric be defined as an ability, in each particular case, to see the available means of persuasion" (Aristotle 37).

Aristotle used the word *persuasion*. What does that word mean to you? I've found it useful to think of rhetoric as the study of how attitudes are influenced by words—that's persuasion to me. Our attitudes are *judgments* about things. Judgments are products of experience: what we see, hear, and feel. Each day we're making and keeping judgments, and those judgments become attitudes. We use persuasion when we want to influence the attitudes of others.

Remember the guy I mentioned in the first chapter who sat in front of me during that meeting when I was rude? I'm sure he left the meeting feeling like I was an annoying jerk. He had a bad attitude about me, formed by his judgment of my behavior. But that's not the end of the story. When I saw him in the hall a week later, I went straight up to him and said, "I'm sorry I was so annoying during that meeting. I just wasn't thinking." He seemed surprised, and then *he* apologized to *me* for turning on me so sternly. Apparently we'd both been concerned about the attitude the other guy had for us, and we both apologized in order to improve that attitude. Maybe subconsciously I thought that tweaking his attitude about me would help me achieve my goal for living harmoniously with others and not getting punched in the face. That's the goal of rhetoric: influencing attitudes through communication to achieve our goals.

This turns out to be tricky. Our attitudes, especially for things about which we care deeply, are hard to change. In *The Righteous Mind*, psychologist Jonathan Haidt explains that our moral judgments (about abortion, for example) are often formed by subconscious emotional responses we make rapidly and without much thought (40). Once these judgments form, they can become immune to change, even when good reasons to change are presented. If we have a strong intuition about something— say, that the federal government should redistribute wealth—anything that tells us differently creates what social psychologist Leon Festinger called "cognitive dissonance." Cognitive dissonance makes us uncomfortable because it makes us feel inconsistent inside; we don't want to be wrong or look stupid. That's just human nature. So we avoid considering evidence that runs contrary to our attitudes. (A college education, by the way, is supposed to help us get over the cognitive dissonance problem and actually embrace full-on frontal assaults to our attitudes through reason, rhetorical analysis, and reflection. Thanks, college!)

What powerful rhetoric can do is trigger a re-evaluation process in an audience; it can trigger "new intuitions" that help us see things "in a new light or from a new perspective" (Haidt 47). Rhetoric is most effective, writes Haidt, when laced with empathy—when a speaker can make an emotional connection with an audience through goodwill and love (68— more on empathy in chapter eight). Of course there are many issues about which we do not care so deeply. When we moved into a house in Provo, Utah, a guy came around selling water softeners. He told me that a water softener system would help keep our pipes from calcifying and would reduce soap scum in showers and on washed dishes. And I said, OK, then: Give me some of that soft water magic. That's how easy it was to sell me on a water softener. I didn't have a strong opinion (or any opinion) about it. *And* I thought his reasons were good reasons.

People who understand how rhetoric works (the theory) and can use it effectively (the art) are powerful people. They influence the attitudes of other people and change the course of history. By signing up for this writing course, you've accepted the challenge to become one of those people. This chapter is about how rhetoric works (the theory), and subsequent chapters will help you improve the way you use it (the art).

The Rhetorical Situation

Since I've already told you one embarrassing story about myself (i.e., the time I talked through that one meeting), I'll tell another.

In sixth grade I had a friend named Jesse who was the youngest of four kids. One spring day I was over at his house after school, just lounging around on the living room carpet doing nothing, like we usually did, while his mother and father helped his oldest sister Sheri inspect a beautiful black dress she planned to wear to her senior graduation. Sheri twirled in the dress in front of a tall, slim living room mirror and beamed at herself, her parents beaming next to her. I don't remember how it happened, but suddenly all three looked down at us, as if asking for our opinion, as if twelve year-old boys could have meaningful opinions about graduation dresses.

And without thinking, I said: "Looks like you're going to a funeral."

I think I was trying to make a joke through associational thinking: Black dress = funeral. Yeah, it's not funny now, and it wasn't funny then. Jesse's dad—a tall, bald, goateed, muscled veteran of the Vietnam War who was fond of martial arts weaponry—gave me the most caustic scowl I've ever received. His mom and sister blasted me with crusties, too. And I felt my smile fade and my cheeks light up with shame.

How can rhetoric help us understand this disaster?

Let's start with the proposition that rhetoric occurs in *situations* or contexts where various aspects create meaning for all those involved. Let's call this instance from my childhood a *rhetorical situation*. The secret to understanding rhetorical thinking is understanding rhetorical situations. Each rhetorical situation has six interconnected forces:

Exigence

Usually rhetoric doesn't just happen—it's *called forth* by what rhetorical theorist Lloyd Bitzer calls **exigence**. (Notice that this term is *exigence*, with an "e" at the end, not *exigency* with a "y." Both mean essentially the same thing, but exigence is a rhetorical term, so let's geek out and go with it.) Bitzer defines an exigence as "an imperfection marked by urgency," which "strongly invites utterance" (Bitzer 5–6). Simply put, the exigence is the invitation to speak because speaking might solve a problem. When Jesse's father, mother, and sister looked down at us, they invited us to say something about the dress that might help Sheri feel confident and attractive. Exigences can be more or less demanding: If you receive a text from a friend accusing you of something you didn't do, you've received an exigence that demands a quick response. If a teacher asks the whole class, "What do you think about what we read for homework?", that's more of an invitational exigence, one that perhaps you can ignore and let someone else respond to. There are millions of heated online comment threads we can, and should, ignore; sometimes, though, we see an exigence and we write a comment.

At any rate, the exigence is the invitation to speak, the wrinkle in the universe that calls for someone to say something, to make something with clever words, to patch up the problem with prose. The exigence is the call to rhetoric.

Kairos

Connected to the idea of exigence is *kairos*, another aspect of a rhetorical situation. *Chronos*, as you probably know, is a Greek word meaning "time" (think of the word chronology). Kairos is different: it's a Greek word meaning "the opportune or fitting moment" for action. Kairos is less about minutes and hours and days and so on; it's about opportunity, timing, and desire—it's more about "psychological time" (Hauser 40). You're in the woods alone with your special someone. The moon floats full and luminescent above you, the snow crunches beneath your feet, and your conversation is intimate and free. Do you reach out for his hand—for the first time? Any moron can see that the moment is kairotic. But maybe he's shy. Maybe he has a funky skin disease and would be mortified. What about a kiss? If it's a first date? At what point in the conversation do you lean in? What in your history together leads you to this moment? Timing is everything! The student of rhetoric understands how the right words at the right time can influence the right people.

Rhetorical situations have life cycles that we create with our words, our arguments, our actions. When Civil Rights activists were pushing for racial equality in the United States in the 1960s, many sympathetic Southern white citizens felt that black leaders like Martin Luther King needed to cool their political activism and wait for racist attitudes to change, which they thought they would—eventually. White citizens felt that the moment wasn't kairotic to push for equal rights for African Americans. They feared pushing civil rights through even peaceful protests would lead to civil unrest, even violence, which it did. King and his associates disagreed; in fact in 1963 King wrote a book called *Why We Can't Wait* explaining why racial equality was an important kairotic rhetorical issue that, yes, could not wait—the opportune, fitting, appropriate rhetorical time, for King, was right then. Kairos, as you can see, is psychological rather than chronological in the sense that it is *debatable*: It is contested and determined by words rather than solar or atomic increments, or the face of a watch or cell phone.

You make an issue timely when you write about it; you just have to be sure your rhetorical watch is set to everyone else's, or you have to invite your audience to set their rhetorical watches to yours. You're also responsible to acknowledge what has been said before. Think, for example, about how timing plays a role when you enter a conversation at a party by listening to what other people have said before you to set the stage.

Rhetor

The third element in the rhetorical situation is the ***rhetor*** (pronounced like it rhymes with *better*)—the speaker or writer or creator of the message. In the case of my funeral comment fiasco, the rhetor is a twelve year-old white middle-class male—a fan of Bermuda shorts, Bon Jovi, and the 8-bit Nintendo, and friend and neighbor to Jesse. Now, Lloyd Bitzer thought the rhetor was significantly constrained by "the power of the situation" (11). For Bitzer, rhetors have to act within the bounds imposed by an exigence. Bitzer's critic Richard Vatz, on the contrary, believed that exigence was not an objective blunt force; its meaning and urgency are in fact interpreted by the rhetor who then helps the audience understand the exigence. When you are a rhetor, you analyze the situation and craft the message, but you're just one part of the rhetorical situation, as I discovered when I said Sheri's dress made her look like she was headed for a funeral. Being a rhetor gives you rhetorical power, but it's power only to the degree to which the message is kairotic (i.e., a fitting, timely response to the exigence) and the audience is open to the message.

The rhetor is the voice of the message—the perspective, the identity, the voice, the stance, the bias. In chapter 8, we'll talk more about how as rhetor you can wield convincing power by constructing a Self that your readers will recognize, and accept. There's this great moment early in the Broadway play *Hamilton* when Alexander Hamilton makes his grand debut in the late eighteenth century intellectual scene by answering the question, "Who are you?" with, "I'm just like my country, I'm young, scrappy, and hungry, and I'm not throwing away my shot." He wastes no time establishing himself as a formidable voice, a rhetor worthy of attention.

Purpose

Fourth, the rhetor has a *purpose*—what he or she intends to achieve by speaking or writing. It's been a while so my memory is foggy, but I think I was trying to be funny by saying Sheri's dress was funereal. To be clear, I was not trying to make fun of her dress. I wasn't that kind of kid. (The only person I made fun of, unfortunately, was my brother.) My twelve-year-old brain must have intended to make a connection with Jesse's family by pointing out what should have been obvious to everyone—that Sheri's dress was black, like the lacy dark shroud of Death itself. I wanted to enhance Jesse's family's attitude about me by making them see how clever I was, how quick with the "fun" associations. I did not suspect that my message would not achieve my purpose.

You can understand purpose by asking the following questions: How does the rhetor want to influence attitudes? What does he/she want the audience to feel, think, or do? What does he/she want to achieve? Why is he/she speaking/writing/composing? One way to discover a rhetor's purpose is to look carefully at the message and make assumptions about why the rhetor chose the strategies he/she did.

Genre

Which brings us to the fifth element, the **genre**. As we've already discussed, genres are not merely rigid forms of writing. They represent a sociological need. Let's go back to Professor Carolyn Miller's definition we saw on p. 20: Genres are "typified rhetorical actions based in recurrent situation." Let's unpack this definition from back to front.

Recurrent situations: Genres emerge from rhetorical situations that happen over and over in life. Someone has money; someone else wants it. The someone with money asks for a proposal arguing for the best way to spend that money. Someone dies. His loved ones gather to speak of his life and accomplishments. A dramatic political event occurs. Someone writes to the newspaper arguing a perspective on that event—a perspective the writer hopes will help other citizens make better judgments. Someone finds a cute way to decorate a cake. That someone shares a how-to video on YouTube.

Culture is all about patterns of behavior and experience. We've found that certain events—all with unique exigences—happen regularly.

Rhetorical actions: Recurring events call for responses. Writers use strategies they hope will be suitable to the situation. Funeral eulogies often call for rhetorical actions meant to inspire the living to live better. Grant proposals include budgets and schedules and arguments for financial need. Genres reflect rhetorical strategies meant to answer situational exigences. (And now you know what that fancy sentence means.)

Typified: We organize the world in patterns, or types. Genres harden into recognizable forms because those forms serve purposes for us. Websites include "About Us" links. Wikipedia entries begin with a summative paragraph on the topic. Academic essays blend outside sources with the writer's own voice. Some genres have fairly rigid formats (scientific journal articles); others breathe with creative life (personal essays). Genres represent fairly typical responses to everyday situations. They are texts in context.

Audience

Finally, and most importantly, we have the **audience**—the people who, according to Bitzer, "are capable of being influenced by discourse and of being mediators of change" (8). I say audience is the most important element because the audience holds what the rhetor wants to influence, the thing in which the entire rhetorical process culminates—the attitude. One of the cardinal principles of rhetorical theory is *Know Thy Audience*. If you understand what motivates your audience, what makes them tick, what their interests and needs and attitudes are, why they need the genre you're going to present them, then you'll have rhetorical power as a rhetor.

As a twelve-year-old, I had a pretty weak understanding of Jesse's mom, dad, and sister; and in fact, we'd been friends for just a few months, so they really didn't know me either and so they couldn't read my "funeral" comment in the way I intended it. I thought my audience would think better of me if I cracked a joke right then. But I also made this error: I assumed I understood enough about a teenage girl in a new dress to make a joke about said dress without sounding like a jerkface. Wow, I was dead wrong. And I didn't know *that* teenage girl at all. I'm surprised Jesse's dad didn't throw a ninja star into my forehead.

The idea of audience should be straightforward. You imagine someone speaking at a banquet, and the audience sits at round tables, their soiled cloth napkins crumpled next to empty plates, their heads nodding in agreement (or sleep). In such a case, the audience is clear. (The word audience comes down to us from the Latin word *audire*, to hear.) You send a text message to a buddy on his birthday, and he's your audience.

You talk to a friend at a party, and you look at her right in the face, and the audience smiles right back atcha.

But let's say, hypothetically, that you're in Mrs. E.'s third-grade class and you write a note intended for (let's make up a name) Stephanie Martinez praising (let's say) her curly brown hair and asking for her eternal affections, and then, hypothetically of course, while the folded-up letter is being passed from student to student to Stephanie, who sits on the other side of the room so that the outside light gives her chestnut skin an ethereal and sumptuous glow, it is intercepted by Mrs. E. who, let's pretend, is old and cranky all the time because of a spastic colon, and she opens your epistle of love while walking back to her desk and she decides—we'll just pick a likely punishment—to make you write your name with a check mark next to it on the board.

Is Mrs. E. now the audience for the love note? Yes. Was she the intended audience? Certainly not. She was, in fact, the last audience the (ahem, purely fictional) writer imagined would read the letter. What does this complication do to our theory of audience?

There are two problems with the concept of audience. First, it's hard to anticipate the way people will respond to anything we say because they're *not us*. Other people have different brains, chemicals, histories. Jim Morrison of the rock band the Doors said it best when he sang, "People are strange." Inventing things to say takes guts and imagination; we assume other people will appreciate what we have to say because we assume they're like us in some fundamental way. Rhetoric invites us to accept as an article of faith that other people are, to some degree, predictable enough that we can use strategies of persuasion with confidence. But still, rhetoric is a leap of faith we make with language; we hope that by some miracle we'll be not only understood but influential.

The second problem with audience is a problem related to the medium of writing. When we speak to someone, our eyes track their faces for responses. We look at their eyes, their lips, and their body. We can tell if they're interested or bored, or if we've offended or disgusted them or if they disagree with us, and we make little conversational adjustments to get back on track (Pinker 27). When Jesse's dad scowled at me, I felt it on every inch of my skin. We are exceptionally good at reading faces; we've been doing it since we were babies.

But when we write, we don't have that kind of feedback loop. When we write, our recipients "are invisible and inscrutable," writes Harvard psychologist Steven Pinker, "and we have to get through to them without knowing much about them or seeing their reactions. At the time that we write, the reader exists only in our imaginations" (28). We have to guess how a reader might respond, and sometimes we might guess wrong. Sometimes we'll never know whether or not we guessed wrong. As we discussed in chapter two, advanced writers can hold in their heads simultaneously their own ideas, the words they want to clothe those ideas in, and their "imagined reader's interpretation" of those ideas (Kellogg 5). Well, that kind of rhetorical thinking takes time. And it takes—make me proud, beat me to it!—metacognition.

So, when you write, you're challenged to hold in your mind an image of your readers, the kind of readers you hope will read you *and* read you the way you want to be read. Your text will reveal rhetorical decisions based on your assumptions about your audience—what you think about their attitudes, their desires, their judgments, and what you assume about your shared interests with them. The concept of imagined audience helps us accept the fact that sometimes we really don't know what an audience wants; in other words, that cardinal virtue we mentioned above (*Know Thy Audience*) is difficult to enact. We're trapped in our own bodies, with our own perspectives and prejudices. Who knows what will influence someone else's attitudes? When you write to apply for a job or for college admission or a scholarship, you're writing to people whose faces are blanks to you. And yet, you go ahead and make your best guess anyway.

Imagining audience, even audiences that we invoke or invent in our minds (see Lunsford and Ede; Ong), is a creative act, a "mark of cognitive maturity," as Irene Clark put it (111). Novice writers write "writer-based prose" (Flower)—that is, prose that represents the interests and needs of the writers themselves—because they can't represent in their minds or their texts the interests of the audience, or they choose not to (Kellogg). Writing is often boring because the writer isn't thinking about audience. The writer is like the one guy at the party, drink in hand, prattling on and on about trivia related to the new *Star Wars* movie, and he doesn't even notice that we've slipped into a coma. Imagining audience—and writing *reader*-based prose—is not only an act of cognitive maturity; it's an act of goodwill. (And we'll talk more about goodwill in chapter eight.)

However, it's worth noting here that online and social media writing has changed the way we think of audience. Now, more than ever in history, we get some sense of how audiences respond to our writing by comment threads, retweets, likes, stars, linkbacks (sometimes called pingbacks or trackbacks), text backs, and other connective love. But even then, we're still writing in the shadows. How representative of your full audience is a "like" or two?

Okay, you just leveled-up your game as a writer. We defined rhetoric as the study and art of effective communication. (You're studying it right now, so you can be more artful at it.) Effective communication, I suggested, is *persuasive*, which means that it influences someone's attitude and therefore behavior. Attitude is a *judgment* about something. Judgments are hard to change, but you're the kind of person to take on Mission Impossible.

Rhetorical thinking begins and ends in rhetorical situations: exigence, kairos, rhetor, purpose, genre, audience—all connected, all depending on each other to create meaning, all necessary for your success as a writer (i.e., a rhetor). By the end of this class, you should be able to rattle off these six parts of the rhetorical situation in your sleep. You now have a simple theory of communication that you can apply to any situation that calls on you to speak, write, create, act.

How are we feeling about all this? Good? Good.

Audiences—Take Your Pick

We're going to end this chapter by expanding on the notion of audience by addressing, briefly, nine kinds of audiences you may find in various rhetorical situations. Understanding these audiences will help you write to them, if the situation arises.

- **Discourse communities**—Various social groups have different ways to make knowledge and get stuff done. Discourse communities are composed of people with common interests, goals, vocabulary, and processes of inquiry (i.e., how they make knowledge through research, experiment, analysis, argument, etc.). When your college professors write articles, they're writing to specific discourse communities (like the American Psychological Association or the Society for French Historical Studies). When you advance in your major, you'll be asked to write as a member of a discourse community oriented to a discipline (like exercise science). Effective rhetors will know when they need to write in the language and style of a particular discourse community.

- **Publics**—As I wrote this chapter, a twenty-nine-year-old woman named Brittany Maynard, who suffered from malignant brain tumors, ended her life by drinking a lethal mixture of water and sedatives. A doctor in Oregon had prescribed the medication legally as part of a death-with-dignity treatment for the terminally ill. Before Brittany died, media outlets lit up with arguments about whether or not ending your life should be a right of all those who suffer terminal illnesses. Brittany's case became an exigence that various citizens responded to with their own arguments, directed to each other in blog posts, op eds, TV interviews, and dinner table conversations. A *public* is this collection of citizens (sometimes called stakeholders) that emerges through rhetorical exchange about a particular problem or issue. Since publics are rhetorical (rather than merely political or geographical), they form, function, and disappear as important issues are discussed and then discarded.

- **Users**—This term comes to us from computer science and refers to people who will interact with the text you have made, especially when a genre has an interactive component (like a website), some kind of navigable dimension (like a table of contents), or instructions to perform some kind of action (like the manual for your car).

- **Incidental or secondary audiences**—Back to the Mrs. E. incident I totally invented earlier. Remember, she was not the intended audience; she intercepted ~~my~~ the love note intended for Stephanie Martinez, the primary audience. Sometimes people overhear things not intended for them. Boyfriends get dragged to so-called chick flicks. Atheists stumble into evangelical tent revivals. Children play violent video games rated M by the Entertainment Software Rating Board. One time a girlfriend of mine wrote me a mushy email and sent it to her ex-boyfriend. (True story!)

We're going to call such audiences *incidental* or *secondary* audiences. Even though incidental audiences are not part of the original rhetorical situation, once they experience the text they form a *new* rhetorical situation, with a new exigence and kairos. If as a student you read Martin Luther King's "I Have a Dream" speech, you become a new audience, inviting King to influence your attitude from the grave.

The concept of incidental audience is especially important for us as readers because it invites us to stand in judgment of the enduring rhetorical value of a text. Perhaps King's call for racial justice can be kairotic over and over each time racial strife draws us into debates about race.

- **Decision-makers**—Straightforwardly: those who have power to act to do something the rhetor wants done. Think proposals (for grants, or for marriage).

- **Universal audience**—Immediate audiences often share the prejudices of the rhetor, and, in turn, the rhetor will often play directly to their prejudices by making arguments that no one outside a particular in-group would accept. You see this happen on talk radio and political programs and websites. However, a rhetorician named Chaim Perelman argued that sometimes people craft their rhetoric for a *universal audience*, meaning an imagined audience made up of "competent and reasonable" people who care whether or not an argument is valid for any thinking person, not just a biased in-group (14). The idea of such an audience is useful for saying something like, "Well, such-and-such message would persuade other members of the National Rifle Association, but it wouldn't convince a universal audience of smart, unbiased people!"

- **Evaluators**—are like teachers or peer tutors. Evaluators, though secondary audiences, help rhetors achieve their purposes. They help rhetors imagine how immediate or imagined audiences may respond to their genres. Your writing instructor, for example, will assign you a grade based on your rhetorical performance. I hope this is a relief to you because some writing students tell me that they feel like grading is an arbitrary whim of the instructor, based on whatever the instructor "likes" or their glucose levels. But an evaluator-audience is supposed to dramatize what reading your work would be like for your intended audience. My sense is that they can do that more effectively if you tell them, in a reflection, who you're writing to and what you're trying to do.

- **Friends/followers/fans**—New media and social media make it possible for us to create networks of people who are guaranteed to have only one thing in common: You. When you post a status update on Facebook, you're writing for an audience of (sometimes) hundreds of people with a variety of interests. It's hard to read this audience, for some people. (Ever unfriend someone because they post annoying or offensive things that do nothing for you as an audience?) And yet social media networks can lead to rhetorically rewarding exchanges motivated by interests that have nothing to do with school projects. And this is an audience that can flip the rhetorical situation by becoming rhetors and making *you* the audience.

- **Skeptics**—To sharpen your critical thinking as a rhetor, it's useful to think of your audience as people who may disagree with you or who aren't easily convinced by what you have to say. Their attitudes bend slightly away from you; you have to bend them back. How will you do that? Imagine your audience with a wry smile, their eyebrows pointing down in skepticism, an expression that seems to say, "I doubt it, but convince me!" Or: Maybe you imagine your audience being completely unmoved, but you're willing to at least chip away at their bias by presenting the best possible case for the opposition.

All this talk about audience is meant to get you thinking about your own rhetorical situations, both in school and out of school. You already know this, but it's challenging to think about rhetorical situation when you write for teachers. When you get an assignment to write something, you feel you've been placed in an artificial situation in which your purpose is to get an A on the paper, and the genre is a "research paper," and your audience—everyone knows—is the teacher who will grade the paper. It turns out that most writing assignments in secondary school and college are informative (as in, present some data about this or that) and written to "teacher-as-examiner" (Melzer 28). But even with these limitations, you can use your rhetorical knowledge and hold in your mind a vision of your audience, beyond your instructor, that works for your purposes. Every time you write, write to *engage* someone else in ideas and arguments that matter, even if your understanding of that "someone else" is a little fuzzy.

Rhetoric Goggles

My goal for this chapter was to define rhetoric and introduce you to a theory of rhetoric that will help you communicate more effectively by influencing the attitudes of others. I hope I've given you *rhetoric goggles*: You put 'em on, and everywhere you look, you see purposeful communication from rhetors trying to influence an audience with a well-crafted, and timely, genre meant to achieve some kind of purpose.

Frankly, I hope rhetorical theory will help you live better. When someone is trying to influence you, I hope you'll put on your Rhetoric Goggles so you can see the rhetorical situation more clearly.

I'd go even further to say that if you take only *one thing* with you from this book, I hope it would be a habit of rhetorical thinking. The next time an exigence creeps up on you and calls you to speak or write or create or compose or collaborate to make a text, I hope it'll be automatic for you to ask:

- Who am I as a rhetor?

- What is the exigence?

- What would be a fitting, timely, appropriate response?

- What is my purpose?

- What kind of a genre am I being asked to create?

- Who is my audience? What kind of audience are they?

Works Cited

Aristotle. *On Rhetoric: A Theory of Civic Discourse.* Trans. George A. Kennedy. 2nd ed. NY: Oxford, 2007. Print.

Bitzer, Lloyd F. "The Rhetorical Situation." *Philosophy and Rhetoric* 1 (1968): 1–14. Print.

Clark, Irene L. *Concepts in Composition.* NY: Routledge, 2012. Print.

Ede, Lisa and Andrea Lunsford. "Audience Addressed / Audience Invoked: The Role of Audience in Composition Theory and Pedagogy." *CCC* 35.2 (1984): 155–171. Print.

Flower, Linda. "Writer-Based Prose: A Cognitive Basis for Problems in Writing." *College English* 41.1 (1979): 19–37. Print.

Haidt, Jonathan. *The Righteous Mind.* NY: Pantheon, 2012. Print.

Hauser, Gerard. *Introduction to Rhetorical Theory.* 2nd ed. Prospect Heights, IL: Waveland, 2002. Print.

Melzner, Dan. *Assignments Across the Curriculum.* Logan: Utah State UP, 2014. Print.

Ong, Walter. "The Writer's Audience is Always a Fiction." *PMLA* 90.1 (1975): 9–21. Print.

Perelman, Chaim. *The Realm of Rhetoric.* Notre Dame UP, 1982. Print.

Pinker, Steven. *The Sense of Style.* NY: Viking, 2014. Print.

Vatz, Richard. "The Myth of the Rhetorical Situation." *Philosophy and Rhetoric* 6.3 (1973): 154–161. Print.

07

WRITING RHETORICALLY— ARGUMENT

Rhetorical Decisions Matter

In the last chapter, I told you about a friend of mine who was called by the military to serve in Iraq before he completed his schooling to become an army chaplain. I sort of left the story hanging there, so let me finish it. My friend decided to write the required petition letter asking the Army to defer his tour of duty so he could finish his degree. He sat down at the computer, like you yourself have done many times, and, like a good soldier, he *strategized*. With each sentence, he made rhetorical decisions that he thought would best help him influence his audience (i.e., change their judgment about the timing of his tour of duty). Maybe he wondered if he should play the sympathy card: *My family will suffer if I don't finish this degree!* Or perhaps he thought of appealing to the Army's self-interest: *Let me wait, and I'll be a more experienced and credentialed chaplain.* He probably chose his words and evidence carefully, proofreading his finished letter with precision so he wouldn't look sloppy.

Whatever he did, it worked. The Army granted his petition, and he completed his Master of Divinity and became a full-fledged chaplain when he deployed to Iraq months later.

This anecdote illustrates a great truth about rhetoric: Rhetorical decisions matter. They make a difference in the world. Rhetorical strategies open doors, soften hearts, change attitudes, loosen up funds, provoke minds, secure justice or mercy, entertain the bored, inform the ignorant, convince the skeptical, energize the faithful. Or, they don't. It's up to you.

In this book we discuss a variety of rhetorical strategies you'll want to consider when an exigence calls you to action. While there are many situations in which deliberate rhetorical thought is not required (at lunch with a best friend, perhaps), most opportunities to speak and write are opportunities to choose strategies mindfully that help you achieve your goals and make the world better.

Yes, I just said that rhetorical strategies make the world better. I can't help myself. Too many people believe that rhetoric is a tool for Voldemort-like evil. When graduate student Shannon Soper and I studied English corpora (a *corpus* is a collection of texts; *corpora* is the plural), we noticed that at least 75% of the time, the word *rhetoric* means unethical speech that is weak, false, or inflammatory. I call this the "rhetoric-as-poison" perspective, and I don't really know how rhetoric changed in popular usage from a powerful tool for communicators to a weapon of mass deception. When politicians talk about an opponent's "rhetoric," it's not a compliment.

But now you know better. And now you can help me spread the word. For starters, every intelligent person should understand that they use rhetoric all the time, and not just when they're being sneaky. Earlier I said that rhetoric is like dance in some ways—it's a universal human activity you find in nearly every culture, and it can be used for any purpose, good or ill. A few classical rhetoricians even argued that when you study rhetoric, you necessarily study how to be a good person and use rhetorical strategies for good in the world. (The missing *Avenger* superhero is Captain Rhetorician.) The Greek rhetorician Isocrates (436–338 BCE), for instance, believed that by practicing rhetoric, we "cultivate intellectual and moral character" based on "the values of the good and useful citizen" (Walker 121). Whether or not that's *necessarily* the outcome of studying rhetoric, it's certainly empowering to think of ourselves as moral agents learning to use strategies that will promote virtue and happiness.

What is needed the most, said the Roman statesman Cato (234–149 BCE), is the good person skilled in speaking (*Vir bonus, dicendi peritus*). That's you: Captain Rhetorician, defender of truth and justice.

Anyway, the strategies we'll talk about in the next few chapters represent centuries of experience with rhetorical influence. I'm not just making them up or passing along fossilized rules that worked for some tunic-wearing Greek guy 2500 years ago. The Roman orator Cicero (106–43 BCE)—perhaps the most famous rhetorician of all time—explained in his dialogue *On the Ideal Orator* that strategies find their way into textbooks like this one because "certain people have observed and collected the practices that eloquent men [and women] followed of their own accord. Thus, eloquence is not the offspring of art, but art of eloquence" (Cicero 90). In other words, the strategies I present in this book are tried-and-true influence strategies that come from actual practice. They're *useful*, in all kinds of settings. You'll find these strategies celebrated across cultures and disciplines. Modern science supports them as well. (Check out Robert Cialdini's book *Influence*, for example.)

Can you think of a more important subject to study, or art to master?

Selecting Appropriate Strategies

So, which strategies do we use—and when, and why?

Repeat after me: It depends on the rhetorical situation (your audience, purpose, exigence, etc.). My man Aristotle (384–322 BCE) defined rhetoric as "an ability in each particular case, to see the available means of persuasion" (37). Your means of persuasion are dizzyingly vast; even a font type speaks to your audience. If you want rhetorical vertigo, visit Gideon Burton's website *The Forest of Rhetoric* (rhetoric.byu.edu) where you can choose from hundreds of cool rhetorical moves to master.

Your instructor can walk you through this forest of rhetoric some time. In this text, I'm going to share with you the four *Biggies*; when you enter any new rhetorical situation, you'll want to **pull out your ACES:**

Argument

Character

Emotions

Style

Okay, acronyms are corny, and mostly forgettable. But let's give this one a go anyway. We'll spend some time on all four of these strategies because they're so useful. Anytime you sit down to solve a writing task, you'll want to have these strategies at your command. And: ACES will help you understand how other people use rhetoric as well.

The first three—the ACE of ACES—correspond to what you may know as *logos, ethos,* and *pathos*. These Greek terms come to us from Aristotle's *On Rhetoric*, a series of lectures he gave at the Lyceum, his school in fourth-century BCE Athens. In *On Rhetoric*, Aristotle argues that we're most persuaded "when we suppose something to have been demonstrated" (33). And how do we demonstrate something to the satisfaction of others? By using artful strategies (*pisteis* in Greek, meaning something like "proofs"—the "means of persuasion"): Logos (words or language—here we're calling it argument), ethos (character), and pathos (emotion) are, for Aristotle, the fundamental strategies of persuasion, and you should learn how to use all three to your rhetorical advantage in writing and speaking.

The rest of this chapter is about *argument*, the first of our ACES. (I actually recommend not using the term logos because students often confuse it with logic—another term I don't recommend we use because of its quasi-mathematical connotations—or facts.) Then we'll spend one chapter on character and emotions, and one on style. In some ways these four rhetorical strategies are *generic*, meaning that they teach you broad principles you can apply in any setting. However, we must always remember that rhetorical situations create their own ecologies for persuasion. While Aristotle's pisteis can be deployed in some fashion in most situations, the way they're applied is situation-specific, contingent on exigence, kairos, rhetor, purpose, genre, and audience.

Argument

The word **argument** has negative connotations. Say the word out loud—what's your first impression? An uncomfortable disagreement, maybe. Fighting? Political adversaries on the streets with forehead veins pulsing? A domestic disturbance? If you write "argument" in Google Images, most of the pictures you'll see are of people getting in each other's faces, shouting at each other with their teeth clenched, spit flying, eyeballs almost popping out.

Well, that's one definition. We're going to focus on another, more useful definition.

The word itself comes from from the Latin word *arguo*, meaning "to prove or demonstrate"; related is the Latin *arguere*, which means something like "to make clear." Those words suggest that an argument is a kind of test in which language is used to clarify, prove, or assert something. An argument, then, can be a *process* through which this happens. Two people can *have an argument*: They can go back and forth trying to test out the strength of an idea. Think of it as an intellectual process.

In a female dorm room, for example.

Let's set the stage:

It's late on a Sunday night. Three roommates in for the night. Homework's completed. Television comedy streaming on a laptop open on a coffee table, and everyone's huddled under blankets on a couch.

Roommate 1: Last night my sister set me up on a blind date with this loser who just plays video games all day.

Roommate 2: Is he cute?

Roommate 1: What does it matter if he's cute? All he wants to do with his spare time is play Xbox!

Roommate 3: What's wrong with playing Xbox?

Roommate 2: Wait—you didn't answer me. Is he hot?

Roommate 1: I did answer you. Hotness doesn't matter if all he's interested in is playing Call of Duty on his Xbox with his roomies. I'm not interested in someone who can't talk about anything except one thing that I don't care about.

Roommate 3: Well, if all he wanted to do was play basketball, would you be interested then? Or do you want your dates to be, like, always going to art galleries or museums or something?

Roommate 2: If he was hot, you wouldn't care if he Xbox'd, so he's obviously not hot.

Roommate 1: Are you kidding me? He *is* hot—*really* hot actually—and *no*, I don't expect my dates to "like" go to art galleries all the time! I just want to date a guy with more than one interest and definitely more interests than video games! That's so one-dimensional!

A million arguments like this one happen all around us, all the time. We dismiss them as the flatulence of culture—the crackling social static, the dorm room back-and-forth, the sports bar jabber, the comment thread flame-outs, the playground throw-backs, the white noise of modern life. It's easy to dismiss if you think of it as meaningless chatter, but take a closer look at our script and you'll see some interesting intellectual gymnastics going on in this argument. Gerald Graff would call it "hidden intellectualism" (214)—it's an argument, and it takes critical thinking to have one.

An argument is an intellectual process, as we said. Having an argument is an act of critical thinking because critical thinking means taking propositions (i.e., statements that represent some kind of judgment) and testing whether or not we should accept them. American philosopher John Dewey (no, not the Dewey decimal guy) thought of critical thinking as "active, persistent, and careful consideration of any belief or supposed form of knowledge in the light of the grounds that support it, and the further conclusions to which it tends" (Dewey). Science grows from this kind of thinking. "Why does an apple accelerate as it falls from a tree?"

wonders Isaac Newton. And he figures out why. "Why do I have a cur-few?" asks my thirteen-year-old son Ben at the dinner table one night. "None of my friends have one!" My wife Amy's eyebrow goes up. "*None*?" she asks. "Not a single one of your many friends has a curfew?" See, she's testing a proposition through argument.

An argument is also a *thing*, a product. One of the most popular rhetorical strategies in the universe has a simple anatomy: make a point and support it with some kind of evidence. We call this an argument, too.

Let's walk through an example.

One time I was at the Monterey Bay Aquarium, in California, and saw this sign on a paper towel dispenser in the bathroom:

PAPER TOWELS = TREES

Mysterious! That's bizarre math. Paper towels equal trees? What do you think I was being told? I'm thinking the sign was a gentle reminder that paper towels come from a natural resource (trees, dude!) that human beings generally want to protect and conserve.

So the sign was giving me an argument: A point (*You should not use more paper towels than you need…*) with supporting evidence (*…because paper towels come from a natural resource*).

We'll call these two parts the **claim** (the point) and the **reason** (the support).

But there's a third part. Notice that the *strength* of the argument depends on an unspoken something that passes between me and the aquarium people as I stand there, hands dripping, reading the sign. They *assume* that I'm on board with the idea that we should conserve our natural resources to the point where I'm willing to use fewer paper towels when drying my hands in a public restroom. They don't need to say that because that part of the argument is built into the air, like electricity. They assume I accept the reason as valid evidence to support the "further con-clusion to which it tends," in Dewey's words.

(Some folks want to separate reasons from evidence because they assume evidence means something like *fact*. Since facts can be presented as rea-sons for claims, I call *reasons* anything used as the supporting "stuff" of a claim.)

Now we have three parts to our argument anatomy: **claim, reason,** and **assumption.** We'll have more to say about assumptions later, and while they often go unspoken, as they do in the paper towels example, they are essential to our discussion because they're what make arguments *rhetorical*. An argument, of course, is audience-based. We provide reasons we hope an audience accepts. When I say to you, *Take my umbrella because it's raining outside*, I'm assuming you're the kind of person who doesn't like to get wet. I'm assuming you're like me in that respect, and I don't need to add, *and I assume you're like me and you don't like to get wet unless you want to.* And if I say to you, *I don't want to date guys whose only real interest is video games because they're so one-dimensional*, I'm assuming you accept the idea that being one-dimensional is a bad thing. (Is it? Always?)

So, an argument is an assertion—a claim—that is accompanied by an attempt to prove or support the claim—the reason (Arg = C + R). When a parent asks a teenager why she is coming home late and she says, "I lost track of time," she is providing an argument: I am late (the *claim*) because I lost track of time (the *reason*). From the parent's perspective, it's a lame argument (the assumption = losing track of time is a legitimate reason for being late), but it has the essential elements of our definition of argument: a claim supported by a reason to accept the claim.

To understand how arguments work as rhetorical strategy, we need to understand the relationship between claims, reasons, and assumptions.

I once overheard a female student talking on the phone about a romantic movie she had seen the night before called *The Vow*. It was clear by her tortured voice that she had been disappointed by the movie. She even said as much: "I was so looking forward to it, and it was just really disappointing!" Had she made an argument? Nope. Not yet, at least. All I had heard so far was a claim: *The Vow* is disappointing. We have a C, but no R.

Any time you hear a claim dangling out there, you can ask, *Why?* or *So what?* Global warming is a myth. *Why?* Global warming is real, and man-made. *So what?* You should clip your toenails. Textbooks are too expensive. Prostitution is wrong. Video games make you smart. Gluten-free diets. Apple products. Viral cat videos. College tuition. CIA torture memos. Texting while driving. Police and racism. *Why? Why? Why?* An argument just ain't an argument without a reason. To paraphrase the female vocalist Pink, just give me a reason—just a claim is not enough…to call something an argument.

So this student's claim that *The Vow* was a disappointing movie was *not* an argument—until she provided a reason. Which was this: "The ending was so bad! It totally didn't resolve anything and just kinda left you hanging." The *reason* completes the argument. It invites us—the audience—to accept or reject the claim and agree with the arguer. Is it a *good* reason?

What do you think?

There is power in argument. In fact, there is scientific evidence that arguing is a healthy trait we humans have developed to help us deal with the truckload of information dumped on us each day. We use arguments to justify who we are and what we do. We come up with claims and reasons to support our decisions and encourage others to see things our way. We analyze arguments that challenge our beliefs, values, or well-being. Recently in the journal *Behavioral and Brain Sciences*, Hugo Mercier and Dan Sperber argued that argument is central to the way we think. In fact, they *argue*—fittingly!—that the primary function of thinking itself is to produce and analyze arguments to defend our behavior. Apparently, argument comes as natural to us as sleeping.

One last note on the idea of argument before we move on. It has no doubt occurred to you that argument is central to rhetoric—the art of persuasion and social cooperation. It is also central, as rhetoric itself is, to democratic life. Democracy depends on the judgment of the citizens. It's a scary thought, I know, but we're all we've got. And we cannot exercise good judgment to make good decisions about life if we do not hear arguments—not only good ones, but bad ones as well—about what we should be doing and why we should be doing it. All the crucial political questions that almost flummox us and grind the gears of government to a halt—like *What should we do about the nation's uninsured? What if an enemy of state produces a nuclear weapon? How should the wealthy be taxed? How do we improve the schools? How do we get more people into college? How much should the Internet be regulated? What do we want from our media?*—need answers, and those answers take the form of arguments: claims, supported by reasons, backed by assumptions.

Finding Claims

In the course of your life, you will be asked to make arguments about this and that. Sometimes you'll have to make an argument in the spur of the moment without much preparation. One time while my wife and I were on a walk, she told me she wanted to replace the windows on the house, and she asked me what I thought about it. She might as well have asked me what I thought about carbon nanotubes or gluten-free diets or Sumerian architecture or anything else I had spent exactly zero minutes thinking about. Any argument I could make in that moment would be on the fly, without any analytical thought or research. We all have to make such arguments from time to time, and it's a bummer because sometimes we sound uninformed when we do.

In writing classes, you have the luxury of crafting your arguments in advance by going through a rigorous writing process involving *rhetorical invention*, which we talked about in chapter three.

How does one *invent* arguments? You've learned about rhetorical situations already. The kinds of arguments you make will depend on the rhetorical situation you find yourself in and the genre the situation demands. (And, yes, some rhetorical situations don't call for *arguments*. They might call for genres that inform—like a brochure on an illness at the doctor's office—or delight—like a good slasher movie. There's a textbook called *Everything's an Argument*. Do you think that's true?)

Once you feel like you understand your situation, you're ready to go looking for an argument that you hope will be suitable for your audience and purpose.

So let's assume you have a sense of your audience, and you understand your purpose and topic. One way to invent claims is to think about them as answers to questions—very big questions, in fact.

Questions like:

- What exists? And what kind of *stuff* is it made of?

- What is good?

- What should we do?

I'm willing to bet that almost every claim you hear is going to fall into one of these three categories, so they can be useful to know. Let's give them specific names and flesh them out a bit.

What exists? And what kind of *stuff* is it made of? Let's call this kind of claim a *substance* claim. Substance claims make claims about the nature of reality, about facts, about the status of things, about history and events, about definitions and essences. If I make the claim that humans cause climate change by burning fossil fuels, I'm making a substance claim. If I argue that political campaign contributions are "free speech," that's a substance claim, too (definitions are about substance or essence). If I claim that bicycle riders on campus pose a danger to other students, or that baseball is a religion, or that no cinnamon gum lasts longer than Big Red, or that it is impossible to balance the national budget without raising taxes, or that the public schools are in crisis, then I'm making a substance claim.

What is good? This kind of claim is a *value* claim. Value claims are statements about what is good or bad, right or wrong, ought or ought not, moral or immoral, effective or ineffective, best or worst, righteous or wicked, dumb or smart, cool or lame, ethical or otherwise. It's wrong to eat animals for any reason, says a value claim. And a value claim answers right back: Eating beef is a good old-fashioned American tradition! A value claim calls a movie—like *The Vow*—disappointing, or an action—like downloading copyrighted music outside legal channels—immoral. This candidate is better than that one. Vampires are not as cool as werewolves. It's justifiable to start a war if there's a credible threat. The cost of parking on campus is a scandal. Sexist remarks online are cowardly. Tax cuts for the wealthy are good for the economy. You get the point.

What should we do? My wife argues that we should replace the windows in the house. I argue that we shouldn't. At least we agree on what we disagree about, and what we disagree about is what we should do, which we call a *policy* claim. Policy claims are statements about things that should be done. Think of the way legislatures (ideally!) approach public problems. What should we do about rising health-care costs? Require everyone to have insurance, answers one group; another claims that we should reduce frivolous malpractice lawsuits. Should the university prohibit skateboards on campus? Should your instructor give everyone A's this semester?

In argument practice, reasons also can be categorized in these three ways. Someone, for example, might use what we call a substance claim as the reason to support a policy claim. An example: We should remove the emergency phones on campus because nearly every student now has a cell phone. Since arguments are made up of two assertions—we've been calling them claim and reason—the two parts can be categorized differently, and most likely are. You can support a policy claim with a policy reason (*We should replace the windows because we should conserve energy*), but it might be more effective to support a policy claim with a substance reason (*We should replace the windows because the cheap ones we now have lose 45% of the heat in the house, costing us over $100 in unnecessary heating bills*).

What's the unspoken assumption behind this argument about replacing windows? Remember, the arguer often doesn't speak the assumption because he or she assumes the audience accepts the assumption already. In this case, maybe the assumption is: *It's bad to lose 45% of the heat in the house*. We'll talk more about assumptions in a moment.

We've talked about three ways claims, reasons, and assumptions can be categorized. What's another way to invent an argument?

In *Teaching the Argument in Writing*, argument scholar Richard Fulkerson uses the acronym GASCAP to teach a structured method (see chapter three) for inventing arguments. Now, let's pretend we want to write an argument on health issues for students. Let's say we want to look into the nutrition and dietary behavior of freshmen on college campuses. Here's an example of how the GASCAP principles can help you generate arguments. (You can apply this to your own topic.) As you read these examples, think about what makes this kind of argument strong and what might make it seem weak.

G is for *generalization*. If a sample group has X trait, then the bigger group has X trait. This kind of argument depends on whether the sample is really representative of the population. (If you go on a date with a loud, obnoxious male student, are you justified in thinking all male students are the same? Would that conclusion be justified after two, three, ten similar dates with different men?)

> *Example:* If students at State U. eat more empty calories during finals week than they do at any time in the semester, then we can assume college students nationally do the same. OR, to put it in our C + R structure: (C) College students eat more empty calories during finals week than any other time in the semester, because (R) students at State U. do.

We're pattern-seekers. Scientists can't study every single stork or volcanic rock or television viewer, so they take samples. We can't judge the behavior of every single toddler; your nephew represents them all. We abstract from small samples to large populations. That's how we advance in knowledge. It's also how prejudices are formed (*I don't like this race or sex or religion or age because of the few I know*). So you can see how generalizing can make effective arguments, but my guess is you can also see its weakness.

A is for *analogy*. X and Y are alike enough that if X has Z traits, then Y likely has Z traits. Like generalization, this argument's strength rests on similarity—this time between two alike things or groups. For you poets out there, metaphor functions like this (see chapter eleven). If I compare thee to a summer's day, I'm arguing that summer's days have certain qualities that you, too, possess.

> *Example:* If students at the University of Wherever eat more empty calories during finals week, then we can assume that State U. students do the same.

Fulkerson explains that "an analogy is made stronger by a greater number of *relevant* similarities, and it is weakened by dissimilarities" (31). As I write this, the creators of the movie *Selma*, a critically acclaimed historical drama about the Civil Rights movement in Alabama in the 1960s, are being criticized for portraying President Lyndon B. Johnson as an enemy of the Selma campaign, which some historians say is not true. One editorialist compared *Selma* to another movie—*Zero Dark Thirty*—that depicts C.I.A. agents using testimony taken from torture to find and kill terrorist Osama bin Laden, which, some historians say, didn't happen. The argument goes like this: (C) The movie *Selma* should be criticized because (R) it's like *Zero Dark Thirty* in its historical inaccuracies. The strength of the argument, of course, depends on the similarities.

S is for *sign*. X means that Y is the case. If there's smoke, there's fire. If she doesn't call you back, she's just not interested. If a straight-A student starts blowing off class and assignments mid-semester, I may suspect that something has gone wrong in his or her personal life—but then again, I may be reading the signs incorrectly. Acts are signs of character. We believe that a person's acts reveal a coherent character hiding underneath. (We'll talk about that when we talk about ethos, in the next chapter.)

> *Example:* State U. freshmen tend to gain around seven pounds during their freshman year. (This may or may not be the case, by the way; I made it up.) The weight-gain is a sign that the students' diets change significantly once they move away from family and common routines.

C is for *causality*. X caused Y, or Y is a consequence of X. A tricky one sometimes. After a horrible school shooting in Columbine, Colorado, in

1999, journalists tried to argue that hard-rock music, video games, bullying, or parenting caused two young men to bring guns to school and murder their classmates. Was that really the case? Causal or consequential arguments appeal to us because they suggest sequences that seem to make sense. Our brains demand connections. Some of them are sound, some are not.

> *Example:* Students who play more video games than other students tend to be less healthy than other students. OR: (C) Students who play more video games than the average student are more unhealthy because (R) video games lead to a sedentary lifestyle.

Can you think of a reason why such arguments might not work? Sometimes it's hard to determine the actual *cause* of something. In the Columbine case, it was clear from investigations after the tragedy that the two shooters were bullied at school. Did the bullying push the two students over the edge? Is it accurate to say that no bullying = no shooting? But other students were bullied at Columbine High and didn't go on a murderous rampage.

A is for *authority*. If an expert on a given issue says X, then X is probably true. Well, who's an expert? Someone who knows quite a bit about a subject or who has spent a significant amount of time working in a particular field, OR someone who has intimate experience with the subject, OR someone who has some kind of credential related to the subject (like a PhD in microbiology), OR someone who is nationally recognized as an authority on a subject.

> *Example:* The *New England Journal of Medicine* reports that college students who play two or more hours of video games a day consume three times more soda than the national average. (Yeah, I made that up, too. But doesn't it sound authoritative?) So, the argument looks like this: (C) College students do X, because (R) the *New England Journal of Medicine* says so. And we assume the *NJM* did some kind of scientific study to come to that conclusion.

Authorities are strong insofar as the audience accepts them as legitimate. How do audiences come to accept authorities as convincing? Well, think about it for a moment and you tell me. Another question: Is the authority *alone* in this perspective? Do other authorities agree or disagree? Is *this* authority—in this example, the *New England Journal of Medicine*—stronger or more convincing than another authority—let's say *Lancet*, the premiere medical journal of the United Kingdom—that may say something different?

P is for *principle*. X is true or just or right or moral. These kinds of arguments depend on what values are shared between the writer and the audience. Think about the various ways of thinking that create moral judgments: religion, politics, philosophy, culture, intuition. Things can get tricky in there. Psychology professor Jonathan Haidt has argued that moral judgments, though powerful, are sometimes difficult to defend because they come from deep within the strange mazes of our intuition. And yet, so many of our public arguments come from the moral or ethical realm.

> *Example:* (C) State U. should provide healthier options in the cafeteria (R) because colleges are responsible for the health of their students.

The principle in this argument is represented in the reason provided: Generally, we believe that universities are morally obligated to help their students stay healthy. The power of the argument rests on whether the audience accepts this principle or cultural value.

Anatomy of Arguments: A Closer Look

How do you know what makes an effective argument for your audience? Or: How do you know if an argument for which *you* are the audience should be convincing?

This is quite a vexing question. What do I mean by the word "effective"? One answer might be, "Whatever persuades your audience!" *Effective*, in other words, is *audience-specific*, based on what rhetorical theorist Gerard Hauser calls "local norms of reasonableness." An argument that might convince a convention of evangelicals in Texas might not convince readers of a physics blog. Each **discourse community** has a different way of creating knowledge and making arguments, and sometimes those ways are very specific, even exclusionary.

However, this answer, though probably true to the way rhetoric works much of the time, is in some ways unsatisfactory. For one thing, it seems to suggest that the point of rhetoric is to use whatever arguments will convince a specific audience, and no one else. If it works to scare people, whip up the mob, make wild and unsupportable claims, stereotype, lie, attack others, reinforce ignorant prejudices, or distort an opposing view, well...then it works! While it is true that very specific discourse communities will have their own way of arguing, in public discourse we are *ethically obligated* to pursue the public good through our arguments—in other words, to make arguments with good reasons that help to refine, rather than dull, public judgment. Team Rhetoric fights for truth and justice! Your challenge is to grow in rhetorical knowledge by devising reasonable, emotionally salient arguments that even people who disagree with you might accept as respectable.

In that spirit, then, we can say that there are ways we evaluate arguments that depend on general principles of reasoning—principles that, though general, work in specific situations as well. We can think of arguments as *strong* or *weak*, depending on whether they have certain virtues of good thinking—critical thinking.

If arguments were like mathematical equations, then the problem of persuasion would be solved: As long as the audience accepts the definition of the numbers and other math symbols, then the conclusion is inevitable. The same goes for logical *syllogisms*. A syllogism is a logical statement of two claims, called premises, and a conclusion. If the premises are true, then the conclusion is true. Here's an example:

- Premise #1: All humans will die.

- Premise #2: You are a human.

- Conclusion: Therefore, you will die.

Bad news, I know. Someone tell Alphaville that we're not gonna live forever or be forever young. If premises #1 and #2 are true—and I'm pretty sure they are—then the conclusion follows. In fact, it follows with a kind of *violence* because there's no way for you to reject it and remain a rational person. Face it: You're gonna die.

But everyday arguments don't really take the form of a syllogism, nor are they *logical* in the philosophical sense of that word. Rather, they are *rhetorical*. Take our movie critic. Her first premise (her claim) is: The Vow *is a bad movie*. Well, maybe! Unlike in the *All humans will die* example, we need to be *persuaded* with good reasons before we will accept that *The Vow* is a bad movie and get on the same page as our arguer. Master writers understand how this process works; they can analyze arguments by dissecting claims, reasons, and assumptions. They also invent arguments with these three parts of argument in mind.

Your goal as a writer of arguments is to write good ones. As you construct claims and reasons, you'll want to analyze them through "active,
persistent, and careful consideration…in the light of the grounds that
support" them, as Dewey put it. Let's go back to the PAPER TOWELS =
TREES argument for a moment. How could we analyze the argument as
we reconstructed it earlier? We can't just confront the claim because a
claim by itself isn't an argument (remember?). So let's take a closer look
at the other parts of the argument:

1. The first thing we could do is **question the reason.** Notice that the
    reason (*paper towels come from a natural resource*) to accept the
    claim (*You should not use more paper towels than you need…*) is
    a fact-based claim—a substance claim. The arguer is telling me, as
    my drippy hands reach for the dispenser, that to make paper towels
    for restrooms, someone has to go out and chop down a tree. Is that
    really true? Who knows! Maybe paper towels are made from recycled
    materials or cloth or wood pulp, or maybe very few trees are used
    in the process, or maybe trees are used to make paper towels but
    not "these towels"—the ones in the Monterrey Bay Aquarium, which
    are actually made out of shredded wheat. The point is that you can
    begin analyzing an argument by checking to see whether you'd call
    the reason a *fact* we can depend on. In this case, since I have nothing
    but the Monterrey Bay Aquarium authorities to rely on, I'm going to
    go ahead and assume they're right about where paper towels come
    from. (Do you agree?)

    Granted, assessing the reason might be easier when you have a state-
    ment like "these paper towels are made from a natural resource" than
    when you have, as in our movie critic example, a statement like "the
    ending doesn't resolve things." Seems like a subjective statement to
    me. If *I* were to throw caution and good taste to the wind and go see
    The Vow, would *I* think that the ending didn't resolve things? When
    it comes to these kinds of judgments, sometimes we must depend on
    the *ethos* or authority of the speaker to help us determine whether or
    not to accept this reason. (More on ethos in a later chapter.) But in
    sum, your first task as a critical thinker is to analyze the reason and
    determine whether the reason is a fact—something you could look
    up and confirm—or some other kind of assertion.

2. The second, and more challenging, way to assess an argument is to
    look at the *assumptions* that make the argument possible. But

assumptions are hard to "look" at, because usually they're not there. Assumptions are the (often) unspoken values, beliefs, or principles that arguers assume they share with their audience. In the case of the movie critic, the unspoken underlying assumption could look like this:

> *Assumption:* Movies that have endings that don't resolve things are bad.

You may have thought of other ways to express this assumption that go deeper into underlying assumptions. You could say that as movie audiences we expect a certain structure to our movie plots, and the structure gives us a kind of pleasure, which drives us back to the theaters. When a movie violates that structure contract—say, by concluding in a manner that leaves too many loose ends—it should be condemned. We've gone way beyond where I think the student movie critic was going, but these assumptions seem to underlie her argument. She means to express them without saying them because she assumes that her audience assumes them, too. And it's our job as the audience to analyze whether her assumptions are legitimate.

Analyzing assumptions is challenging, but sometimes it's the only way we can assess whether or not an argument is strong or weak. Let's go back to the paper towels argument:

> *Claim:* You should not use more paper towels than you need…

> *Reason:* …because paper towels come from a natural resource.

What does the speaker/writer/aquarium staff assume is true in this case? One way to express the unspoken assumption might be:

> *Assumption:* Natural resources should be conserved or used sparingly.

With the assumption now on the table, can we say whether this is a good/bad, strong/weak argument?

It depends. It depends, of course, on the audience and whether the audience accepts the reasons, data, and assumptions. But in this case I'll take a chance and say that this assumption probably enjoys quite a bit of *adherence* in public discourse. Adherence in argument studies means *agreement*. Many people, I'd guess, agree that natural resources should be conserved or used sparingly. So maybe I want to conclude that since the assumption is strong—i.e., enjoys widespread adherence—then this argument is strong.

But not so fast. A rhetorical critic doesn't let assumptions off the hook that easily. We may go further and ask this assumption a "why" question: *Why should natural resources be conserved?* What if trees are so plentiful that they don't need to be conserved? Now we're getting into a third strategy for inventing and analyzing arguments.

3. Finally, you can rebut the claim by **coming up with a counter-claim**. We've looked at the reason and the assumption, and now we should test the argument by coming up with possible rebuttals. We've already done some of that work above by asking whether the paper towels in the dispenser actually come from trees. Think about rebuttals as "unless" statements that cast doubt on the argument:

> You should not use more paper towels than you need because paper towels are made from a natural resource.
>
> ...*unless* they *aren't* made from a natural resource.
>
> ...*unless* we don't need to conserve trees because there are so many of them.
>
> ...*unless* conserving trees will be too expensive or have other negative consequences—on the economy, for example.

Argument as Strategy, as Critical Thinking

As a budding rhetorician, you should practice identifying claims, reasons, assumptions, and counter-claims in the arguments you write and the ones you hear each day. Philosopher Stephen Toulmin created a simple chart to teach the anatomy of argument, and it looks something like this (and you should already know what each letter stands for):

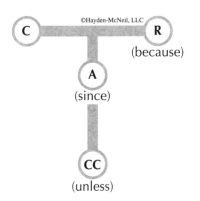

Toulmin here rediscovers Aristotle's understanding that argument (he called it *enthymeme*) is a human practice that follows ordinary patterns of thinking. It's just that in ordinary practice, we often don't think much about these patterns, nor do we stop to test the strength (through critical analysis) of arguments we or other people use.

Armed with this layout, you can invent convincing arguments when arguments are needed. When people talk about critical thinking, they're talking about learning how to apply C + R + A + CC thinking so you can understand, analyze, evaluate, create, and judge meaningful arguments in daily life. Of course, "daily life" arguments are quite complicated and tangly. We've talked as if CRA are easily discovered in the arguments you encounter. Sometimes you have to reconstruct CRA from what's been given you. You'll also notice that many written arguments look more like CCCRRRRRAAAAAA: multiple claims and sub-claims, backed by several reasons and assuming a dozen assumptions. Your job as rhetorical critic is to disentangle this mess o' argument as best as you can, using the critical thinking skills you've mastered, ever keeping your eye on whether the arguments are persuasive for intended audiences.

I believe that if we would all get better at this kind of thinking, our public discourse would improve, as would our judgments.

Works Cited

Aristotle. *On Rhetoric*. 2nd ed. Transl. George A. Kennedy. NY: Oxford, 2007.

Dewey, John. *How We Think*. Project Gutenberg eBook. 14 September 2011. Web. 28 March 2015.

Fulkerson, Richard. *Teaching the Argument in Writing*. Urbana, IL: NCTE, 1996.

Hauser, Gerard. *Introduction to Rhetorical Theory*. 2nd ed. Prospect Heights, IL: Waveland P, 2002.

Mercier, Hugo and Dan Sperber. "Why do Humans Reason? Arguments for an Argumentative Theory." *Behavioral and Brain Sciences* 34.2 (2011): 57–74. Web. 8 May 2015.

Toulmin, Stephen. *The Uses of Argument*. Updated Ed. Cambridge: Cambridge UP, 2003.

WRITING RHETORICALLY—
CHARACTER

In this chapter we'll cover the C of ACES: character as rhetorical strategy. You won't go far as a writer unless you understand how you can present a convincing *ethos* for your audience.

Ethos: Who We Are (to Audiences)

Something bizarre happened at the 2009 MTV Video Music Awards. (Something bizarre *always* happens at these shows, which is why we watch.) When singer-songwriter Taylor Swift, then only nineteen years old, waltzed out to accept the VMA for Best Female Video (for the syrupy-sweet country pop song "You Belong with Me"), rapper Kanye West jumped onto the stage and snatched the microphone out of her hand in the middle of her acceptance speech. Apparently he had a speech of his own to give:

> "Yo, Taylor, I'm really happy for you and I'mma let you finish, but Beyoncé [another female vocalist up for the award] had one of the best videos of all time. One of the best videos of all time!"

Then West shrugged, handed the mic back to a stunned Swift, and walked off. Swift was so shocked she couldn't finish her speech.

Wikipedia tells me that retribution for Kanye was swift—pun intended. The audience booed him off the stage. In the weeks that followed the VMAs, other celebrities like Janet Jackson, 50 Cent, Pink, Kelly Clarkson, and Donald Trump publicly condemned Kanye's actions. Even President Barack Obama threw him under the bus when he told a reporter he thought Kanye had been a "jackass." Ouch. Kanye did his best to make amends. He wrote a blog post and a few tweets, went on Jay Leno and said how ashamed he was, even contacted Taylor Swift personally to apologize. The public was not impressed. *Forbes* magazine reports that Kanye's earnings dropped from $25 million to $12 million in the year following the event (Greenberg). Ticket sales for a music tour with Lady Gaga were so low he had to cancel.

Take a moment and think about what's going on here. What did Kanye do wrong?

97

It's hard to feel bad for Kanye West: Two critically acclaimed smash-hit albums later, he's back on top of the world. In some ways the vitriolic response of the public to his stunt with Taylor Swift seems like an over-reaction—I mean, was what he did really *that* bad? Like, $13 million dollars bad?

Mr. West learned a difficult lesson: *our character influences attitudes.* Remember that the goal of writing is to influence the attitudes of others. In the last chapter, we talked about how you can influence attitudes by providing compelling reasons for the claims you make. You can also influence attitudes, in good or bad ways, by the way you present your Self—in writing, certainly, but also in public speaking and interpersonal communications, in the clothes you wear, in the way you treat other people, your likes and dislikes, what you know and don't know, who you associate with, your accent and word choices, your Facebook posts and photos, who you listen to, what games you play, your sense of humor. Like it or not, all these things lead your audiences to make judgments about you. If we're mindful about it, the person we present to other people can be a rhetorical strategy. We call it ethos.

Ethos is another funky Greek word, yes, but like kairos, it's quite a useful word. "Since rhetoric is concerned with making a judgment," says our Grandpappy Aristotle, "it is necessary not only to look to the argument [like we did in last chapter]...but also for the speaker to construct a view of himself [or herself] as a certain kind of person" (112). Aristotle used the word *ethos* to describe this act of construction—how the speaker, in the speech, presents a persuasive self to the audience. He also, and somewhat confusingly, thought of ethos as the character of the audience itself; he encouraged his eager students to study psychology to understand the way people behave and their likes and dislikes in order to appeal to their collective ethos in speaking. Maybe in making this argument, Aristotle was remembering what Socrates, the noble philosopher, said about rhetoric in Plato's dialogue, *Phaedrus*: "Oratory is the art of enchanting the soul, and therefore he who would be an orator has to learn the differences of human souls." Rhetorical power comes from understanding what makes a persuasive character for various audiences.

It may surprise you to hear that Aristotle believed that "character is almost, so to speak, the most authoritative form of persuasion" (39). Maybe he's right.

How Character Persuades

So: How does character persuade? If it's true that when you write you bare your soul, what kind of soul is the most convincing? And how do we use writing to establish our ethos?

Let's go back to chapter six for a moment to remind us of the big, universal determiner of any rhetorical strategy: the rhetorical situation. Whether or not you're successful using any of our ACES strategies depends on your exigence and purpose for writing and, of course, your audience. Genre matters, too—significantly. Think about cover letters for jobs. When you write a cover letter, you have to present yourself as a certain kind of person—professional, experienced, responsible, creative—and avoid looking like another kind—unskilled, entitled, conceited, clueless. Rhetorical situations are culturally contingent as well, meaning that the kind of character some cultures or discourse communities might find persuasive may not persuade other cultures or communities. For example, my acquaintances from Korea are far more respectful and deferent to people over forty than the Americans I know, especially the younger Americans I know.

Ethos, then, must be appropriate for the rhetorical situation. (You should have this kind of thinking seared into your brain by now: rhetorical strategy depends on rhetorical situation!) Sometimes we bring our ethos with us into a rhetorical situation, so that our character persuades before we even say anything. Let's call this *established ethos*.

When a five-star general steps up to the podium to address issues related to national defense, his character already is convincing us before he says a word. Or if an internationally renowned psychologist has something to say about bullying, we lean into her message more than we would if she were an accountant or just an angry parent (Aronson 77). Even good looks can convince: legal studies have shown that "attractive defendants are twice as likely to avoid jail as unattractive defendants," regardless of the gender of the defendant, judge, or jury (Cialdini 147).

Established ethos also works against folks: Past misdeeds, guilty associations, ignorant comments, obvious self-interest, or perceived prejudices can kill a message. Kanye West will wear the Taylor Swift incident around his neck for as long as cultural memory preserves it. When he was caught visiting prostitutes and forced to resign as governor of New York in 2008, politician Eliot Spitzer found audiences reluctant to accept his arguments about the economy, even though he knew quite a bit about how the economy works.

It may be that we're convinced so easily by established ethos (the decorations on a general's uniform, a doctor's lab coat, a distinguished title, the relative hotness of a defendant) because it saves us time and cognitive effort. In *Thinking, Fast and Slow*, Daniel Kahneman, a brilliant Princeton psychology professor and winner of the Nobel Prize, explains that we often make errors of judgment because our minds work in two speeds: fast and slow. Fast judgments come from our intuitions and take very little effort. Slow judgments require "effortful mental activities," like calculations, analysis, or careful attention (Kahneman 21). Both judgments are necessary for a good life, but slow judgments often correct the errors our fast judgments make. Prejudice, for example, is often a result of fast judgment ("I don't like Catholics—my aunt is Catholic, and she's a monster!"). Established ethos is powerful because our brains don't really want to listen carefully to someone's argument to find out if we should be convinced; we'd rather just see a white labcoat and say, "She's a doctor. She's right. I don't have to think now."

If you want to learn more about the potential pitfalls of established *ethos*, Google "Stanley Milgram."

On a less sinister note, established ethos is useful for us as writers. When you use sources to support an argument (in a research paper, for example), you want your audience to know if your sources have established, convincing characters. Look two paragraphs up. What did I tell you about Daniel Kahneman? Did I need to include that bit about him being a Princeton psych prof? See how I threw in his Nobel Prize, too? Did you find yourself leaning more willingly into his argument about fast and slow thinking because I established his ethos? Can you imagine being equally persuaded if I'd written, "My uncle Roger thinks our brains work in two speeds"? I doubt it.

What do we do when we have to write and we don't have some hoity-toity established ethos to slap down on our readers? Well, we need to *invent* an ethos, then, with our words. (Thanks to Sharon Crowley and Debra Hawhee for teaching me about this distinction between established and invented ethos.) Aristotle teaches us that persuasion through character "should result from the speech, not from a previous opinion" (39)—that's what we mean by invented ethos. While established ethos does, indeed, work wonders (in spite of what Aristotle may think), much of the time when we write, we write without commanding credentials, and we write to total strangers who often don't care who we are or what we've done. In those situations, we'll have to win them over with an invented ethos. We'll have to construct for them a convincing ethos through our words.

I must stress one last thing here. For Aristotle, ethos is an *argument*—it's an argument connecting claims and reasons by connecting character to actions. While we may say that "actions speak louder than words," it turns out that words are, in fact, actions, and word-acts invoke character. As audiences, we look for patterns in the characters of others. We read rhetorical action as evidence of character, and we expect rhetorical acts to be consistent with what we understand of someone's character. We get suspicious when people say or do things that seem "out of character" because inconsistency seems inauthentic. When politicians reverse course, we think they're just weather-vaning (i.e., turning any way the wind blows) their way to getting elected. However, a supporter might argue that reversing course is an *act* that represents *wisdom* or *intellectual engagement* or *pliability*. Rhetorical acts argue for character; they are the signs of character.

We've covered five principles of ethos I want you to remember:

1. Character convinces—in fact, it's one of the most important rhetorical strategies we have.

2. Character is argument—i.e., the relationship between acts and character is like the relationship between reasons and claims.

3. The convincing power of ethos depends on the rhetorical situation (kairos, exigence, rhetor, purpose, genre, audience) and the shared culture of writer and audience.

4. Character can be either already established (think white lab coat), or invented.

5. We can—and should!—invent convincing ethos in our writing.

Strategies for Inventing *Ethos* in Writing

Keep in mind that the word "invented" doesn't imply imaginary or phony ethos. It refers to the ethos you must construct in the act of writing. For the rest of the chapter, we'll cover three major strategies for inventing ethos in your writing: credibility, relationship with the audience, and other virtues.

Credibility

As I write this, *NBC Nightly News* anchor Brian Williams is under fire for lying about being, well, under fire. For years, Mr. Williams has claimed that while covering the war in Iraq in 2003, his helicopter was shot down by a rocket-propelled grenade and made a dramatic emergency landing. Earlier this week, several military veterans who witnessed the event came forward, after over a decade of silence, to say that Mr. Williams' story is bunk: the helicopter he was in was actually *behind* the one shot down, and it took no enemy fire. After the story broke all over the media, a news analyst said that Williams' lie "raises serious questions about his credibility in a business that values that quality above all else" (Mahler, Somaiya, and Steel). Maintaining credibility can be a tricky business.

When we believe someone is credible, we trust them; we find them believable. We find what they have to say convincing because they create a sense of *gravitas* with their words. Credible people speak with authority; they've either done their homework on a topic or they have personal experience that gives them an edge over others who don't. Their credible acts cue us to their credible characters, and we move in their direction. We know how this works with established ethos (i.e., we respect recognized authorities with credentials like academic degrees, or prestigious job titles, or relevant experience, or fame). But inventing a credible ethos in writing can be a challenge, especially when you're a first-year writing student trying to edge your way into conversations already controlled by published experts and commentators.

So how do you convey credibility in writing? There are three methods you'll want to learn:

1. **Look smart, be smart.** The first method is to demonstrate, simply, that you know what you're talking about. You want to convince your audience that (a) you've done your homework on the issue—i.e., you're in command of the relevant facts, events, and players (like other credible sources—just make sure your audience understands

why they're credible); (b) you have kairotic awareness of what makes your topic timely, interesting, of the moment; (c) you know the lingo (the key terms or concepts, the "lexical field") of the discipline or subject you're writing in, and you're all about the details, the how-to, of academic writing; (d) you understand the conventions of the genre— in other words, you're an insider, someone who knows what you're supposed to do in situations like these; and, (e) you know how to use the English language really well, avoiding obvious errors that might slow down the reading experience and lead audiences to form unflattering judgments about you. (A quick note about (e): Mistakes are a fact of life, sure, but it's also a fact that they can tarnish your credibility. In one research study, business executives surveyed felt that errors convey the message that the writer is hasty, careless, uncaring, uninformed, or poorly educated [Beason]. While not all errors are equally egregious to audiences, and some aren't even noticed, they can still chip away at your ethos.)

In looking smart, do you risk looking *too* smart? Yes. No one likes a smarty-pants; Hermione Granger learned this over the course of the *Harry Potter* books. That's why you study the third strategy for inventing *ethos*—the virtues—which we'll discuss soon.

2. **Use personal experience.** When it's appropriate to the genre you're writing, use relevant personal experience to demonstrate that you've been there, done that. In *My Age of Anxiety*, writer Scott Stossel introduces us to the history and science of anxiety and panic disorder through his own experience. "I struggle with emetophobia," he writes, which is "a pathological fear of vomiting, but it's been a little while since I last vomited. More than a little while, actually: as I type this, it's been, to be precise, thirty-five years, two months, four days, twenty-two hours, and forty-nine minutes" (65). Stossel's personal struggles with anxiety give him a unique perspective that boosts his credibility, especially when he supplements his experience with significant research on anxiety.

But be careful. Personal experience sometimes can't be generalized (see chapter seven about *generalization*). Just because you take better notes on a laptop than a notepad doesn't mean everyone else does. There's another danger, too: Audiences can sniff out a fake (take note, Brian Williams!). If you're an Amazon reviewer, one of the best ways to sink your ethos with me is to admit you've never actually used the product you're reviewing. (Amazingly, this happens all the time.) Men get themselves into trouble by assuming they understand the experience of women; adults often are not fully empathetic to the pain and suffering of children. ("It's just a scrape—quit your whining!" "So your balloon popped—big deal, we'll get you another one!") Writers can project cultural insensitivity or a lack of empathy by assuming that their own experience is the right experience, or by dismissing the experience of others. To sum up: use personal experience, but be authentic and empathetic.

3. **Show balance.** One of the easiest ways to win people over is to project a fair and balanced *ethos*. Aristotle tells us that "we believe fair-minded people to a greater extent and more quickly than we do others, on all subjects in general and completely so in cases where there is not exact knowledge but room for doubt" (38). Social psychology backs this up: We trust people more when it looks like they're not pushing their own agenda. Self-interest is a turn-off when it's too obviously in play (Aronson 78–81). While it may be true that we all have biases, wearing them on our sleeves can destroy our credibility.

You build credibility by showing that, though you have an argument to make, you've looked at the issue from multiple sides and weighed evidence for and against your proposal. In a massive study of the most successful businesses, Jim Collins and his research team discovered that the most influential leaders were not afraid to confront the "brutal facts" or invite others to criticize their management practices (69). This approach projects not only fair-mindedness but confidence. When in our writing we give a full hearing to opinions that go counter to ours, we show we have nothing to hide. We tell readers we want them to judge for themselves whether or not we've made a convincing case. (This is an especially strong move for well-informed audiences; it's not as strong for audiences who have already made up their minds. See Aronson 94.) When we take seriously alternative viewpoints or weaknesses in our own perspective, we convey wisdom. We create credibility by acting, by doing, by speaking and writing.

Credibility convinces. Enact yours, and your audience will lean into your argument.

Relationship with the Audience

Back to T-Swift: What was Taylor Swift planning to say before Kanye West ripped the mic out of her hands? Later she told the press that she just wanted to thank the fans for voting for her video. She wanted her words to create a connection with her adoring audience—she wanted to bring the love. That's a great rhetorical move. Audiences lean in when they feel a writer has their interests and needs in mind. If writing is a social, other-directed activity, as I've argued, then we do it better when we form constructive relationships with readers.

In the literature about rhetoric, this ethos strategy is often called *goodwill*. As a writer, you want your audience to feel like you have their best interests in mind. You want to demonstrate that this whole writing thing is really all about them, not you. Maybe that's a stretch, but it's a stretch worth making.

So, how do you get perfect strangers to like you?

1. **Be kind.** One way to convince others is to be *kind* to them. Psychologist Jonathan Haidt argues that when it comes to reasoning, we're like a rider on an elephant's back—and the elephant is our intuitions, passions, and biases. "When discussions are hostile," he writes, "the odds of change are slight. The elephant leans away from the opponent, and the rider works frantically to rebut the opponent's charges. But if there is affection, admiration, or a desire to please the other person, then the elephant leans *toward* that person and the rider tries to find the truth in the other person's arguments" (68). He concludes that good reasons can, in fact, persuade, but "especially when reasons are embedded in a friendly conversation" (71). Show respect for adversaries. Assume that your readers are smart and willing to weigh the evidence. Demonstrate that you want what's best for the community or public. Avoid sounding smug, condescending, or holier-than-thou.

2. **Give awesome content.** Quality writing is a compliment to your reader. By writing a witty, smart, polished, well-argued paper, you've created a good experience for someone else. By sharing engaging links through social media, you give gifts; when you share lame-o stuff, you waste everyone's time. Imagine your writing instructor, slogging through a neck-high stack of papers, finally taking your paper from the stack and finding, to her joy, a masterpiece, a genuinely pleasurable reading experience, an experience created by your best thinking and writing, by stylistic and design pizzazz, by your persistent

acts to minimize static by avoiding errors and design problems. Quality builds ethos.

3. **Connect with your audience.** Yet another reason why you need to know your audience as well as you can. As Robert Cialdini explains, the social science research is clear: "We like people who are similar to us" (148). The rhetorical theorist Kenneth Burke called this principle *identification*. You persuade someone, reasoned Burke, if you show you talk their language and identify your interests and purposes with theirs (55). One way to do that is to suggest that your writing has implications for a shared issue; in other words, your writing is meant to chip away at problems in the community at large. Let me share a brief example from the world of psychology. When psychologist Timothy Wilson wrote a book on how interpretations of the world can influence our well-being, he wrote:

> Our interpretations are rooted in the narratives we construct about ourselves and the social world, and sometimes, like the pessimistic calculus student, we interpret things in unhealthy ways that have negative consequences. We could solve a lot of problems if we could get people to redirect their interpretations in healthier directions. (Wilson 10)

Notice that Wilson uses the first-person plural to connect with the audience: *our* interpretations, the narratives *we* construct, *we* interpret things. In essence, he suggests that his scholarship will help us solve these problems of interpretation and make us healthier. By writing in this way, Wilson builds a relationship with us by saying, in essence, "My concerns are your concerns, and my project your project, my culture your culture, my solutions *our* solutions."

If at the end of your text a reader has to ask, *What does this have to do with me?*, then you've missed a chance to build *ethos* by creating a relationship with your audience.

Other Virtues

We've covered *credibility* and *relationships* as rhetorical strategies. I conclude here by suggesting that there are other convincing character traits that can be conveyed in writing. Certain *virtues of character* endear us to other people and prepare our attitudes for adjustment.

I'm not competing with *Us Weekly* for celebrity coverage, but let's go back—for the last time, I promise—to Kanye's stunt at the Video Music Awards in 2009. He said, you'll remember, that Beyoncé's video "All the Single Ladies" was one of the best videos of all time. Clearly he felt that some injustice had been done when Taylor Swift won the VMA over Beyoncé. (He did the same thing, though off-stage to *E!* reporters, after the 2015 Grammy's when the musician Beck won Album of the Year over Beyoncé.) Later in the broadcast, though, Beyoncé herself, the reigning pop diva, asked Swift back to the stage. She gave Swift a big hug and invited her to finish her speech.

Now, how about *Beyoncé's* ethos? She could have been upset, like Kanye, about losing to Swift. Instead, she turned the awkward moment into a classy, gracious redress for a wronged sister musician. Her ethos capital soared to new heights, if that's even possible for someone as universally well-liked as Beyoncé. Her gracious acts reinforced our perception of her character.

Beyoncé gained rhetorical power by being gracious in that moment. You, too, can gain rhetorical power in your writing by demonstrating that you have certain virtues of character respected and admired by your audience. In *On Rhetoric*, Aristotle suggests that people who possess *arete*—virtue—are more persuasive than those who don't (112). Virtue here means *excellence* (not merely sexual purity), and it was a big deal to the Greeks. It's a big deal to us, too. We listen to people we admire, people who we think of as *good people*: funny people, courageous people, humble people, passionate people, just (as in *fair*) people, ethical people, self-reflective and self-sacrificing people (see Brooks), complimentary people, talented people, charitable people.

How do you project all that in writing? By performing rhetorical acts that reflect good character. Telling stories about yourself helps. Expressing appropriate emotional responses to situations can signal certain convincing qualities about yourself (see next chapter). Showing you have a sense of humor, or that you're a sensitive and just person, or that you're up on recent news stories or pop culture trends, or that you want what's best for the community—those moves present to readers a writer they can respect and trust, even like.

In her memoir *Bossypants*, comedian Tina Fey talks about her body— "wide German hips that look like somebody wrapped Pillsbury dough around a case of soda"—in such a self-effacing, humble, and hilarious way that we can't help but like her:

> I would not trade any of these features for anybody else's. I wouldn't trade the small thin-lipped mouth that makes me resemble my nephew. I wouldn't even trade the acne scar on my right cheek, because that recurring zit spent more time with me in college than any boy ever did. (25)

We admire people who don't take themselves too seriously, so long as their joking is appropriate to the situation and they don't come off as being full of themselves.

Though in person we can create convincing character with nonverbal vibes, writers can still invoke an ethos audiences can connect with. When that connection is made, your audience will lean more readily into your argument.

Works Cited

Aristotle. *On Rhetoric*. 2nd ed. Transl. George A. Kennedy. NY: Oxford, 2007.

Aronson, Eliot. *The Social Animal*. NY: Worth, 1999. Print.

Beason, Larry. "Ethos and Error: How Business People React to Errors." *College Composition and Communication* 53.1 (2001): 33–64. Print.

Brooks, David. *The Road to Character*. NY: Random House, 2015. Print.

Burke, Kenneth. *A Rhetoric of Motives*. Berkeley: U of Cal P, 1969.

Cialdini, Robert B. *Influence*. 5th ed. Boston: Pearson, 2009. Print.

Crowley, Sharon and Debra Hawhee. *Ancient Rhetorics for Contemporary Students*. 5th ed. Boston: Pearson, 2012. Print.

Fey, Tina. *Bossypants*. NY: Little, Brown, 2011. Print.

Greenberg, Zach O'Malley. "The Strange Symbiosis of Taylor Swift and Kanye West." 25 August 2014. Web. 3 Feb 2015.

Haidt, Jonathan. *The Righteous Mind*. NY: Vintage, 2013. Print.

Kahneman, Daniel. *Thinking, Fast and Slow*. NY: Farrar, Straus, Giroux. 2011. Print.

Mahler, Jonathan, Ravi Somaiya, and Emily Steel. "With an Apology, Brian Williams Digs Himself Deeper in Copter Tale." *New York Times*. 5 Feb 2015. Web. 6 Feb 2015.

Stossel, Scott. *My Age of Anxiety*. NY: Knopf, 2014. Print.

Wilson, Timothy D. *Redirect*. NY: Back Bay, 2011. Print.

WRITING RHETORICALLY—
EMOTION

Rhetoric sets up relationships. Knowing someone's ethos helps us know how much attention we should pay to them. Rhetoric orients us to each other, invites us to lean in, to bond, to identify with each other, to like and trust each other. Since emotions function like a glue for these bonds, then emotions are inherently rhetorical. So let's talk about them.

You may not have spent much time thinking about the relationship between schooling and poverty, but educator Jonathan Kozol has. Consider the following excerpt from his book *Savage Inequalities*, a book about the public school system in the United States. Kozol is in the middle of describing the rough conditions kids face in low-income areas of East St. Louis. I want you to make sure you're in a quiet place, leaning over the page, letting the full impact of the words work on you:

> As in New York City's poorest neighborhoods, dental problems also plague the children here. Although dental problems don't command the instant fears associated with low birth weight, fetal death or cholera, they do have the consequence of wearing down the stamina of children and defeating their ambitions. Bleeding gums, impacted teeth and rotting teeth are routine matters for the children I have interviewed in the South Bronx. Children get used to feeling constant pain. They go to sleep with it. They go to school with it. Sometimes their teachers are alarmed and try to get them to a clinic. But it's all so slow and heavily encumbered with red tape and waiting lists and missing, lost or canceled welfare cards, that dental care is often long delayed. Children live for months with pain that grown-ups would find unendurable. (Kozol 20–21)

Unless you have a heart of stone, you'll be moved by this account. Poor children with bleeding gums! Sitting in their little wooden chairs at school—in the kind of pain that would double over a grown-up! And we can't get them relief because of bureaucratic red tape! If you're like me, you feel empathy mixed with pity mixed with frustration. Kozol is inviting us to develop an attitude, and therefore a judgment, about the moral consequences of America's unequal education landscape.

I've said before that studying rhetoric increases your social intelligence—i.e., your ability to understand and intervene in situations in which working with others is necessary to get things done, situations for which writing can be a catalyst for change. We've talked about how you can increase your rhetorical power by using claims, reasons, and assumptions your audience will accept (*logos*, in Aristotle's language). We've talked about how establishing a convincing character in writing gives you rhetorical power (*ethos*). In this chapter, we'll talk about the E in ACES: emotion (*pathos*). Your quest to be a rhetorical superstar must include some understanding of how emotional appeals work, and why. Even mild emotions have "a highly significant influence on the way people form, maintain, and change their attitudes" in social situations (Forgas 149).

Emotions Are Rhetorical

What are emotions? You know, I know, everyone knows—things like anger, sadness, fear, joy, surprise, shame. But what, exactly, is the emotion itself? Is it the feeling that comes over us when our brain registers that our dog just got run over by a car? Is emotion the unstoppable tears streaming down our face, the impulsive quaking in our arms, the heavy downturn of our mouth and eyebrows? Or is emotion the conscious *attitude* we form as we think about poor Rover, our beloved pet, squashed like a pancake in the middle of the road? (Did I go too far there? Disgust, too, is an emotion.) Or to put the question more simply: Is emotion an involuntary physiological response to what happens to us, or is it a culturally formed judgment about what happens to us? Or maybe both?

Think of surprise. Have you ever jumped at something that happened in a movie, or had a practical joker startle you? Did you make a conscious decision to jump, to exhale or shout, to bring your arms up close to your body in a defensive gesture, to pop your eyes open, to race your heart? Nope—your body decided to do that on its own. The stimulus jumped out, and your brain—in neuroscience-speak, the "limbic system circuitry, the amygdala and anterior cingulate" (Damasio 133)—sent signals to your body at lightning speed and everything just did its thing without any help from conscious You. Evolution has equipped us with those reflexes for good reason: When the beast jumps out of the bushes, you don't want to have an internal dialogue about how you should respond.

Now think of someone you love whom you haven't seen in a long time. Imagine some crazy coincidence of seeing this person unexpectedly in a public place, across a crowded room. Imagine the face of that person turning to look at you—the wide eyes, the smile, the most happy surprise imaginable. You run across the room and embrace. What's the feeling now? Surely you don't feel the same feelings looking at the faces of the strangers in the room; the face of the person you love carries all the experiences and conscious decisions you've made over the years in your relationship. Unlike being startled, this time the stimulus leads to a *judgment*, whether obvious to you or not, about that person and what he or she means to you, *before* (somehow) your heart races and your mouth shoots upward and you feel like a million bucks. The emotion—joy—is the result of a social judgment.

The Oxford English Dictionary defines *emotion* as "natural instinctive affections of the mind (e.g. love, horror, pity) which come and go according to one's personality, experiences, and bodily state; a mental feeling." But let's channel the corny classic rock group Boston and say that emotion is *more than a feeling*. The philosopher Robert Solomon tells us that emotions are not "just" feelings; they represent "sophisticated and subtly structured perceptions of the world" (138, 141). Emotions are far more important than chemical responses in the bloodstream. They are "*strategies* for getting along in the world" and "means of motivating, guiding, influencing, and sometimes manipulating our own actions and attitudes as well as influencing and manipulating the actions and attitudes of others" (Solomon 3). In other words, emotions are *rhetorical phenomena*.

Aristotle's got Robert Solomon's back on this one. Here he is again, speaking across the centuries in his tunic and sandals:

> The emotions [*pathe*] are those things through which, by undergoing change, people come to differ in their judgments and which are accompanied by pain and pleasure, for example, anger, pity, fear, and other such things and their opposites. [...] I mean, for example, in speaking of anger, what is their *state of mind* when people are angry and against *whom* are they usually angry and for what sort of *reasons*. (Aristotle *Rhetoric* 113)

Remember that attitudes lead to judgments lead to behavior. As Aristotle says, we "come to differ" in our judgments because of the "state of mind" they put us in. Emotions lead to attitudes lead to judgments lead to behavior.

Is this a good thing? I mean, aren't emotions irrational? Don't emotions lead to sloppy thinking and manipulation and brain-dead citizens and propaganda and the rise of fiery demagogues who become tyrants and bestride a blood-soaked earth with the fury of hell in their crazed eyes?

Let's not get too carried away. Yes, over the centuries since the Enlightenment, Western thinkers have often championed what we call rational thought over emotions. Since emotions often begin with physiological reactions over which we have little control, and since emotions often seem to "hijack" the rest of our brain with alarming force (Goleman 14), it's reasonable to be suspicious of them. Some people believe that objective thinking *requires* that we become, somehow, dispassionate, devoid of any emotional experience, like Spock on *Star Trek* or maybe Sherlock Holmes the way Benedict Cumberbatch plays him.

Such thinking, we've come to discover, is impossible. Current neuroscience tells us that "emotions drive the brain" (Franks 59). In other words, the high-order functions of the brain (thinking, reasoning, analyzing, etc.) are connected to, and depend on, what happens in the lower brain regions (called subcortical) where emotions are generated (Damasio 128). Emotions are tied up in our thinking and decision-making; without them, we'd lack a profoundly important mechanism for acting in the world. So like it or not, emotions are central to our being in the world.

They're also a pain in the neck. They can be unruly, just as the rationalists feared. They can move quickly to hijack a moment and render us helpless victims. Fear keeps us from living, loving, risking, connecting. Anxiety clouds our judgment, rendering even the most harmless situation terrifying. Anger makes us say or do things we regret later. Shame leads us to doubt ourselves, devalue ourselves. Surprise leaves us speechless. Even happiness can be a trap: When we like or dislike something, we use that feeling as a lazy shorthand for making decisions, sometimes "with little deliberation or reasoning"—that's called the *affect heuristic* (Kahneman 12). When it comes to living with emotions, there be dragons, my friends.

That's where this chapter comes in. In this chapter, I want nothing more than to boost your EI—your emotional intelligence—so that you can motivate, guide, and influence the emotions of your audience. When Daniel Goleman wrote *Emotional Intelligence* in 1995, he believed EI constituted two general abilities: identifying emotions (in self and others) and influencing emotions (also in self and others) (43). Identifying emotions can be easy if we're looking at faces—even little babies know when someone's making an angry face at them. (What twisted goon makes an angry face at a little baby?) Goleman argues that emotions circulate more obviously in face-to-face interactions in which as much as "90 percent or more of an emotional message is nonverbal" (97). It takes mindful effort, and not a little imagination, to work with emotions in writing. Because of spatial and temporal distance, you'll find it hard to analyze a rhetorical situation to decide how an audience feels now and how it *should* feel after reading your writing. This looks like yet another job for Captain Rhetorician. (That's *you*.)

Robert Solomon concluded that "we can create better lives for ourselves only if we create better emotions as well" (215), especially if we are committed to being the Good Guys. Since we assume that good people respond with appropriate emotions because of a habitually moral way of life, emotional appeals are intimately tied up in ethos as well. Emotional appeals, then, work to create better lives. They're a necessary ingredient in any rhetorical strategy, since research demonstrates that arguments with emotional appeals are more effective than primarily or exclusively logical arguments (Aronson 85).

Let's talk first about how emotions are *appropriate* in rhetorical situations, and then we'll talk about some methods for making emotional appeals. I'll conclude with some dangers you'll want to consider as you analyze other rhetors' attempts at emotional appeals.

Appropriate Emotions

In the chapter on rhetorical situation, we talked about how kairos means using language at the opportune, fitting, appropriate rhetorical time. The ancient Greeks believed that speech should "address recurring topics and occasions properly," since "on certain occasions and before certain audiences only certain utterances are appropriate" (Poulakos 60). The Greeks called this virtue *to prepon*; in Latin, the word is translated as *decorum*. Effective emotional appeals invite audiences to feel appropriate (i.e., opportune, fitting, proper, suitable) emotions.

In his book on ethics, Aristotle teaches that we can experience emotion too much or too little, depending on the situation: "but to feel them at the right times, with reference to the right objects, towards the right people, with the right motive, and in the right way, is what is both intermediate and best, and this is characteristic of virtue" (*Nicomachean Ethics* 340). Keeping our emotions suited to the moment is a balancing act between too much and too little—we're looking for the Goldilocks dose of emotional response. Even anger, an emotion we usually associate with Hulk-like destruction, can be fitting if the person "is angry at the right things and with the right people, and, further, as he ought, when he ought, and as long as he ought" (389). How do we know when we're evoking the right kind or amount of emotion? It ain't easy, says Aristotle. (Gee—thanks, Aristotle!)

A brief political anecdote might teach us about this rhetorical principle. On April 20, 2010, an oil rig drilling in the Gulf of Mexico exploded, sank, and started gushing oil into the ocean. Before it could be capped, several months later, the rig had spilled around 5 million barrels of oil into the Gulf, the largest oceanic oil spill in history. In June of that year, a Washington Post–ABC News poll revealed that 75% of U.S. citizens believed the spill was a "major environmental disaster" ("Washington Post").

Now, imagine you're the President of the United States. How do you respond to this? What is the emotion most fitting for a disaster like this?

President Barack Obama first decided to play it cool. In May he called a press conference to update the public on plans to clean up the spill and actions taken against BP, the company responsible for it. In measured language, he explained what the U.S. government was doing to manage the crisis. Near the end of the speech, Obama noted that citizens were angry about the spill: "Every day I see this leak continue," he said, "I am angry and frustrated as well" ("Remarks").

For whatever reason, that anger and frustration seemed to many to be inappropriately muted. One journalist present at the press conference summarized this disconnect in these words:

> As I sat in the fourth row on Thursday, I was struck by the weirdly passive figure before me. He delivered lawyerly phrases and spoke of his anger about the oil spill but showed none in his voice or on his face. He was, presumably, there to show how aggressively he has handled the disaster, but he seemed cool, almost bloodless. (Milbank)

Even Obama's supporters felt that he had not been "angry enough" in a situation that seemed to call for righteous indignation (Hertzberg). To some of his audience, Obama's coolness made his arguments less convincing because the coolness suggested a detached character, a character out of touch with the needs of the moment. After mounting criticism,

Obama tried to show a little more spit and vinegar, but by then it was too late—to some, the kairos for expressing anger had come and gone.

So: Where are we? We've learned the following principles:

1. Emotions are not just feelings—They're social *judgments* emerging from situations, habits, and social experience.

2. Emotions are not irrational—Emotional experience is necessary for rational thought, and emotional appeals are necessary for convincing audiences.

3. However, emotions *can be* dangerous—they can hijack rhetorical situations, if we let them.

4. Emotionally intelligent people can identify and influence emotions in themselves and others.

5. Emotions are signs of character—they reflect a habitual way of being in the world.

6. Like any appeal, emotional appeals should fit the rhetorical situation (purpose, audience, kairos, etc.).

Tattoo these principles on the fleshy tables of your heart, and you'll be a more effective rhetor.

Emotional Appeals

Now we get down to pragmatics—the "how-to" of emotional appeals. Like ethos, pathos concerns both the rhetor and the audience, both the emotions you *express* as a writer and the emotions you *evoke* in your readers.

Expressing Emotion in Writing

How do you tell someone how you're feeling in writing without saying something banal like, "I am sad about this"? We mock emoticons and emoji for being too cute or overused, but they are useful for conveying emotions to audiences who may otherwise have to guess at how you feel. Am I right or am I right? ☺

As the Obama oil-spill example revealed, people care how you ought to feel. They want to see, in writing, that your own emotional state is fitting for the moment, that your judgment is appropriately conditioned for the kairos at hand. (Sounds a lot like ethos; well, you've noticed already, no doubt, that rhetorical strategies bleed together.) In the last chapter, we talked about writing cover letters. Potential employers want to see that you're emotionally mature enough to have confidence in your relevant abilities ("I'm particularly confident in using JavaScript, Flash, and Python, and I'm excited to learn more programming languages in my career"). They want to see your passion for the content of the job ("Though I'm not yet a professional web designer, I've been creating web content eagerly since I was in grade school"). These moves are subtle, but they convey emotional content to readers.

Expressing emotion doesn't have to be as subtle. Consider this excerpt I took from a 2008 blog post by Michelle Malkin, a professional conservative blogger. She's writing about how young female celebrities often transition quickly from innocent child stars to sexualized, troubled young adults:

> First Britney. Then Lindsay. And now: Miley Cyrus. Do they ever learn?
>
> By "they," I don't mean the girls. I mean their parents. Where are they? What the hell are they thinking?
>
> I don't know how many times I've asked those questions over the years as a parade of young Hollywood starlets has burst onto the scene with wholesome charm, achieved dizzying fame and fortune, and then crashed back to Earth half-naked with corrupted souls and drug-glazed eyes.

Are parents without scruples more likely to sacrifice their daughters to the wolves of the entertainment industry? Or does show business sap all the common sense out of mothers and fathers who should know better? Either way, they are guilty of child abandonment. (Malkin)

How do you read this language? How does Malkin convey her own emotional state in this excerpt? Is it over the top, or appropriate to the situation she's responding to?

Political bloggers like Malkin seem to be in a perpetual state of outrage, which is one of the reasons why they're popular—we're drawn to passionate people, to the scrum of politics. We're used to the idea that some issues are worth getting mad as heck about—remember Aristotle's Goldilocks principle for fitting emotions. On the other hand, we may find the Perpetual Outrage Machine a drag. I find it hard to take comment threads seriously when every post spits venom at strangers. But that's beside the point. I wanted you to see in Malkin's post that the emotional state of the writer can be expressed in the words and phrases of the writer.

You might think certain genres don't lend themselves to emotional appeals. Lab reports, for example, or professional memos seem like bloodless documents. But consider, for a moment, how less conspicuous emotions (like optimism or frustration or satisfaction) could be woven into even the most straightforward of genres. When science writers end science reports by calling for more research, they are expressing curiosity, expectation, maybe even hope.

Evoking Emotion in Readers

Of course, bloggers like Michelle Malkin hope *her* outrage will become *your* outrage. (Maybe you're outraged at her outrage!) Ultimately, the reason we express appropriate emotions is to invite others to accept our judgment of the situation and match their emotions with ours. In a cover letter, you want to convey your own enthusiasm for the job so that the employer will feel "mirror enthusiasm" about hiring you. But you don't need necessarily to wear your emotions on your sleeve to evoke emotion in your audience.

Here are five tried-and-true strategies for evoking emotion in your audience:

1. **Give concrete details.** In *Made to Stick*, Chip and Dan Heath describe a study conducted by Carnegie Mellon University that tested how audiences respond to requests from charities. The researchers gave participants five bucks to complete a survey on technology, and then unexpectedly they asked participants whether they'd donate some of their money to a charity called Save the Children. For one group, the request letter gave statistics for the sad state of children in Africa, like "Food shortages in Malawi are affecting more than 3 million children" and "More than 11 million people in Ethiopia need immediate food assistance." Participants in this group gave on average $1.14 in response to these dramatic stats. However, another group's request letter introduced them to Rokia, a "desperately poor" seven-year-old girl from Mali, facing "the threat of severe hunger or even starvation." Participants who learned about Rokia contributed twice as much—$2.38 on average—as the group barraged with facts (Heath and Heath 166).

   Vivid examples have more persuasive power than a barrage of statistics; we have an "insensitivity to quantity," making it difficult to be touched by large, abstract numbers (Aronson 92–93; Greene 112). Tangible, concrete language creates images in the mind, which in turn act on our emotional imagination. It's hard to picture 11 million people starving in Mali; the magnitude, while certainly evocative, can't touch us as much as a single face: seven-year-old Rokia's face, for example. This bias for the concrete, for the viscerally evocative, can be problematic if it leads us into thinking that Rokia's face is somehow "more real" than relevant statistics (Kahneman 130). And yet the power of concrete imagery remains. Words and phrases that evoke sensory experiences in readers can lead them more effectively to emotional judgments. Think of Jonathan Kozol's poor children with bleeding gums and rotting teeth.

2. **Tell stories.** Why do we like stories? We're wired for them. For millennia, we've told stories to each other—stories about gods, devils, fairies, imps, spirit creators and tricksters, nature, great heroes and villains. We live in story while we sleep. As pattern-seekers, we use story to explain the unexplainable—from haunted houses to conspiracy theories. Nursery rhymes and fairy tales teach kids to beware the Big Bad Wolf. We tell stories in movies, TV shows, popular songs,

video blogs; we tell stories at camp, around the cooler, in the locker room, around the kitchen table. We even tell stories about ourselves—psychologists call them "core narratives" (Wilson 52)—and those stories influence how we feel, what we understand, and what we do with ourselves. "If you want a message to burrow into a human mind," writes Jonathan Gottschall, "work it into a story" (118).

Stories, of course, are *rhetorical*—we tell stories in particular situations for particular audiences and purposes. The emotional appeal of story is almost automatic; when we hear or watch a story unfold, our bodies respond as if we're part of the story (Gottschall 62–63). Some psychologists believe stories function like simulators of social life—the vicarious emotional experience teaches us something about how to live with other people, and how not to (Gottschall 58).

What goes into a story? In a way, a story is just a sequence of events: Yesterday I went to work until noon, then went to lunch with a friend, then came back to work and answered some emails, then went to a banquet with my wife, and then came home and read *Madeline and the Bad Hat* to my daughter. Call that a story if you want, but it's an incredibly boring story. Good stories, on the other hand, are almost always about *trouble*. It's the "universal grammar" of all stories (Gottschall 52). To tell a good story, put a person in some kind of predicament and then tell us what happens. Storytelling experts have diced the elements of a good story in all kinds of ways, but the four most useful elements are *character* (the protagonists in the tale), *scene* (the location of the action), *conflict* (trouble!), and *resolution* (how it all ends). Resolutions, which don't have to be happy and are often better not so, can be closed or open: closed endings answer all questions and curiosities and satisfy "all audience emotion"; open endings "leave a question or two unanswered and some emotion unfulfilled" (McKee 48).

When should you tell a story in writing? Let us repeat our rhetorical anthem: *It depends!* It depends on the situation, purpose, audience, and genre. Personal narratives are nothing but story, but even the stodgiest of technical grant proposals must tell the tale of how past attempts to solve a problem have failed and failed miserably. Research papers can begin with a story to hook readers emotionally; argumentative papers can use stories as evidence to accept arguments.

Where do you get stories? Four places: from your own life, from the lives of others (in your social circle, or in history or the news or biographies), from your imagination, or from existing fiction (novels, movies, folk tales, etc.). When I was young, my church pastor would tell the same story at Christmas every year: the story of George Bailey, banker of Bedford Falls, who learns from divine intervention to value his own life after trying to commit suicide. And every year, as he told the story, my pastor would sob—and the congregation would sob right with him—even though everyone knew he was just rehashing the plot from the Frank Capra movie *It's a Wonderful Life*.

3. **Tap shared values.** We talked about this strategy in reference to *ethos* and the relationship you build with your readers. One way to evoke emotion in your audience is to express support for something valued by the discourse community to which you and your readers belong. And conversely, you can evoke emotion by shouting "boo-hiss," so to speak, at the Bad Guys. This kind of rhetorical move was called *epideictic* in classical rhetoric: you praise the praiseworthy, or you blame the blameworthy (Aristotle *Rhetoric* 48). Value talk is central to public discourse, which often calls upon us to make moral judgments about how to get all the stuff to all the right people.

4. **Amplify with word choice.** You'll learn more about the term *diction* (meaning word choice) in the next chapter on style. For now, just think about how different words create different emotional buzzes in audiences. Think of the difference between the words *cheap* and *inexpensive*. If your friends told you that your dress looks *cheap*, would you take it as a compliment? But would you shy away from telling them it was a *bargain*?

Words have *denotations* (their standard dictionary definitions) and *connotations* (all the thoughts and feelings associated with a word in a context). The word *communism* may denote a political ideology, but in the United States the word evokes negative feelings beyond the word's definition. Some words evoke vague, but real, emotions because of the bundle of impressions they create in the minds of readers: words like *freedom*, *family*, *justice*, *love*, and *democracy*. Sometimes words used as metaphors can evoke powerful judgments. In 2005 *The Independent*, a center-left British newspaper, ran an online opinion article titled "The Rape of the Rainforest," about a Brazilian soybean farmer whose company worked to clear 10,000 square miles of Amazon rainforest in 2004 (McCarthy and Buncombe). How does the word *rape* work in the title? How are we meant to judge the Brazilian farmer's actions? Surely the word *rape* upgrades the act of cutting down trees to a violent crime.

Sometimes people use *euphemisms* to mute the emotional blow of something unpleasant. Employees are "let go" when their bosses fire them, and companies "downsize" when they fire a whole bunch of people; a man run over by a cement truck "passes away"; "pork" is the remnants of a pig that's been slaughtered, gutted, and sliced into pieces; your dog Rover is "put to sleep" when a vet injects him with massive amounts of pentobarbital; "having a drink" could mean slamming shots of Kentucky bourbon; a sexually promiscuous person has "been around the block"; an ugly person has a "sweet spirit"; thugs "talk some sense into him" by beating him senseless; a "slight delay" means she won't get on her plane for another three hours. All these euphemisms attempt to manage the emotions of the people hearing them. Certain words carry more emotional power than others.

5. **Call your audience to action.** Somewhere in your writing, you'll want to tell readers why what you've written matters. You'll suggest *implications* for your argument that answer the audience's burning question, "So what?" You want to convey to your readers that your ideas have consequences—and those consequences matter. You want them to feel a sense of urgency from the things you've said. One way to do that is to suggest that audiences take action. Even stodgy academic writers do this when—say, at the end of an article on the mating practices of the slipper limpet snail—they call for further research on the issue. Many genres invite this kind of move. At the very least, you can ask your readers to think differently about the issue you've addressed. Sometimes it's appropriate to suggest some kind of collective action ("As Group X, we need to do Y"). You may also find it appropriate to tell the government or some other organization to change its ways ("It's time for the state legislature to provide equal housing opportunities for everyone, regardless of sexual orientation"). Once you've invoked emotion, it's your rhetorical responsibility to help readers think about what to do with those emotions—in other words, how to act appropriately.

Decorum Is All

Undoubtedly it will have occurred to you—because you're wicked smart—that emotional appeals can be used to manipulate other people. You may feel that some of the strategies I've talked about sound like a recipe for bewitching people against their will. Am I asking you to play your audience like a two-bit piccolo? No.

Remember two things about pathos from our earlier discussion:

(1) You need some kind of emotional appeal, even when writing genres that seem formal or stuffy or official or otherwise all-too-rational; emotions, remember, drive the brain, and they help us form judgments, which is the whole purpose of rhetoric; and,

(2) emotional appeals, like all other appeals, should be *appropriate to the situation* you're writing in. They prepare your audience for appropriate action.

Yes—decorum, my friends, is all! When you're preparing to write, think about what kind of emotion is fitting for the situation. Overkill turns off your audience, especially if they don't share your opinion about the issue or see your emotional appeals as a fitting response or sign of good character. Emotional appeals can be subtle; at some low-burn level, comprehension itself (i.e., merely understanding something and feeling that knowledge work in you) delivers an emotional fix that invites us to judgment. But emotional appeals should be there each time you write, and they should be fitting.

I'll close with Daniel Goleman's words on emotional intelligence. Skill with emotional appeals allows writers "to shape an encounter, to mobilize and inspire others, to thrive in intimate relationships, to persuade and influence, to put others at ease" (113). That's powerful stuff.

09

Works Cited

Aristotle. *Nicomachean Ethics*. In *Introduction to Aristotle*. Ed. Richard McKeon. NY: Modern Library, 1947. 297–543.

Aristotle. *On Rhetoric*. 2nd ed. Transl. George A. Kennedy. NY: Oxford, 2007.

Aronson, Eliot. *The Social Animal*. Eleventh Edition. NY: Worth, 2012. Print.

Damasio, Antonio. *Descartes' Error: Emotion, Reason, and the Human Brain*. NY: Penguin, 1994.

Forgas, Joseph P. "The Role of Affect in Attitudes and Attitude Change." *Attitudes and Attitude Change*. Ed. William D. Crano and Radmila Prislin. NY: Psychology P, 2008. 131–158.

Franks, David. "The Neuroscience of Emotions." *Handbook of the Sociology of Emotions*. Ed. Jan E. Stets and Jonathan H. Turner. NY: Springer, 2006. 38–62.

Goleman, Daniel. *Emotional Intelligence*. NY: Bantam, 2005. Print.

Gottschall, Jonathan. *The Storytelling Animal*. NY: Mariner, 2012. Print.

Greene, Joshua. *Moral Tribes*. NY: Penguin, 2013. Print.

Heath, Chip and Dan Heath. *Made to Stick*. NY: Random House, 2007. Print.

Hertzberg, Hendrik. "Spilled Oil." *The New Yorker*. 28 June 2010. Web. 16 Feb 2015.

Kahneman, Daniel. *Thinking, Fast and Slow*. NY: Farrar, Straus, and Giroux, 2011. Print.

Kozol, Jonathan. *Savage Inequalities*. NY: Harper Perennial, 1991. Print.

Malkin, Michelle. "The Seduction of Hannah Montana." 29 April 2008. Blog post. Web. 19 Feb 2015.

McCarthy, Michael and Andrew Buncombe. "The Rape of the Rainforest." *The Independent*. 20 May 2005. Web. 22 Feb 2015.

McKee, Robert. *Story*. NY: Harper, 1997. Print.

Milbank, Dana. "Obama's Oil Spill Response." *Washington Post.* 30 May 2010. Web. 16 Feb 2015.

Poulakos, John. *Sophistical Rhetoric in Classical Greece.* Columbia: U of South Carolina P, 1995. Print.

"Remarks by the President on the Gulf Oil Spill." The White House. 27 May 2010. Web. 18 Feb 2015.

Solomon, Robert C. *True to Our Feelings.* NY: Oxford, 2007. Print.

Washington Post–ABC News Poll. 3–6 June 2010. Web. 18 Feb 2015.

Wilson, Timothy D. *Redirect.* NY: Back Bay, 2015.

WRITING RHETORICALLY—
PRINCIPLES OF STYLE

We've made it to the S in ACES (Go, Team Rhetoric!). We've covered

Argument
Character
Emotions,

and in the next two chapters we'll cover

Style.

Style—When You Do That Thing You Do

Every year, usually in the middle of Fall semester, my wife asks me about the new styles on campus. "What are students wearing these days?" she wonders. "What's trendy?"

And I answer, "I have no idea—I'm an absent-minded professor with more important things to worry about!"

But I'm lying. Like most everyone else, I'm not beneath noticing the trends hanging on the bodies of everyone on campus. Last year I noticed male students pegging (i.e., rolling up) their skinny jeans, which is something my friends and I did in sixth grade, back in 1986. One year, the galoshes came out—in all kinds of colors and styles—and replaced the sheepskin boots that passed for *Arctic chic* for a while. Popped collars come in and out. Having come of age in an era when hip-hop culture merged with Seattle grunge in an unholy alliance of baggy, sloppy, and flannel, I'm amused to see hipsters pulling off the sloppy but tightened-up lumberjack look. And this year the galoshes have been replaced by knee-high dressy leather boots, which soon will be replaced by herringbone combat boots with SmartBoot® wearable technology built into the shoelaces. (I made up that last part.)

And I know that everything I just said will be woefully out of date in five minutes.

How do you define style? When you say someone is *stylish*, what does that mean? If I wear jeans, a faded green t-shirt, and my University of Arizona hat (Go Wildcats!), do I have *style*? When do you know something's *out of style*?

Style means a *manner* of doing something. Our dictionary definitions talk about style as a *particular way* of doing something, a manner or characteristic habit or practice. Style, then, is unavoidable. You have a style of walking, talking, dressing, dancing, playing sports, eating, or brushing your teeth—even if you're not trying to. When you walk, you choose, consciously or otherwise, how to put one foot in front of the other and how to swing your arms or hold your head. All those decisions add up to your style of walking. (Wanna go insane? Focus deliberately on the way you walk for an entire day.)

But I bet you know someone with a *distinguished* walk, a walk that really sticks out in your mind, because somehow, compared to other walks, it has its own special step, swing, or swagger. In this sense, then, style is more than manner: It's about distinct individual expression—it's about grace, purposeful self-expression, elegance, flamboyance, skill, spunk, a unique voice.

When I think about style as a quality of writing, I like to think of it in both these ways. Every time you write, you write with style. You can't help it. Each sentence you write reflects a series of rhetorical decisions, a sensibility, even if the writing seems straightforward and unadorned. Paul Butler defines style in this way as "the deployment of rhetorical resources, in written discourse, to create and express meaning" (Butler 3). That pretty much sums up all the writing we do. But writing with style also means writing with a distinct voice that conveys a distinct personality to the reader, a personality that seeks to make an impression, to make the reading experience pleasurable. Novelist Mary McCarthy defines style more in this second sense as voice: as "the irreducible and always recognizable and alive thing" (Yagoda 23). Sounds like ethos, doesn't it? Style is ethos.

This "always recognizable and alive thing" we call style is a big part of what keeps a reader reading your work, or not. With each sentence, you take shape in the brain of the reader, taking the cerebral stage as a character in a rhetorical drama. That character becomes recognizable and real to readers through style, and style makes the reading experience what it is.

In this chapter and the next, I want to help you improve how you write with style in both senses of the word—rhetorical choice *and* compelling voice. To make that happen, though, we need to get to work: There are things you need to *do* to improve your style, and there are concepts you need to *understand* to be a lifelong stylistic writer. We'll talk about both in this chapter. We'll save the nuts and bolts of style strategies for the next.

Your Stylistic Workout Regimen

If you want to master rhetorical choice and compelling voice, you'll have to hit the exercise equipment. Let me be your personal trainer for a moment. I suggest a regimen of seven exercises that will help you develop your writing style:

1. **Read good writing.** Good readers can become good writers in part because they internalize the language of writing. They see how the pros use prose. Your universe is full of amazing writers writing in every genre imaginable. Find some really great writing and read it. Try poetry. I'm not a natural poetry-lover, but I try to read at least one book of poetry each year from contemporary poets. Find an essay writer that makes you laugh (I like David Sedaris and Mary Roach). Look for a compelling ethos emerging from a blog or Twitter feed. Read online magazines and news outlets. Don't always settle for a quickie skim of the headlines; burrow into an article that takes more than five minutes to read. Read the National Book Award or Pulitzer Prize winners.

2. **Keep a journal.** You should have a special writing space where you can write whatever you want, capture cool quotes and sentences, wax bold and eloquent, make mistakes, and experiment with style. These writing spaces are often called *commonplace* books, described by one scholar as "blank bound volumes in which one writes down vivid images, great descriptions, striking turns of phrase, ideas, high points from one's life and reading" (Richardson 19). You don't need a pretentious moleskin notebook. You can use a note-taking app on your phone (if you have thumbs of fury) or an online notebook (blogs or Google Docs make good commonplace books); it's nice to be able to cut and paste. Become a sentence hunter: While you read, look for amazing sentences and jot them down. I have about 120 sentences in my collection, with writers ranging from Ray Bradbury to J.K. Rowling.

3. **Imitate cool sentences.** If you make sentence-hunting a habit, you can *imitate* some of your favorites so you can learn new strategies. Imitating sentences is old-school: kids in ancient Greece and Rome learned to speak and write with power by imitating the work of the masters (Clark). Imitation (the Greeks called it *mimesis*) has a bad reputation because everyone wants to be An Original these days. But originality is overrated—maybe even impossible, considering that creators influence each other all the time. As Kirby Ferguson points out,

everything is a remix. To imitate a sentence, try this method: (a) find a cool sentence you like—more complex sentences work better; (b) write down the sentence *exactly as you see it* in your journal; (c) study for a moment the way the writer has combined phrases and clauses or used punctuation; and then (d) write your own sentence using the same grammatical structure (same noun and verb phrases, same order and type of phrases and clauses). Try on the voice of another writer to get a sense of your stylistic range. Someone—it might have been Pablo Picasso—once said, "Good artists copy; great artists steal."

4. **Combine sentences**. Imagine two sentences: "I'm a writer" and "My mother is proud." How many different ways can we combine those two sentences to make meaning? Here are the first three I thought of: "My mother is proud that I'm a writer," "I'm a writer—my mother is proud," or "My mother, because I'm a writer, is proud." What choices did I make to combine these sentences? How does each new sentence convey a unique meaning different from the others? For years, research has shown that doing such exercises strengthens your ability to write compelling sentences (Dean 87; Strong 2). Your instructor can help you find sentence-combining exercises, and you can find more online.

5. **Learn some grammar terms**. Yep, I said it. You can't fully analyze a person's style, including your own, until you've figured out the way the English language works on the page. You don't need to go all out and memorize the hundreds of terms you find in a book on English grammar. In fact, packing your head with all that stuff might *hurt* you as a writer (Graham and Perin). At the very least, you probably should know something about *syntax*—how words, phrases, and clauses pile up in a sentence to make meaning—and *modification*—how words, phrases and clauses enhance the meaning of other words, phrases, and clauses. If you don't know how sentences work, you and your instructor won't be able to talk as freely and usefully about the sentences you write. We'll talk more about syntax and modification in the next chapter.

6. **Rewrite**. I learned to develop my style by rewriting the heck out of my own writing. And you can, too. Take a short paragraph of your own writing and see if you can rewrite the entire thing without looking at the earlier draft. Get in the habit of reworking sentences until they *zing*—rewording, combining, rearranging, deleting, destroying, garnishing. Remember that "a difference of style is always a

difference in meaning," even if the shift is subtle (Beardsley 7). You have options—use them. As you learn different sentence types and methods of modification, you'll have more moves to make as a writer. As you rewrite, you'll feel more freedom to play with language; novice writers often feel that when they write sentences, they carve them in stone. Without play, you can't develop your style.

7. **Compose out loud, revise out loud.** Sometimes when I'm in a conference with a student and we're stuck on a funky clunky sentence, I'll say, "Why don't you just tell me what you were trying to say here." Nine times out of ten, whatever they say, right there on the spot, is better than what they were trying to say in writing—and by "better" I mean clearer, more concise, more interesting, more voiced. In *Vernacular Eloquence*, Peter Elbow teaches writers that we have "a rich store of eloquent linguistic resources" from our everyday speech that often goes untapped in writing (7). As I've said before, speech is natural but writing requires explicit motor practice. Because writing is not natural, students often write in a stilted, stuffy, and formal way because they think that's what a teacher wants. We denigrate the way we speak as sloppy when in fact our speaking can be clearer, easier to process, more lively and diverse, and more emotionally engaging to audiences than our writing.

So Elbow suggests we use our natural speaking abilities at various stages in the writing process. For example, in the early stages we can try "unplanned speaking onto the page," by which he means talking through what we plan to write or using freewriting as a way to capture ideas that might otherwise be roadblocked by the fastidious editor in our brains (Elbow 139). He also recommends reading drafts aloud. Reading your drafts out loud is a revelation. I've rewritten many a sentence that looked fine on paper but sounded like a train wreck when I read it out loud. I find, too, that if I read out loud to my wife Amy, editor and friend now for fifteen years, I'm more attentive to the way I sound to someone else. When we read writing out loud, we develop empathy for our readers because we can *hear* how we sound in a reader's head.

Writers get better when they're mindful about getting better. Remember that Great Truth from Chapter One? Writers get better *at their style* when they *become mindful apprentices of style*. I'm inviting you to join me in becoming a Style Apprentice. We don't have uniforms or sashes or t-shirts or cookies or anything, but we do have rhetorical power!

Okay, we've talked about what you can *do* as a Style Apprentice. For the rest of the chapter, we'll talk about what you need to *know* about style.

The Virtues of Style

What makes a date a *good* date? When I was in my early twenties, a few of my family members and friends were foolhardy enough to set me up on blind dates. And after each one, I thought, "Does [fill in the blank with name of guilty family member] know *anything* about me?" It seemed that my date and I were about as compatible as a smartphone and bathwater. (I blame myself.) So maybe one cardinal virtue of a good date would be compatibility—that click-y "goes together nicely" feeling we get when we're with someone with whom we share a certain affinity.

What makes a writing style a good writing style?

According to the philosophers of antiquity, the Four Cardinal Virtues of the Soul are prudence, justice, temperance, and courage. The ancient rhetoricians had Four Cardinal Virtues of Good Style, too, and they still resonate today: Good writing is fitting, clean, clear, and compelling. As a writer, you should cultivate these four virtues as you write.

First: Good style—and here, surely, I'll shock the pants right off you—is **fitting.** Yes, my friends, style, like any other rhetorical decision, should be a welcomed guest to the rhetorical situation (see chapter six). You've seen this come up before in previous chapters. I don't want to oversimplify things, but in essence rhetorical choices are effective when they are appropriate, full-stop. In one of his dialogues, the Roman rhetorician Cicero has one of his characters say, "there is really no rule that I could give you at this point"—about style, he means—only that "we should see to it that [the style] is adapted to the problem at hand" (290).

Style is most effective when it's appropriate for the targeted audience. For example, I have had writing projects rejected by academic journals because the reviewers said my style was too casual for the venue. And I'm pretty sure if I'd written, as I did in the last paragraph, "here, surely, I'll shock the pants right off you" in a manuscript for a scholarly journal, I would have been rejected in one hot minute. But I think of you as friends (really!), so I thought it would be okay (i.e., fitting) in this setting. Your genre will guide your stylistic decisions, as will your audience and purpose. This Cardinal Virtue reminds us that style is not necessarily something you find in a text; you find it in the *context*, in the interaction between writer and reader as mediated by the text. As two writing scholars have said, "style embodies or defines relationships between people" (Holcomb and Killingsworth 4). Style, then, is fitting when it's appropriate for the genre.

The reading experience creates an ethos that is either fitting or not-so-fitting for the work that needs to be done to respond to the situation's exigence. Your goal as a Style Apprentice is to imagine how your rhetorical choices influence a particular audience through the sound of words on the page or screen. Let the style fit the situation. You don't wear the wild Hawaiian-print shirt to the business interview (unless you're interviewing with a flakey tech start-up run by brilliant, iconoclastic college dropouts). Consider aspects like *level of formality, familiarity with the audience* (e.g., strangers often misread sarcasm), *idiomatic phrases, jargon or insider talk, allusions, contractions, slang, sexist language* (e.g., avoid the indefinite masculine), and what Holcomb and Killingsworth call "*the interplay of convention and deviation*" (39). This last consideration is important. Each situation has certain constraints and certain freedoms; it's important to know the difference.

I can't help but add one more thing about the concept of "fitting." I have many students who believe that the most fitting style for academic writing is a stuffy, formal, rhetorically-distant tone that approximates (at least the writer imagines it does) a scholar scholarizing. When we get to college, we have to write our way through it, and we often default to a formal tone—without warmth, full of jargon, and needlessly complicated. Though I've said that your style should fit the situation and genre, we have more latitude as writers than we think to write reader-friendly prose. I love how John Trimble says it in *Writing with Style*: "View your reader as a companionable friend" and "write like you're actually talking to that friend" (73). There's rhetorical space even in technical documents for a warm, simple, and direct style to be fitting.

Second, good style is **clean**. By *clean* I mean as free as possible from errors in grammar, spelling, punctuation, diction, mechanics, document design, and fact.

Look: I've said before that errors happen. We make them, no matter how careful we are. And William James is right:

> Our errors are surely not such awfully solemn things. In a world where we are so certain to incur them, in spite of all our caution, a

certain lightness of heart seems healthier than this excessive nervousness on their behalf. (James 470)

In addition, language changes somewhat. It's flexible; it's our tool. There are varieties of English, from a variety of cultures, and we should celebrate that. We ourselves shift registers when speaking to different audiences; we present different selves in language, depending on rhetorical situation (Gee 87). Linguists think of grammar as a way to describe what we do with language, not as a system of rigid laws carved on the tablets of humanity. So you might as well criticize "the song of the humpback whale" or the spider's web as criticize the way we use language (Pinker 383). Some rules are solid and hardwired: the standard English subject-verb-object (SVO) formation tells me that writing *high grammar learned school you in* will cause serious problems for readers, even those readers who respect Yoda, the grammatically creative Jedi in *Star Wars*. Other rules are more like *conventions* of usage commonly accepted by People Who Seem to Know (like teachers). Sometimes those conventions make no sense. *Don't split infinitives*, they say. *Don't begin sentences with conjunctions like* and *or* but. And (ha!) these conventions get flaunted by professional writers all the time.

But (double ha!) here's the thing: Errors, insofar as readers notice them, create static. Readers see them—not in any predictable fashion, sometimes, but they see them. Error, it's true, is mostly in the eye of the beholder, i.e., the reader, and if the reader doesn't see them, then they might as well not exist (Williams). However, we've already established in chapter seven that errors mar credibility; alas, they make us look dumb. One of the earliest and most charitable scholars of writing error, Mina Shaughnessy, writes that errors are "unintentional and unprofitable intrusions upon the consciousness of the reader." Often they "carry messages which writers can't afford to send" (12). Perhaps Cicero (first-century rhetorician) said it worst: "Nobody has ever admired an orator for speaking correct Latin; if he doesn't they actually make fun of him, and not only consider him no orator, but not even a human being" (238). It's mean to dehumanize people for their writing skills—and it reveals elitist thinking and ignorance of the dynamics of language. But, okay, Cicero may be right at least this far: Error has social consequences.

What I emphatically *don't* want to do is perpetuate the equally ugly idea that error-free writing is the end-all, be-all of learning to write. Many a student's writing spirit has been crushed in the claws of school teachers who treat learning to write as the art of not making mistakes. Forgive the soapboxing, but I feel that it's particularly cruel to mark up an elementary school child's writing with red ink for not getting the commas in the right place. If we fixate on error when learning to write, we become like a centipede overthinking where to put its feet while walking. (Thanks, Francis Christensen, for that metaphor.) When we write, we want to be treated like someone with ideas and thoughts and arguments and interesting things to say. Having our errors called out often feels like our ethos has been demolished because we have a slightly crooked tooth. Writing classes should be safe places to make mistakes and learn from them.

So: Where does that leave us on the whole *clean* issue? Remember, first, that you should attend to *surface-level issues* late in your drafting process, as we talked about in chapter three. In the drafting stage, you should just write with unfettered ecstasy and leave the problem of error to later reviewing, revising, editing, and polishing. But keep your audience in mind! Prepare your drafts so that peers or instructors will not get caught up in speed bumps that might be avoided with a quick proofread. As reluctantly as I might say it, you need to understand that your stylistic decisions constitute an *ethos*; with each sentence, you invite the reader into a reading experience. Glaring errors make both efforts rough rowing, especially when you're in the professional world. (I've seen hundreds of blog posts about how errors in business and social media writing can damage brands or reputations.) One last thought: many errors are actually *patterns* of error that show a kind of logical thinking about language (Shaughnessy). Look for patterns of error in your work when you're revising, and consult a handbook if you're not familiar with some of the more popular, and rhetorically important, conventions.

The third Cardinal Virtue is this: Good writing is **clear**. Clarity is one of those virtues that textbooks throw out there with great centrifugal force, as if divine beings had commanded that we be clear in our writing. The word is also an abstraction—what does it mean? In the field of writing studies, it is somewhat controversial (Butler; Howard; Lanham). Some scholars feel that those who focus so enthusiastically on clarity as a cardinal virtue ignore not only the virtue of complexity and eloquence but the value of context. They make clarity sound Puritan; nobody wants to party with that boring stick-in-the-mud *Clarity*! Shakespeare is hard to read, and yet he is considered one of the five most important people in the last millennium.

Richard Lanham, one of clarity's skeptics, gives us a working definition: "clarity indicates a successful relationship between reader and writer" (57). Its first job "is to make us feel at home" (50). I like that metaphor: As readers we slip into a clear style like we slip into Grandma's comfy chair. That's what we want the reading experience to be like for our readers. We want our writing to be understood. We don't want to waste our readers' time or confuse them. In *Performing Prose*, Chris Holcomb and Jimmie Killingsworth help us understand that clarity is a "convention of readability" that exhibits five attributes: it's active (meaning, subjects and verbs are clear—more on this in the next chapter), it flows, it's organized for emphasis, it uses familiar language, and it's concise (41–48). We live in a saturated world. Your writing competes with a deluge of other activities people could be doing, like playing video games on their phones. When you write clearly, you set up the relationship quickly and smoothly, therefore advancing your purpose to influence attitudes.

I know this principle may sound abstract at this point. But there's a simple idea behind clarity: Most of the time, we want our readers to understand what we're saying without having to work too hard at it. There are exceptions, absolutely. Sometimes we want readers to lean over the page with scrunched eyebrows and struggle with us as we struggle with complex ideas. When we write stories or poems, we may be more interested in giving readers a profound (and confounding) experience than in delivering a simple message. In the busy flow of practical language, however, clarity is key. In 2010, the United States Government passed Public Law 111–274, titled the "Plain Writing Act of 2010," in order "to improve the effectiveness and accountability of Federal agencies to the public by promoting clear Government communication that the public can understand and use" ("Plain Writing"). The spirit of the law is instructive: When the stakes are high (imagine legal or medical writing), we are responsible to write in a language our readers understand.

Finally, good writing should be **compelling**. Let us, for a moment, consider the termite, as it appears in the language of Wikipedia (I've done some editing for length here):

> Termites are eusocial insects in the cockroach order Blattodea. Like ants, termites live in colonies where labor is divided in castes. Termites feed mostly on dead plant material, mostly in the form of wood, leaf litter, soil, or animal dung. As pests, they can cause serious structural damage to buildings, crops, or forests. Termites are major detritivores, particularly in the subtropical and tropical regions. Their

recycling of wood and other plant matter is of considerable ecological importance.

Ah, the language of science! This is, I'd say, a perfectly respectable paragraph. It's simple. It contains factual information (as far as I know—I'm no entomologist). You could say that it's *correct* and *clear*—two of our cardinal virtues. Maybe it's fitting for a crowd-sourced world encyclopedia used by strangers for quick factual information. But what happened to you as you read the paragraph? Did you feel yourself slipping into a familiar role as "reader of encyclopedic information"? Each sentence sounds about the same as the others. No ethos emerges from it except maybe an *ethos* interested in sharing somewhat disconnected facts about termites.

Now let's look at the way science writer Natalie Angier tackles termites:

> Or consider termites, the primary groundskeepers of tropical rainforests. They gnaw through dead or rotting trees and return much of the woody wealth back to the forest floor. What is a termite but a set of jaws joined to a petri dish, its gut a dense microecosystem of many hundreds of strains of microbes. Bacteria allow termites to wrest sustenance from sawdust and, like Gepetto, give dead wood a voice. (Angier 185)

I'd argue that Angier's writing is more lively than Wikipedia's (no offense, I hope, to the hundreds of people who may have crowd-sourced that paragraph). In the first example, termites are "eusocial insects in the cockroach order"; for Angier, they're "groundskeepers," a term which personifies termites, making them sound like little squishy helpers taking care of business. Whereas the first example talks of "their recycling of wood," Angier uses her *W*s and *F*s in the sonorous "woody wealth back to the forest floor." She also plays with sound when she says "wrest sustenance from sawdust," an unusual and interesting phrase. She exaggerates the termite's anatomy, or underplays it: a "set of jaws joined to a petri dish." That's a fascinating image. Notice, too, the Pinocchio allusion at the end: comparing termites to Gepetto, creator and father of the magical wooden boy, is both weird and wonderful. It surprises and delights. It's playful.

Both excerpts demonstrate rhetorical choices. The second one alone shows how writing can be that "always recognizable and alive thing"— a distinguished and unique voice meant to create a pleasurable reading experience. Writing can be, and most always should be, compelling in this sense. In the words of Aristotle, compelling prose makes "language unfamiliar"; as pattern-seekers, we pay attention to variations, surprises, delights (Aristotle 198). Classical rhetoricians often called this virtue *ornamentation*, but that word implies cosmetic frippery, making style seem like a fancy sweater on a ferret or something. Instead, I like the word *compelling* for the power it invokes. A reader admires a compelling prose style almost in spite of herself. It invites attention, interest, admiration, joy. It breaks the boring plane of row upon row of words and says, "Hey! I want you to *really enjoy* what I'm telling you!" Compelling prose is pathos, as well as ethos.

How do you make your writing compelling? I'll share a few ways in the next chapter, but here are a few strategies, for starters: metaphor, proverbs, schemes (clever language patterns, like repetition), humor, hyperbole, analogy, allusion, imagery, sentence variation, surprising use of words, irony, satire, sentence fragments, parallelism, rhythm, poetic patterns (like alliteration), questions, direct address, emphasis. Sometimes these strategies will just tumble out of you while writing. At other times, you can revise them into your drafts, always keeping in mind how your specific audience might respond to your stylistic invitation to dance. I'm not suggesting you choke your sentences with piled-up purply tricks that will weary the reader because they're too obviously playful. You still have to be fitting, clean, and clear. But you don't have to be *ordinary*. That's why we often encourage writers to avoid cliches—those tired phrases that are like beating a dead…well…that are overused.

May I be frank here? So much of what we read in our lives is boring. And I say that as someone with great respect for anyone who tries to get things done with writing. In spite of my best efforts to engage you, I'm sure from time to time I've bored you in this book. (If that's the case, please, for the love of Aristotle, don't tell me.) Learning to persevere through boredom is a life skill; at times we must work through boredom to find meaning and use in the texts we read. Smartphones have made boredom even more painful because we know we can reach in our pockets at any time and find instant delight in text messages, video games, social media feeds, or photos. But you, my friend, do not have to be boring when you write! Each time you write, you take the stage. You open a relationship. You tell another human being, "Come, sit down. I have something to tell you, and you're gonna like this." You create an experience rich with meaning, with possibility. You make *contact*. Even the most technical and seemingly boring genres have room for distinction.

Welcome to your style apprenticeship!

10

Works Cited

Angier, Natalie. *The Canon*. Boston: Houghton Mifflin, 2007. Print.

Beardsley, Monroe C. "Style and Good Style." *Contemporary Essays on Style*. Ed. Glen A. Love and Michael Payne. Glenview, IL: Scott, Foresman, 1969. 3–15. Print.

Butler, Paul. *Out of Style*. Logan, UT: Utah State UP, 2008. Print.

Cicero. *On the Ideal Orator*. Trans. James M. May and Jakob Wisse. NY: Oxford UP, 2001. Print.

Clark, Donald Lemen. *Rhetoric in Greco-Roman Education*. NY: Columbia, 1957. Print.

Dean, Deborah. *What Works in Writing Instruction*. Urbana, IL: NCTE, 2010. Print.

Elbow, Peter. *Vernacular Eloquence*. NY: Oxford UP, 2012. Print.

Gee, James Paul. *Social Linguistics and Literacies*. London: Routledge, 2012. Print.

Graham, Steve and Dolores Perin. *Writing Next: Effective Strategies to Improve Writing in Adolescents in Middle and High School*. Report for the Carnegie Corporation of New York. 2007. Web. 2 March 2015.

Holcomb, Chris and M. Jimmie Killingsworth. *Performing Prose*. Carbondale and Edwardsville: Southern Illinois UP, 2010. Print.

Howard, Rebecca Moore. "Contextualist Stylistics." *Refiguring Prose Style*. Ed. T.R. Johnson and Tom Pace. Logan, UT: Utah State UP, 2005. 42–56.

James, William. *Writings: 1878–1899*. NY: Library of America, 1984.

Lanham, Richard A. *Style: An Anti-Textbook*. Philadelphia: Paul Dry, 2007. Print.

Pinker, Steven. *The Language Instinct: How the Mind Creates Language*. NY: Harper, 1994. Print.

"Plain Writing Act of 2010." Public Law 111–274. U.S. Government Publishing Office. 13 Oct 2010. Web. 10 March 2015.

Richardson, Robert D. *First We Read, Then We Write*. Iowa City: U of Iowa P, 2009.

Shaughnessy, Mina. *Errors and Expectations*. NY: Oxford, 1977. Print.

Strong, William. *Sentence Combining*. 3rd ed. NY: McGraw-Hill, 1994. Print.

Trimble, John R. *Writing with Style: Conversations on the Art of Writing*. 2nd ed. Upper Saddle River, NJ: Prentice Hall, 2000. Print.

Williams, Joseph M. "The Phenomenology of Error." *College Composition and Communication* 32.2 (1981): 145–168. Print.

Yagoda, Ben. *The Sound on the Page*. NY: Harper, 2004. Print.

WRITING RHETORICALLY— ANATOMY OF STYLE

In the last chapter we covered the exercises of the style apprentice (that's you) and the Cardinal Virtues of Good Style. Now we get down to brass tacks. I hope what I've said so far helps you understand some theory behind style—why it's important, how you can get better at it, what makes it effective. In this final section, I invite you to master a vocabulary that will help you talk about specific surface-level strategies in writing. Without this vocabulary, we end up talking about style in the vague way we sometimes talk about love ("It's a feeling you feel when you're feeling a feeling you've never felt before"). This vocab will help you analyze stylistic strategies in other writers and use style more purposefully in your own writing.

Here I've been selective, and brief. The top shelf in my office is filled entirely with books on style. Handbooks are more thorough than this, websites more expansive (check out Gideon Burton's "The Forest of Rhetoric" website). In the interest of brevity, I don't cover emphasis, cohesion, coherence, metadiscourse, rhythm, various grammatical and visual principles, and a slew of rhetorical terms from *anadiplosis* to *zeugma*. Your instructor will help you prioritize and build on what I'm giving you here, but the following six principles work as a good enough start. (I'd invent a forgettable acronym, but amazingly there are no vowels to play with. How does DSMSPD stick in your brain? Dissim sped? Forget it.)

Six Strategies of Style

11.1 Diction

In an article in *The Atlantic* about a terrorist group called ISIS (Islamic State in Iraq and Syria), Graeme (pronounced "graham," like the cracker) Wood explains how terrorists often speak so intelligently about their cause. Then he writes this sentence:

> If they had been froth-spewing maniacs, I might be able to predict that their movement would burn out as the psychopaths detonated themselves or became drone-splats, one by one. (Wood)

Zow! Ordinary? Hardly. Graeme Wood peppers his sentence with strategic words that catch our attention, creating both meaning and atmosphere.

"Froth-spewing maniacs" combines imagery (someone spewing froth— ew) and moral judgment (we think of maniacs as unbalanced and dangerous). Psychopaths are, quite literally, the mentally diseased whose antisocial behavior is uninhibited and scary; in the context of terrorism, they *detonate themselves*. Finally, he creates the compound phrase "drone-splats" to describe the disturbing result of a military drone strike. It's almost too dismissive—the *splat* sounds gross, even ironically cutesy, which shocks us when we consider the controversial gravity of U.S. drone strikes in the Middle East.

Wood has made some stylistic choices here that we call *diction*. Many of you have heard the word before in English literature classes. It means word choice. It's weird, though, leaving it at that, since *all* the writing we do requires word choice; you can't get around it: you're always choosing words when you write. How else can you write? So how is diction a rhetorical strategy, and what do you need to know to use it effectively?

I have a few ideas, and undoubtedly your instructor will, too. Here are four biggies:

1. **Denotation and connotation**: Words have dictionary definitions. They also have cultural meanings beyond those definitions—meanings and associations evoked by the word but not necessarily synonymous with its dictionary definition. The dictionary definition is the *denotation*. The Oxford English Dictionary defines the word *government* as "the action of governing" or "the governing power in a State." But when we use the word *government* in writing, particularly in political writing, the word evokes certain attitudes and emotions beyond "the action of governing." For many people, like political conservatives, the word suggests overgrown bureaucracy, corruption, lies, strangling regulations (Lemann 108). Another example from politics: In the 1960s the word *liberal* had positive connotations; the politically minded scrambled to look and act liberal because it was popular to be a liberal. (Look up the word in a dictionary to find its denotation.) By the late 1970s, however, liberalism was associated with "spinelessness, malevolence, masochism, elitism, fantasy, anarchy, idealism, softness, irresponsibility, and sanctimoniousness" (Nunberg 43). Because the word has become so toxic, democrats like Hillary Clinton call themselves *progressives* to avoid negative connotations. Good writers are aware of the cultural connotations of the words they use.

Likewise, we often use words or phrases to hide meaning. When we want to conceal the denotative meanings of unpleasant terms, we use *euphemisms* like "passed on" for *died* or "laid off" and "let go" for *fired* or "take a pit stop," "powder my nose," and "see a man about a horse" for…well, y'know. Writers use these terms to soften the blow of certain realities like sex, bodily functions, or war (e.g., "enhanced interrogation techniques" instead of *torture*). Sometimes we create euphemisms to deflect responsibility for terrible things. Euphemisms are rhetorically powerful, and sometimes irresponsible. We also use *cacophemisms* (don't you just love that word?) to do the opposite: make something sound more dreadful than it is. An estate tax becomes a *death tax* and end-of-life medical consultations get called *death panels*. Racial slurs and vulgar nicknames fall in this category, as do words that should be neutral but become derogatory because they're used to cast a negative judgment on something (like calling someone a *hipster* or a *jock* and not meaning it as a compliment).

2. **Lexical field**: Words create rhetorical relationships with audiences. When we write, we create what Jeanne Fahnestock calls a "lexical field," or a reading environment made up of words related to particular topics and ways of speaking (Fahnestock 62). If I were to thumb through a copy of the *Journal of Microelectromechanical Systems* (yes, there is such a journal), I wouldn't be able to make heads or tails of the articles because of all the specialized language related to the topic. I'm not a member of that discourse community, so the specialized words—jargon, we call it—wouldn't make sense to me as it would to engineers or scientists. We use certain words for certain topics to show that we're in the know on that topic. If you're talking about transgenderism, for example, you'll need to know what the term *cisgender* means.

We can also think of lexical fields in terms of formality and informality. When we want to sound more casual, we use allusions (to cultural artifacts, like movies), idioms—phrases not to be taken literally (like "she's just pulling your leg")—or slang or contractions; we create intimacy with our readers that way. (Should you use a casual lexical field in an email to a professor or a cover letter for a job application?) Some words just sound more fancy than others (and I could have said *ostentatious, rococo,* or *resplendent* instead of *fancy*). We use ten-cent words to sound intelligent; sometimes student writers will thesaurize their essays assuming that teachers will be dazzled. Businesses or governments might use the word "containerize" instead of *put in a box* or "consideration of deferred action" for *please don't throw me in jail* (see "WonderMark").

Consider this example of transgressive thesaurus use from Corbett and Connors' book *Style and Statement:*

> After the conflagration had been extinguished, the police obstructed the thoroughfare and forefended all inquisitive spectators from perambulating before the incinerated residue of the pyrogenic catastrophe. (9)

What the writer means to say is...

> After the fire had been put out, the police roped off the street and prevented all sightseers from strolling past the charred ruins. (9)

We're looking at two problems here: (1) the ten-cent words from the first example are just gilding the lily (ever heard that saying?), i.e., clothing simple concepts in too-fancy dress, and (2) the writer chooses clusters of words that could be replaced with one or two ("incinerated residue of the pyrogenic catastrophe" instead of "charred ruins"). The second practice leads to wordiness, a problem not of long sentences but of sentences with unnecessary fluff. Any good handbook will teach you how to reduce clutter. For example, *Rules for Writers* shows you how to eliminate redundancies, avoid unnecessary repetition, cut inflated phrases (like "at this point in time"), and simplify sentences (Hacker and Sommers 156–161). Such practices make your writing concise, which is the opposite of wordy. Being *concise* is often a matter of picking the most fitting lexical field for the job, which reflects the virtue of clarity we talked about in the last chapter.

In sum, a lexical field is composed of all the words, key terms, and phrases you use in your writing. When you analyze diction, you're not analyzing a few scattered words: You're analyzing a constellation of words that create a persuasive atmosphere.

3. **Abstract and concrete**: Some words refer to concrete objects we experience with our senses. Other words evoke emotions or associations that you couldn't really sketch in a game of Pictionary. Take the word *freedom*. What does it mean? For Americans, the word could evoke anything from the end of slavery to ballpark hot dogs to "the

how ya think about ya," as they sing in the musical *Shenandoah*. When we use abstract language, we assume that our audience shares our understanding of the word, when actually there's wiggle room. Abstractions aren't necessarily bad. Rhetorician Jeanne Fahnestock writes that "abstract language can be as rhetorically appropriate and effective as concrete language" if, for example, you want to express grand ideas or shared values (66). When presidential candidates give speeches, they often use abstractions to invoke shared values that are hard to capture in words.

But abstract language can be too vague, too general, too unfitting for the situation. Write too generally, and your audience might think you don't know what you're talking about or that you're evading the truth. Vague words cause vague thinking. Specific, concrete language adds clarity, a sense that you're in control of the details. Why write the word *government* when you're really talking about the President or the Internal Revenue Service or some other specific government entity?

A particularly useful example of concrete language is *imagery*—another word a high-school literature teacher might have taught you. Imagery is vivid language that stirs our senses of sight, sound, smell, taste, touch. Check out Eric Schlosser's description of his visit to a meatpacking plant:

> A worker with a power saw slices cattle into halves as though they were two-by-fours, and then the halves swing by me into the cooler. It feels like a slaughterhouse now. Dozens of cattle, stripped of their skins, dangle on chains from their hind legs. […] The kill floor is hot and humid. It stinks of manure. Cattle have a body temperature of about 101 degrees, and there are a lot of them in the room. Carcasses swing so fast along the rail that you have to keep an eye on them constantly, dodge them, watch your step, or one will slam you and throw you onto the bloody concrete floor. (Schlosser 170)

Schlosser uses this visceral imagery for both *pathos* and *logos* in his criticism of America's obsession with fast food. He hopes his descriptions of fast food nation will be both emotionally disturbing and logically convincing. He wants to evoke in you a specific sensory experience. Imagery can be powerful; concrete language evokes and provokes.

4. **Amplification**: Some words have more *zing* than others. I wrote "zing" in that last sentence when "rhetorical power" would have sufficed. But zing captures the meaning of amplification—the method of choosing words for their emotional power when less evocative alternatives are available. Surely *drone-splat* is more evocative than, say, *victims of a drone strike*. I love finding examples of amplification because it helps me expand my own writing options. In Helen Macdonald's book on falconry, she writes this sentence:

> Maybe you've glanced out of the window and seen there, on the lawn, a bloody great hawk murdering a pigeon, or a blackbird, or a magpie, and it looks the hugest, most impressive piece of wildness you've ever seen, like someone's tipped a snow leopard into your kitchen and you find it eating the cat. (in Schulz 91)

A common hawk becomes a *bloody great hawk* and then, even more amplified, *the hugest most impressive piece of wildness you've ever seen*. Instead of catching a pigeon, it's *murdering* one, which makes the hawk's predator instincts sound evil. The snow leopard metaphor works to amplify the meaning as well: a ferocious beast in *your* kitchen, eating the cat. Not *a* cat, mind you—*the* cat, as in *your* cat.

Google the word *amplification* for additional examples and tricks. Ever heard of *hyperbole*, or overstatement? That's a form of amplification, too. When someone tells you there were, like, a zillion people waiting in line for the show, you know they're using amplification. The opposite of hyperbole is *litotes*, or understatement. If you called World War II a *skirmish* or *tiff*, you're using litotes for rhetorical effect. Amplification (and its opposite) serves our purposes by inviting readers into the play of language and meaning. In this sense, then, *irony* is a kind of amplification: You intensify meaning by inviting readers to understand that you mean something entirely different from what you're saying. Wink-wink.

11.2 Syntax

(You may want to review online the eight parts of speech and some simple grammar terms before reading this next part.)

The Greek word *taxis* means arrangement or order. In writing, syntax refers to the order of words, phrases, and clauses in a sentence. Earlier I mentioned the SVO arrangement of English sentences:

Charlotte kicked the cat.

Charlotte must have had a bad day. In this sentence, *Charlotte* is the subject; *kicked* is the verb (and it's a *transitive* verb, meaning that it's a verb doing something to something else); and *the cat* is the direct object. That's a pretty simple sentence for us to consider. Turns out there are only about ten ways to write simple sentences like the one above, and they all have to do with how you add verby stuff (like Be verbs and linking verbs and transitive verbs, etc.) to subjects.

Here's the cool part about syntax: You can make all kinds of amazing stylistic decisions by building on simple sentences. You can build in the front, like this:

When she came home from school, Charlotte kicked the cat.

Virginia Tufte calls the new stuff an *opener* (155). By adding a sentence opener, I've added meaning and a little drama to why Charlotte kicked the cat.

You can also build at the end:

Charlotte kicked the cat, **sending it tumbling down the stairs.**

We'll call this a *closer*, for obvious reasons. Now we have a sequence of events that fills out the story of the sentence even more. (I wonder, though, if cats *tumble*. They find their feet pretty fast.)

And you can even build right in the middle of the simple sentence:

Charlotte, **a feisty girl in a bad mood**, kicked the cat.

This new stuff is an *interrupter*. It splits the subject and the verb. Check out how novelist Virginia Woolf splits subject (Life itself) and verb (was enough) in this lovely sentence:

Life itself, **every moment of it, every drop of it, here, this instant, now, in the sun, in Regent's Park**, was enough.

You can also split the verb and the object, but in this instance it sounds a little weird:

Charlotte kicked, **with great malice**, the cat.

If you're in a daring mood, you can use an opener, closer, and interrupter all in the same sentence:

> When she came home from school, Charlotte, a feisty girl in a bad mood, kicked the cat, sending it tumbling down the stairs.

Not every sentence should look like this one, but I like what the syntax creates here. There's a rhythm. Our attention goes on an interesting journey with Charlotte and her feisty violence. (No animals were harmed in the drafting of this book.)

Another interesting choice for you: Sometimes we can move around these little add-ons—let's call them **modifiers**, because they enhance the meaning of the various parts of the simple sentence—to change the meaning we want to convey, like this:

> Charlotte kicked the cat **when she came home from school**. (Notice we don't use a comma here.)

I like the "when" stuff better as a sentence opener because the last part of the sentence gets the emphasis, and the kicking should be emphasized.

So the first thing I want you to understand about using syntax is that simple sentences grow into more complex, interesting sentences when we build on them in various ways.

You should know a few things about these growths called modifiers. First, modifiers can be words, phrases, or clauses. A phrase is a bundle of words that go together in a sentence:

- the big red car (this is a noun phrase)

- under the table (prepositional phrase)

- associate director of lab sciences and author of many articles (appositive phrase)

- his eyes bloodshot from crying (absolute phrase—all it's missing to become a clause is *were*)

- foaming at the mouth (participial phrase)

- would have been killed (verb phrase)

It's useful to understand how phrases work so you can use them to add variety, rhythm, and emphasis to sentences. When you vary your sentence lengths and syntax, you create what we often call *voice*, though I prefer *ethos*. We're not going to dive into all the different phrases and their uses here, but let me show you just a couple of incredibly useful phrase types you can use for rhetorical effect:

Participial phrases start with a verb ending in -ing or -ed, as in this lovely sentence from education writer Amanda Ripley:

> In other places, I saw kids bored out of their young minds, kids who looked up when a stranger like me walked into the room, **watching to see if I would, please God, create some sort of distraction to save them from another hour of nothingness.** (Ripley)

Appositive phrases are used to give more information (like authority) about a noun close by, like this:

> Natalie Angier, **Pulitzer Prize-winning journalist for the *New York Times*,** argues that we should learn about science solely because it's fun.

A *clause*, however, is more than a phrase—it has a subject and verb. So:

> foaming at the mouth

is a phrase, but

> My neighbor's German shepherd was foaming at the mouth

is a clause. Clauses can be complete sentences, but they don't have to be:

> *Since* my neighbor's German shepherd was foaming at the mouth...

That's a clause—an adverbial clause, actually, because it's giving us a reason or condition for an action—but we call it a *dependent* clause because it can't stand alone as a sentence. It needs to become an *independent clause* to mature into a sentence, like this:

> Since my neighbor's German shepherd was foaming at the mouth, **I decided not to pet it.**

Like phrases, clauses work in a variety of ways (e.g., as adverbials or, in the case of relative clauses, as adjectivals). A good writing handbook will help you sort through the different types and their operations.

We now have several shapes of sentences to consider (the x's represent the stuff we add—the modifiers—to the simple sentence or base clause):

_____. Here's our basic SVO "Charlotte kicked the cat" sentence.

_____, xxxxxxxxxxxxxx. The SVO as clause, with a closer on the end.

xxxxxxxxxxxxxxxxxxx, _____. With an opener.

_____, xxxxxxxxxxxxxxx, _____. With an interrupter.

xxxxxxxxxx, _____, xxxxxxxxxxxx, _____, xxxxxxxxxxx. With the whole funky parade.

If you've ever heard of simple, compound (two independent clauses fixed together with a coordinating conjunction), complex (a dependent clause attached to an independent clause either as an opener or closer), or compound-complex sentences (dependent clause and at least two independent clauses), then you already know something about syntax, which, you now know, is all about building sentences by putting words, phrases, and clauses together in a variety of ways, like my kids build a variety of wooden trains by coupling engines and cars together in different orders. (How would you map out that sentence I just wrote?)

So, who cares? What's the point of this syntax talk? When you know how to use syntax, you add variety and rhythm to your sentences. You build meaning, sending your readers on little jogs of thought. Often I find myself playing with syntax after I've completed a draft. I'll combine two shortish sentences by turning one into an adverbial dependent clause, or, if all the sentences in a paragraph sound about the same, I'll shake things up by adding a subject-verb interruptor (like an appositive) to a sentence. Sometimes I'll change a sentence so that the most important point falls at the end, because the end gets the emphasis.

If you're a committed sentence-hunter, you'll find delightful sentences everywhere you look, in all varieties, like spring flowers, each a one-of-a-kind. Here's one Anne Fadiman wrote in her book *The Spirit Catches You and You Fall Down*, about a three-year-old Hmong girl named Lia whose seizures kept her hospitalized for much of her early life in Merced, California:

> One night, while Lia Lee was in the emergency room at MCMC for the umpteenth time and a translator was present, Dan Murphy, who happened to be on call, brought up the subject of her anticonvulsant medications. (Fadiman 53)

The base clause in this sentence is *Dan Murphy brought up the subject.* Everything else in the sentence is syntactic jewelry, demonstrating Fadiman's options as a stylist. (Can you write your own sentence in imitation of her syntax?)

Passive and Active Syntax

Since syntax depends so much on the verbs you use, we should talk briefly about the difference between *passive* and *active voice*, terms you may have heard in previous writing classes. The idea behind passive sentences is simple: A passive sentence hides the actor that "does" the verb, like this:

> Oxycodone was given to the patient.

Who gave oxycodone to the patient? Nobody knows. Could have been anyone.

Passive constructions like the one above have a bad reputation. You may hear a writing teacher say, "Don't write in passive voice," making that rule sound like the eleventh commandment. I've also seen writing instructors teach students to eliminate every *to be* verb in their writing, even though many *Be* patterns are not passive:

> Brian is a writing teacher.

> Brian is down in the basement playing *BioShock 2.*

> Brian is impatient but handsome.

> Brian is just waiting, with John Mayer, for the world to change.

I suppose if all you've got in your repertoire are *Be* sentences, you're in trouble. But these sentences ain't passive. And sometimes it makes rhetorical sense to use passive syntax. Take the oxycodone example. What if we don't care who gave the patient the oxycodone? In some instances, the actor is not as important as the receiver of the action. What if the sentence read like this:

> Oxycodone was given to the patient, and the patient had a dangerous allergic reaction.

The focus, then, is on the patient's reaction to the medicine and not the giver of the medicine. This sentence would be particularly useful if we were trying to avoid pinning blame on the giver of the oxycodone (Don't sue us, dear patient!), or if we don't know who gave it. (Mom hears a crash, comes running, sees shards of broken flower vase on the carpet, looks at you and your sister, asks, with exasperation, "How did this happen?", and you say, "The ball was kicked into it.") You may also find that passive syntax gives your sentence a particular rhythm that works well. The sentence

> Oxycodone was given to the patient by the doctor.

is still passive, even though now we have an actor (the doctor), but maybe I like this construction better, for whatever reason (see Tufte 78).

So why avoid passive syntax? Several style textbooks encourage us to get actors and actions together as often as possible (Lanham *Revising Prose*; Williams and Colomb). Remember that we're hardwired to appreciate a good story, and sentences tell stories about actors acting (e.g., Charlotte kicking cats); that's how we're programmed to understand sentences. Try to tease out actor and action in this sentence:

> The utilization of offshore banking leads to reductions in taxation collection at the federal level.

We're in luck: I just Googled this sentence and no one, in the Googleverse, has ever written this pile of tripe. What this sentence wants to say is

> When American corporations bank offshore, the federal government can't collect as much tax revenue from them.

And of course this upsets the Citizens for Tax Justice. But what's more upsetting is that the first banking sentence buries actors and actions: In the first part, the actor (American corporations) doesn't even make an appearance, and the verb (potentially, *bank* or *use*) is obscured by what we call a *nominalization*—that's a nouny thing that could be a verb, like "utilization of" instead of *use*. (Did you notice that I just used passive voice to obscure myself as the writer of the bad sentence? The verb "is obscured.") The writer and teacher Joseph Williams made himself famous fighting the battle against these kinds of sentences. Let's join him.

So: When you write active sentences, you do several things. You…

1. bring actors (if at all possible, humans) and actions together in clear S-V format;

2. avoid what Richard Lanham calls "blah blah *is that*" openers, like "The fact of the matter is that…" (12);

3. avoid preposition pile-ups, like "The policy **of** the mayor **from** the beginning **of** her second term **of** office **in** the city **of** Detroit **for** education policy was…." Lanham calls this stuff *lard* (4); and "You," thus: lard (4); and you…

4. avoid nominalizing away perfectly good verbs: They use *present* (not presentation of), *avoid* (avoidance of), *fund* (funding of), *abandon* (abandonment of) (Williams and Colomb 32).

As you can see, there's lots to say about syntax. We've scratched the surface. The books I've cited in this section and, of course, ever and always, your writing teacher will take you further on the path to writing with rhythm, voice, variety, and emphasis by using syntax effectively.

11.3 Metaphors

Rhetoricians in the past define a *trope* as a rhetorical strategy that changes the ordinary, taken-for-granted meaning of words. So technically, irony or hyperbole are tropes (Lanham *Handlist*). I'm going to focus on the kind of tropes that make comparisons—you know them as metaphors, similes, analogies, personifications, synecdoches, parables, etc. Since all these comparisons are, in essence, metaphors, I'm going to talk about metaphor as the general rhetorical strategy.

I've said before that humans are pattern-seekers. We like to see similarities, make connections, find old experiences that explain new ones, use comparisons to make sense of things. Metaphors make these connections for us by spinning meaning in new ways. The Greek word *metaphor* means, quite literally, to carry over or across—meaning, in this case, to carry across meaning or essence from one thing to another. James Geary talks about metaphor, as Aristotle did, as a kind of weird math problem that looks like this:

$$X = Y.$$

The unexpected, almost illogical nature of this equation is part of the fun. So when the blues artist Sonny Boy Williamson bellows out, "Bet you my bottom dollar, I'm not fattenin' no more frogs for snakes," he's saying

> dating a woman who will end up with another guy = fattening frogs for snakes.

You already know how this works. You've been hearing and making metaphors all your life. As Geary writes, "Metaphorical thinking is the way we make sense of the world, and every individual metaphor is a specific instance of this imaginative process at work" (10). It's a mistake to confine metaphors to literary texts: "What we do every day is very much a matter of metaphor" (Lakoff and Johnson 3). They tumble out of our mouths when we talk (*tumble out* is one), even if we're not aware of them ("I've been *down* this week," "Things are looking *up* for me," "I *see* what you're saying," "She's a *bright* kid"). Yesterday I saw the following headlines in two major national newspapers, all of them dropping metaphors:

"Chaos in Yemen **Stymies** Terror Flight"

"**Torrent** of Cash Exits the Eurozone"

"CEO Tries to Put Brand **Back on Track** After Being **Lapped** by Rivals"

"Glenn Allison Still **Splits** Bowling World with Perfect 900"

"The **Soaring** Dollar is **Crunching** Profits"

"U.S. Private Equity Firms Find a **Chilly** Reception in Australia"

"A Story of Rape Keeps **Unraveling**"

"Netanyahu's Likely **Next Steps**"

"Science Museums Urged to **Cut Ties** with Kochs"

I had to look up the word *stymie* because I didn't know if it was a legitimate trope. Turns out *stymie* is a Scots term for when one golf ball blocks the path of another on the green. Maybe that's not well known, but I feel cooler now that I know the origin. The second headline is clearer: Money is leaving the Eurozone like a violent rush of water, like rainwater flushing down a slot canyon or something. Metaphors fill our everyday talk.

Metaphors work rhetorically by both delighting and convincing. Romeo tells us "Juliet is the sun" to amplify her beauty, to convince anyone listening that (a) Juliet is way hot, and (b) Juliet's hotness comes at you like the sun comes out of the east, killing the darkness and the "envious moon." Do we buy this hyperbole? Doesn't matter: it's cool. Metaphors excite, delight, engage, and confuse. They swerve from ordinary meaning. "The mind is a plastic snow dome," writes James Geary, "most beautiful, most interesting, and most itself when, as Elvis put it, it's all shook up" (16). Metaphors shake up your writing.

They also convince us by working on our attitudes and judgments. As Geary writes, readers should know that:

> Metaphorical choices don't just reflect opinions and actions; they help shape them. So becoming aware of which metaphors are at work—and why—provides an essential reality check in political debate. Bringing metaphorical meanings to the surface enables us to evaluate them, and to decide for ourselves the extent of their influence. (Geary 135)

A good rhetorical critic like yourself will pay careful attention to the way writers use metaphors to make comparisons. Ask yourself: Do I really believe in this case that X = Y? In political discourse, illegal immigrants are often compared to pollution, contaminants, infection, disease, flood (Cisneros). What do these metaphors do as arguments? What connections do they ask us to make? What values or assumptions are at play, and do we agree with them?

As a writer, you should make your writing memorably sticky by lacing it with metaphors. You have several options. You've heard, I'm sure, that *similes* use the word "like" to make the comparison direct and obvious. Direct metaphors tell readers directly that X is Y. Here's how journalist Matt Tiabbi described a particularly powerful investment bank in an article for *Rolling Stone*:

> The world's most powerful investment bank is a great vampire squid wrapped around the face of humanity, relentlessly jamming its blood funnel into anything that smells like money. (Taibbi)

Other metaphors are implied, like the "Cut Ties" headline mentioned earlier. For example, *synecdoche*, an implied metaphor, takes a part of something as the whole, like when we call American soldiers "boots on the ground."

Metaphors can be developed beyond phrases or sentences—allegories or analogies are *extended* metaphors.

Here's a brief example of how an extended metaphor—an analogy—works in writing. When I was in graduate school, a campus political group held an "affirmative action bake sale," an extended metaphor in action, in which prices for cookies dropped for minority students. The group wanted other students to see what they thought of as the unfairness of affirmative action, which is a policy by which some institutions change admission or hiring policies to provide equal access to racial minorities. In the student newspaper the next day, a student wrote the following analogy in rebuttal:

> From the beginning, the white males generally have horded all the recipes as intellectual property; owned all the ingredients, the cookie sheets, the ovens, cooling racks and the cookie jars; controlled the flow of cookies to eager hands while eating the majority of each batch themselves.... In essence, white males in general have created the crisis of democracy that affirmative action seeks to address—the wide divide between those who own the means of making cookies and those who don't.

We have here an exciting Battle of Metaphors! The campus political group compares cookies to all the goods and services distributed to racial minorities; the prices, for them, illustrate the unfairness they see in affirmative action. We don't reduce the price of baked goods for racial minorities, they're arguing, so why should they receive preferential treatment in the college admissions process? The student writer, on the other hand, compares the historically situated power of white males to the entire baking apparatus, arguing by analogy that historical inequality makes affirmative action necessary. Whether or not you agree with these metaphorical arguments, you can see how extended metaphors create strong affinities between two things, creating a new way of thinking about them.

A final thought about writing and reading metaphors: Beware of bad metaphors that, upon closer examination, don't really make sense. Because I wrote a letter once to U.S. Senator Orrin Hatch, I get the "Hatch Dispatch," his periodic newsletter describing his adventures as the third-oldest senator in Congress. In one of the newsletters, he compared government spending to a runaway train:

The runaway spending train enveloping Washington, D. C., is threatening to decimate the future of our children and for all Americans for generations to come.

Trains still run away from time to time, so the metaphor has power: Ain't nobody but Superman (or actor Denzel Washington) stopping one. But do trains *envelop*—wrap up, cover, surround, like fog might? Or *decimate* the future—kill, destroy, or remove? Runaway trains can kill, but I'm not sure how the future can be killed or removed, so the *decimating train* idea doesn't really work for me.

Other bad metaphors are more obviously bad because they mix metaphors and thereby cloud the comparison. Here's one from a comment thread on a local newspaper:

Where there's smoke, there's fire…could this be just the tip of the iceberg???

Metaphors, like all rhetorical strategies, should be *fitting*. And they should make sense.

11.4 Schemes

Classical rhetoricians separated *schemes* from metaphors and other plays with words. A scheme is a rhetorical strategy that plays with the arrangement of words through repetition or balance or some other variation from the norm. Schemes are patterns, often across a series of sentences, and you can find types and subtypes online in the *Forest of Rhetoric*. I'll talk about two.

Check out this excerpt from the book *America*, written by comedians from *The Daily Show with Jon Stewart*:

Though the president is very powerful, he cannot make laws. The president can suggest laws. The president can call individual congressmen and threaten, beg, and cajole them to make laws. The president can use the bully pulpit and appeal directly to the people to ask Congress to make laws. The president can promise that if these congressmen pass the laws the president likes he will make them a delicious sandwich. The president can hold his breath and pound his fists and threaten to run away. But the president cannot make laws.

We call this particular scheme *anaphora*—the writers repeat the same word or phrase ("the president") at the beginning of successive sentences.

Also notice that the writers repeat the phrase "make laws" at the *end* of sentences—that's called *epistrophe*. Abraham Lincoln used it at the end of the Gettysburg Address ("government of the people, by the people, for the people…"), and Wikipedia tells me rapper Nicki Minaj uses it in one of her songs. And if you can find another sentence on Earth that pairs up Lincoln with Nicki Minaj, I'll give you a quarter.

This kind of repetition sets up patterns of expectation with readers. It also lets them know that you're a *writer writing* and having a blast doing it. Just for kicks, let's look at another delicious example from David Foster Wallace's essay "A Supposedly Fun Thing I'll Never Do Again":

> I have seen sucrose beaches and water a very bright blue. I have seen an all-red leisure suit with flared lapels. I have smelled what suntan lotion smells like spread over 21000 pounds of hot flesh. I have been addressed as "Mon" in three different nations. I have watched 500 upscale Americans dance the Electric Slide. I have seen sunsets that looked computer-enhanced and a tropical moon that looked more like a sort of obscenely large and dangling lemon than like the good old stony U.S. moon I'm used to. I have (very briefly) joined a Conga Line.

Another scheme is *balance*. Balance shares pattern-passion with repetition, but it's more flexible:

> I am honestly curious about saliva, but I am also curious about obsession and its role in scientific inquiry. (Mary Roach, *Gulp*, 102)

> My feeling is that if more guys would join mellow, purposeless, and semi-dysfunctional organizations such as the Lawn Rangers, then there would be a lot fewer guys getting involved in aggressive, venal, destructive, and frequently criminal organizations such as the U.S. Congress. (Dave Barry, *Dave Barry's Complete Guide to Guys*, 103)

In these two examples, the writers balance grammatical constructions by using pairs like "I am…but I am also…" and "If…then…" That's an interesting trick. Look, particularly, at how humor writer Dave Barry balances multiple parts of his two clauses:

> more guys would join…a lot fewer guys getting involved in…

mellow, purposeless, and semi-dysfunctional...aggressive, venal, destructive, and frequently criminal

organizations such as the Lawn Rangers...organizations such as the U.S. Congress

You can create balance with either/or, neither/nor, not only/but also, from/to, when/then, if/then. Richard Lanham lists thirty-four different ways to create balance. One simple way is to contrast something unfavorable with something favorable, like, "While it may be true that X, it is also true that Y." Here's the delightful science writer Mary Roach, balancing between two ideas—one appealing, and one not so appealing:

> Yes, men and women eat meals. But they also ingest nutrients. They grind and sculpt them into a moistened bolus that is delivered, via a stadium wave of sequential contractions, into a self-kneading sack of hydrochloric acid and then dumped into a tubular leach field, where it is converted into the most powerful taboo in human history. Lunch is an opening act. (Roach 15)

Notice how she sandwiches (a metaphor!) the gross realities of digestion between the two more palatable (zing!) ideas of meals and lunch. That's balance for you.

11.5 Punctuation

Since I haven't written this book as a handbook, I won't go over all the specific rules of punctuation here. If you're after the rules, I would recommend finding a good handbook or a Web source you trust. I'm more interested in the effects of punctuation. Punctuation is a deviling thing, and you'll spend a good part of your writing life figuring out how to use it well. Here I want to say, simply, that stylistic punctuation uses punctuation to create rhythm, interrupt flow, or separate ideas for emphasis. Punctuation helps you create syntax in a variety of ways. And instead of lecturing you about it, I'm going to let you come up with principles yourselves as you look at the examples from my collection of sentences:

The Comma

Commas separate out the various parts of sentences so everything doesn't just slam together. Commas make sentences breathe, but you shouldn't put them in every time you think you should take a breath. Commas space phrases and clauses, they separate items in lists, they tell you what's modifying what, they work to emphasize asides or editorial comments or amplifications. Commas help build associations in the minds of readers.

> The ethos of the Koran, the value system it endorses, was, in essence, the vanishing code of nomadic Arabs, the matriarchal, more caring society that did not leave orphans out in the cold, orphans like Muhammad, whose success as a merchant, he believed, should have earned him a place in the city's ruling body, and who was denied such preferment because he didn't have a powerful family to fight for him. (Salman Rushdie, *Joseph Anton: A Memoir*)

> The universe passed through its unimaginable first moment, first year, first billion years, wresting itself from whatever state of nonexistence, inflating, contorting, resolving into space and matter, bursting into light. (Marilynne Robinson, *Absence of Mind*)

The Dash

Dashes, first off, are not hyphens. Hyphens are shorter; they connect words and parts of words, and often you can just do without them. Dashes, though, are rhetorical heroes. They add drama to a sentence—both graphically and syntactically. You can use dashes much like commas to separate phrases and clauses upon which you want special emphasis. Just make sure you have a clear rhetorical purpose for being dashing.

> Decomposition like this happens to any long-lived and successful style, surely; so the writer's—or critic's, or reader's—task is then to search for the irreducible, the superfluous, the margin of gratuity, the element in a style—in any style—which cannot be easily reproduced or reduced. (James Wood, *How Fiction Works*)

As Smith's memoir demonstrates, childhood—those first, fresh experiences of the world, unclouded by reason and practicality, when you are the center of existence and anything might happen—should be regarded less as a springboard to striving adulthood than as a well of rich individual perception and experience to which you can return for sustenance throughout life, whether you rise in the world or not. (Christina Schwarz, "Leave Those Kids Alone," *The Atlantic*)

The Semicolon

Most of the time, semicolons work like periods in that they separate two independent clauses that could stand alone as sentences just fine. But maybe you want to suggest a more intimate connection, a more casual transition from one sentence to the next. Then drop in a semicolon. You also use semicolons to separate out more complicated parts of sentences with multiple commas in lists, as Bill Wyman does in the example below.

> The one that killed him—a hospital-grade potion called propofol—was used to put to sleep a man who apparently couldn't find sleep otherwise, and it's easy to see why he would need help, his mind full of songs, ideas, melodies, dance moves; of his fantasies and his lies; of the memories of his silly, grasping, toxic family; of the kids who were, or were not, his kids; of the other families whose lives he had touched and made better and the ones he'd beguiled and corrupted; of the giant global scream of an audience that he could no longer face. (Bill Wyman, "The Pale King," an article on Michael Jackson)

The Colon

Colons trumpet what's to come. They announce lists or examples or quotations or summaries. They draw attention to relationships more dramatically than periods.

> In fact a swimming pool requires, once it has been filled and the filter has begun its process of cleaning and recirculating the water, virtually no water, but the symbolic content of swimming pools has always been interesting: a pool is misapprehended as a trapping of affluence, real or pretended, and of a kind of hedonistic attention to the body. (Joan Didion, *The White Album*)

Combinations

> Historical fundamentalism is marked by the belief that a particular and quite narrowly defined past—"the founding"—is ageless and sacred and to be worshipped; that certain historical texts—"the founding documents"—are to be read in the same spirit with which religious fundamentalists read, for instance, the Ten Commandments; that the Founding Fathers were divinely inspired; that the academic study of history (whose standards of evidence and methods of analysis are based on skepticism) is a conspiracy and, furthermore, blasphemy; and that political arguments grounded in appeals to the founding documents, as sacred texts, and to the Founding Fathers, as prophets, are therefore incontrovertible. (Jill Lepore, *The Whites of Their Eyes*)

11.6 Design

We're in the home stretch! (Where does that metaphor come from?) All that's left is a final word about style from the perspective of *design*.

When I visited my daughter Lydia's kindergarten class, she showed me how she could write the sentence, "I like my dad" on a sheet of lined paper. *Awwww!* She leaned over the page, struggling to get each word right, her tongue poking out of her pursed mouth. When she was done, I gushed about her writing skills—it's a miracle, as I've said—and then started packing up to leave.

Lydia grabbed my arm and said, "Wait! I have to draw you!"

Then, underneath the words she'd written with great care, she drew a picture of me—a cute little weird-looking daddy, with black-framed glasses and the kind of legs you'd find on a gorilla.

It dawned on me, then, that for Lydia, writing is only half the message. All her work up till then had been a combination of words and images, sentences and drawings—her syntactic compositions dancing, on the page, with her crayoned compositions. All the books we read out loud to her and her other siblings almost always used this multimodal dance to communicate. That multimodality may very well be trained out of Lydia as she gets older and teachers expect her to read books without pictures and write essays without drawings (Kress and van Leeuwen).

I've written this book without many visuals or colors because I've wanted to keep it cheap. (You can thank me by joining Team Rhetoric for life.) But the Web has blasted away any thought that we live in a strictly *alphabetic* world—a world governed only in words on pages. I don't need to tell you this or describe the multimodal symphony we experience online, because you live it. What I do need to say, though, is that *style* as we've talked about it so far, as something you do in sentences, is insufficiently narrow. New media, social media, and digital composing challenge us to think of style as the *artful* and *rhetorical* combination of various modes like words, images, color, data, feeds, and video.

Style, in this atmosphere, is more about *design* than anything else: How your multimodal message appears to audiences and how you can manipulate its elements to influence attitudes. But design has always been with us. When you make decisions about how a standard essay appears on the page (font, spacing, margins, citation style, headings), you're making design decisions that enhance or detract from the reading experience. A savvy rhetor will understand how to use these principles effectively to create compelling messages that engage audiences on multiple levels of communication. (Find online the brilliant and Pulitzer Prize-winning *New York Times* story "Snow Fall" by John Branch to get a sense of this potential.)

Effective design engages four aspects of communication simultaneously: rhetorical principles, visual principles, modes, and design tools. Entire books are written about these subjects, so I'll leave it to you and your instructor to decide what's important here. I've listed some possible principles in these four domains in Table 1.

Last Thoughts on Style

In *The Sense of Style*, cognitive scientist Steven Pinker argues that style is important for three reasons: It helps us communicate clearly and efficiently, it "earns trust," and it "adds beauty to the world" (9). All three of these benefits are rhetorical benefits. If you can learn to write with style, you'll influence attitudes, and therefore judgments and behavior. Remember that the exercises I suggest in chapter ten have been *proven* to help writers improve their style. I commend them to you, especially when you've written a draft of something and you're wondering how to take it to the next level.

Table 1. Domains of Design

Rhetorical Principles	Visual Principles		Modes and Design Tools	
rhetorical situation	simplicity	contrast	text	font
audience	repetition	alignment	color	shapes
purpose	proximity	empty space	table	chart
argument	order	flow	graph	diagram
character	framing	texture	video	image
emotions	balance	scale	animation	program
genre	texture	hierarchy	background	template
story	layers	transparency	bullets	transitions
style	grid	pattern	line	word process
arrangement	motion	emphasis	cameras	editing
flow	sequence	surprise	social media	design software
implications (so what?)	unity	point	mobile tech	
			(etc., etc.)	

11

Works Cited

Cisneros, J. David. "Contaminated Communities." *Rhetoric and Public Affairs* 11.4 (2008): 569–602.

Corbett, Edward P.J. and Robert J. Connors. *Style and Statement*. NY: Oxford UP, 1999. Print.

Fadiman, Anne. *The Spirit Catches You and You Fall Down*. NY: Farrar, Straus and Giroux, 1997. Print.

Fahnestock, Jeanne. *Rhetorical Style*. Oxford: Oxford UP, 2011. Print.

Geary, James. *I Is an Other*. NY: HarperCollins, 2011. Print.

Hacker, Diana and Nancy Sommers. *Rules for Writers*. 7th ed. Boston: Bedford/St. Martin's. 2012. Print.

Kress, Gunther and Theo van Leeuwen. *Reading Images: The Grammar of Visual Design*. 2nd ed. London: Routledge, 2007. Print.

Lakoff, George and Mark Johnson. *Metaphors We Live By*. Chicago: U of Chicago P, 1980. Print.

Lanham, Richard. *A Handlist of Rhetorical Terms*. 2nd ed. Berkeley: U of Cal P, 1991. Print.

— — —. *Revising Prose*. 5th ed. NY: Pearson, 2007. Print.

Lemann, Nicholas. "The Word Lab." *The New Yorker*. October 16 & 23 (2000): 100–112. Print.

Nunberg, Geoffrey. *Talking Right*. NY: Public Affairs, 2006. Print.

Pinker, Steven. *The Sense of Style*. NY: Viking, 2014. Print.

Ripley, Amanda. Excerpt from *The Smartest Kids in the World*. NPR Books. n.d. Web. 8 March 2015.

Roach, Mary. *Gulp*. NY: Norton, 2013. Print.

Schlosser, Eric. *Fast Food Nation*. NY: Perennial, 2002. Print.

Schulz, Kathryn. "Rapt." *The New Yorker*. 9 March 2015. 90–95. Print.

Taibbi, Matt. "The Great American Bubble Machine." *Rolling Stone*. 5 April 2010. Web. 25 March 2015.

Tufte, Virginia. *Artful Sentences: Syntax as Style*. Cheshire, CT: Graphics Press, 2006. Print.

Williams, Joseph M. and Gregory G. Colomb. *Style: Lessons in Clarity and Grace*. 10th ed. Boston: Longman, 2010. Print.

Wood, Graeme. "What ISIS Really Wants." *The Atlantic*. March 2015. Web. 7 March 2015.

READING RHETORICALLY

HALT! Before you fling your eyeballs on this chapter, I want you to:

1. decide whether or not you're ready to give this chapter your undivided attention (somewhere comfortable but not *too* comfortable? is your cell phone off? do you have enough time—say, an hour—to commit to it? are you ready to focus?); if so, then

2. look up from the book right now and predict what this chapter is about (i.e., what it will cover, what it won't, what it will argue, etc.);

3. ask yourself, "What do I know about reading, or what have I been taught about reading strategies before?";

4. preview the chapter by flipping through it quickly, looking for key terms or concepts (in headings, or in **bold**), reading the conclusion (spoilers!); and, finally,

5. decide what you hope to get out of this chapter (like, "I hope to learn X" or "I hope that by reading this chapter I learn to do Y because Z").

Okay. Fair warning: While you read this chapter, I'm going to interrupt you from time to time and ask you to do stuff. (But since **HALT!** makes me sound more like a police officer or border guard than a teacher, I'll just say **PAUSE**.) What I'll ask you to do will help you become a more effective and efficient reader, and there's research to prove it.

Consider the following reading situations:

1. One time while on an outing to Jackson Hole, Wyoming, with a youth group, the back-right tire of my truck exploded while we drove on an old dirt road. I'd only had the used truck for a few months, so I wasn't familiar with the mechanics of how to get the spare tire off the underchassis. I tried a few things, and failed. So I opened the glove box and found the owner's manual and flipped to the index where I found several topics under "Tire." I flipped to the "Tire" section, read the instructions, and fixed the tire.

2. In fifth grade, I went to my local library and checked out horror writer Stephen King's book *Christine*, the tale of a demonic Plymouth Fury that terrorizes a small town. It was my first "adult" book—before that, it was all Encyclopedia Brown and Choose Your Own Adventure and Dragonlance. *Christine* was scary, and mature; it terrified and excited me. I read it all the way through in just a few days and could barely sleep afterward.

3. A few weeks ago, while in Denver International Airport, I powered up my smartphone and opened my Flipboard app and flipped through a few headlines. Then I thumbed through my Twitter feed.

4. Many years ago, as a young student on a study abroad program in Jerusalem, I received a kind, handwritten letter from a fellow student that I kinda liked. I read the letter carefully and then handwrote her back a letter, complimenting her on several traits I admired in her. To my surprise, she wrote me back a letter I had to read *very carefully* because it seemed to me she was telling me she loved me, without saying it directly. I then had to decide the best way to respond: *Should I dial this back a little or pick up my pen and go Romeo on the situation?* (We're married now, so you can guess what I decided to do.)

5. Several years ago I was writing an article about neuroscience and rhetoric. I know very little about neuroscience, which should have made me think twice about writing the article in the first place. In our university library, I found a book titled *Affective Neuroscience* by American psychologist Jaak Panksepp. I might as well have been reading the book upside down for all I got from it, but I did note how Panksepp defined emotions in the context of brain chemistry. I quoted his definition in my paper, comparing it to definitions from other experts like Joseph LeDoux and Edmund Rolls and a few scholars whose articles I'd found on Academic Search Premiere online. I then added my own definition.

Now **PAUSE**. Before going further, answer these questions: What do you think I'm going to say about these anecdotes? Do you agree with what you think I'm going to say? What anecdotes could you tell me about your own reading experiences?

This process is called "priming" or "generating" by psychologists who study how we learn. By asking you to puzzle out a problem before hearing the solution, I'm hoping the principle will be "better learned and more durably remembered," in the words of one research team (Brown, Roediger, McDaniel 86).

Reading Is Not Reading Is Not Reading

You don't eat a sandwich with a fork. A sandwich requires a different kind of eating than pasta. You wouldn't wolf down a potential mother-in-law's curry with the same sloppy gusto you use on a microwave burrito when you're all alone in the dorms. You (probably, hopefully) don't douse raisin bran with ketchup. You wouldn't lick sauce off a knife while on a date. Just as various foods in various situations require various eating approaches, various texts in various situations require various reading strategies. Think about the five reading stories I just told. When I got a flat tire, I didn't read the entire manual; that would have been a colossal waste of my time. When I got the letter from my friend and future wife, I didn't just read the salutation and the sign-off; I would have missed the juicy stuff in the middle.

Remember what we said waaaaaay back in chapter one about metacognition—that out-of-body awareness of how we're thinking and learning and writing? The same mindfulness should be applied to reading. If we approach reading mindfully, we'll get more out of it. We'll read with purpose. When I buy a used book and find that nearly every sentence in the first chapter—and first chapter only—has been highlighted, I think, "The past owner did not read this text mindfully." Reading is not reading is not reading. One exigence requires one reading approach, another another.

Yes, I just used the word *exigence*. That key term should trigger thoughts about **the rhetorical situation**, which we discussed in chapter six. Like writing, reading takes place in rhetorical situations in which exigence, kairos, rhetor, purpose, genre, and audiences can be identified. Only now, as reader, you're not only interested in the writer/rhetor's exigence, kairos, purpose, genre, and audiences. You're also interested in your own purpose and experience as audience.

Writing is a social act. Texts appear because someone wants to influence someone else in some way. Reading, too, is a social act; as audience you complete a circuit and connect with another person's intentions. When you read, you should read *rhetorically*, meaning that you should read with a mindful awareness of:

- who writers are (rhetors),

- why they wrote *when* they did (exigence and kairos),

- what they hope readers will feel or think or do (their purpose),

- what rhetorical strategies they use when they write (genre + ACES),

- and how they have constructed an experience for a specific kind of reader (audience).

Now, I have to admit something I hope some of you are thinking at this point. When the tire on the truck popped and I pulled out the dusty driver's manual, I didn't take the time to ask myself, "Who are the writers of this lovely instruction manual and what do they hope I feel when I read this?" I didn't give two hoots who wrote the manual. I couldn't have cared less when the writers wrote it or what their emotional appeals were, and I sure as heck didn't care about whether the writers varied their sentences or used rhetorical schemes. However, I was quite grateful to see that the manual was laid out in the genre of manuals, with a thorough index and a "troubleshooting" section for clueless people like me who know little about the cars they drive. In that moment, out there in the sagebrush of Wyoming, I had one purpose for reading: Find out how to fix a flat tire before we're all eaten by bears. That manual, crammed in the glove box with insurance papers and Jiffy Lube receipts, was written for such moments.

Mindful reading means knowing when to turn on the full force of your analytical skills and when to just sit back and enjoy a text for the joy of texts. In this chapter, I hope to help you calibrate your reading mind.

A Note about Literacy, Literacies, and Reading in College

I find reading remarkable. For people with sight who have learned to read, our eyes scan over funny shapes, sending packaged information to be deciphered and given meaning in our brains. (I wonder if the same thing happens through the fingers when the blind read braille.) The eye's fovea—this tiny dimple full of cells in your retina—acts as a fine-tuned instrument, and your retina gets it in the right place by jumping around in almost-imperceptible "jerky movements" called saccades, a few every second we read (Dehaene 13). Everything else fades into the background; our environment disappears. Neuroscientists tell us we can read only 10–12 letters in a single moment. Then our eyes jump to the next bundle, and sometimes back again, every three-tenths of a second (Dehaene 17). We convert what the fovea gathers into internalized speech sounds— even when we read silently, our vocal chords tremble just slightly—that get converted into meanings in various language-ready networks of the brain, called the "visual word form area" by French neuroscientist Stanislas Dehaene (62). Then the information bounces around other parts of the brain that convert those words into meaning.

But that's just the physiological pinball machine at work when we read. Often we have too narrow a view of reading as this decoding process; literacy, for some people, is the act of decoding words, an "individual cognitive tool" (Street 437) you either have (i.e., you are literate) or you don't (illiterate). Literacy is far more than that. British linguist Brian Street talks about literacy as a plural, as *literacies*—all the "social practices" and "cultural concerns and interests" that go into reading and writing (430). A literacy is a social practice that reflects culture. Such literacies begin in families, in the way relatives (like parents and siblings and other kin) value and use language at home. Other institutions (neighborhoods, schools, governments, economies) impose various reading and writing values or practices that we learn to use (or resist) as we grow up. Linguist James Paul Gee reminds us that we learn to think, write, and read as members of communities who think, write, and read in certain ways, with certain values and practices.

Think, for a moment, about your earliest memories of reading and the environment of reading you grew up in.

> **PAUSE. Go ahead—think about it!** Think about specific books or images, situations in which you read or learned to read, people who taught you to read, people who encouraged you to read, people who discouraged it, your early attitudes and practices and struggles.

Perhaps you had family members read picture books to you. When we were little kids, my brother Kevin would stay up way past our bedtimes, huddled under the covers with a flashlight, reading books that he'd then cram in the space between his bed and the wall. Perhaps you saw older brothers and sisters reading comic books or fantasy novels on an e-reading device. Perhaps you never saw a parent read for pleasure, or maybe Dad didn't read anything but *The Economist* magazine. Perhaps you have a learning disability that made reading a struggle when you were a child. Perhaps you read every Harry Potter book twice, all in one week. Perhaps most reading for you feels like staring at the sun: forcing yourself to concentrate when you want nothing more than to stop.

You learned to read—and all the cultural values, benefits, and challenges that come from reading—from people or institutions or tools that Deborah Brandt calls "sponsors of literacy," which are "agents, local or distant, concrete or abstract, who enable, support, teach, model, as well as recruit, regulate, suppress, or withhold literacy" (25). Parents are sponsors of literacy; so are schools, libraries, houses of worship and religious leaders, SparkNotes (don't deny it!), video games, app designers, prize-granting institutions (like Pulitzer or Newberry), various technologies (including print books), or companies like General Mills (I read a lot of cereal boxes growing up). Standardized tests function as sponsors of literacy, a fact lamented by educator Kelly Gallagher who accuses schools of "readicide," which he defines as "the systematic killing of the love of reading" (2). Our reading attitudes and practices come from the "patterns of sponsorship" we're exposed to in our literate lives (Brandt 26).

For the last couple of decades, the most important enabler of new reading practices has been the screen, our ever-present text-delivery device(s). With high-speed connections, we can download entire books to our devices in seconds. We can open up our phones and scroll through social media updates and news feeds while waiting in line for a movie (especially if we want to ignore the humans standing next to us). Digital texts are cheaper to distribute than print texts, and they're cheaper to buy—and more portable, storable, searchable, sendable, and interactive-able. (I had to keep the -able thing going.) They embed images and video. They foster and publish conversations. When we read online, we read *sideways*, jumping from place to place, forming associations and foraging for what's important to us. There's no doubt that digital sponsors of literacy have made the world a better place for reading culture.

But every technology has its drawbacks, its unpredictable constraints. Turns out that the blue light emanating from screens blocks melatonin, the hormone that tells us to sleep (Harvard Health). Though physicians say teenagers should be getting at least eight hours of sleep, around 70% of teenagers say they keep a glowy device on *all night* (Kim); late-night digital reading messes with our sleep patterns. Some research suggests that we comprehend what we read in print more effectively than what we read digitally, though the differences aren't dramatic (Mangen, Walgermo, Bronnick); other studies have found comprehension is about the same (Robb; Rockinson-Szapkiw et al.; Subrahamanyam et al.). A Yale study, published in the *Journal of Experimental Psychology*, revealed that we greatly overestimate our understanding of something when we use search engines as our literacy sponsor (Hathaway). The Web makes everyone an expert. Some scientists think that digital reading fails to "recreate certain tactile experiences of reading on paper" and therefore causes "navigational difficulties" that impede comprehension (Jabr; see also Keim).

Is that why, according to research by linguist Naomi Baron, 92% of college students *worldwide* prefer reading print texts over e-readers (laptops, mobile phones, tablets, etc.) for college classes (Robb)? Maybe. Regardless of the research, it's important to be mindful enough to know what kind of literacy sponsorship helps you grow as a learner and thinker.

Colleges are sponsors of literacy on a grand scale; on a smaller scale, so are your textbooks and teachers and assignments and student newspaper and registration website and class management software and syllabuses and even those spots on campus where people post stuff they want to sell or parties they want you to come to. Some of the most important reading you'll do in college is the unassigned reading you do for your own pleasure or enlargement. Of course you'll have plenty of assigned reading to do, too, as your new sponsors of literacy (a.k.a. your professors) invite you into texts they hope will help you achieve class objectives.

College reading can be a struggle for students. In his book *Engaging Ideas*, writing scholar John Bean lists all the ways reading can be a real challenge for college students:

- our testing culture rewards surface reading rather than deep reading

- students balk at the time commitment to read texts carefully

- professors often lecture over readings in class, making reading unnecessary

- students don't adjust their reading strategies for different situations

- new genres might be unfamiliar, and therefore confusing

- disciplinary terms, concepts, or rhetorical strategies are new and daunting

- students can't see themselves as audiences for difficult texts—audiences with the right to talk back/with professional authors. (Bean 162–6)

It may sound odd at first to say that college students need to learn how to read, but it's true. Like writing, reading is an iterative skill strengthened by mindful, deliberate practice. It may be a challenge for you to learn new study strategies, but you can do it! We're here to help. For the rest of this chapter, I'll share a process with you that will help you read more purposefully, effectively, and rhetorically. You'll notice how this process follows the steps in our learning model for writing tasks from chapter two.

PAUSE. Look up from the book and summarize, in your own words, what you've learned so far in this last section on literacy, literacies, and reading in college. Use specific key terms from the chapter.

OR, if you're feeling really ambitious, try this: Get out a piece of paper and draw three columns. (You could use a digital table, too.) Label the first column "my summary," the second column "my uses," and a third column "my questions." In the first column, write a brief summary of this last section, with key terms and ideas. In the second column, explain in writing how you might use this material in this class or other classes you're taking, or in your personal life. In the last column, write down 2–3 questions you have about what you've read.

Reading Rhetorically: The Strategies

I've been as obvious as I can about the mindfulness theme of this book. Real learning and growth come from mindfulness. Rhetorical thinking and acting require mindfulness. If we think about how we're approaching our learning, we act with greater purpose and skill. Our powers of rhetorical influence grow. Our model for writing tasks, based on research about "self-directed learning" (Ambrose et al.), walks us through the writer's mindful journey from the exigence (the "call" to write) to the moment the writer reflects on how things went: from planning, through practice (the writing process), revision, and reflection. You can go through the same process with reading tasks.

As with anything else I've said in this book, I encourage you to work with your instructor to build a reading process that works for you. Not everything I'm about to say will be useful to you in every situation.

I. Plan

In the planning stage of reading, you assess your task and set goals. Frankly, this might take five minutes. What you *don't* want to do is look at the syllabus the night before class, look at the page count, crack open your book, and start reading from the first word till the side of your face rests gently on the page.

No drooling on books! When you get a reading assignment, and after you've taken a brief look at the text, ask yourself the following questions:

1.   Why am I reading this? What does my instructor want me to get from it? What do *I* want to get from it?

2.   What is the specific assignment here? Am I being asked to *remember the content* of this text, or will I be asked to *respond to this text* in class discussion or in writing? (Your purpose will influence the reading strategy you take—and this one, between content and conversation, is essential to remember.)

3.   Who wrote the text? Why? What are the credentials, authority, or affiliation of the author(s)? What potential biases or perspectives should I be aware of? What's the *established ethos* (chapter eight)? What kind of audience is intended?

4.   What *kairos* or *exigence* does this text respond to? What conversation is it joining? Who or what is the text responding to? When was the text written? Why was it written when it was? What value does the text have now, in the rhetorical situation you're reading it in? Is it still timely?

5.   What genre is this text? What is the purpose of the genre? What discourse community is served by it? Why do people write texts like these?

6.   What do I already know about this topic and its key terms and moves? How is this text like texts I've read before? What background knowledge from my previous learning or experience do I bring to this text?

When you've sized up your task and purpose, you can set some self-regulating goals. At the beginning of the chapter, I asked you to

> decide whether or not you're ready to give this chapter your undivided attention (are you sitting somewhere comfortable? is your cell phone off? do you have enough time—say, an hour—to commit to it? are you ready to focus?).

Self-regulation, my friend. Discipline is painful. There is, in fact, such a thing as "willpower fatigue," according to Stanford psychologist Walter Mischel, the man most famous for torturing small children by putting marshmallows in front of them and then telling them not to eat them (Urist). (YouTube it. But not right now: You're reading. Ah—feel that? Now you know what Mischel's subjects felt like, staring at that marshmallow!) Research from a Vancouver psychologist revealed that when adults read, their mind wanders somewhere between 15–20% of the time; high school students daydream even more while reading (Winifred Gallagher 149). So, the trick here is to set reasonable goals to help you focus while you read. As you learned in chapter two, self-regulation is the process by which we "suppress brain activity that conflicts with current goals" (Posner 73).

In chapter two, we talked about three kinds of self-regulating goals: environmental, personal, and social:

1. *Environmental* goals for reading might include deciding when and where and under what conditions you'll read. You want to eliminate distractions and find a quiet place and time to read. While the jury is still out on whether background music helps or hurts reading comprehension, studies have found that loud or fast or lyrical (i.e., non-instrumental) music creates a cognitive challenge for readers. But music can put you in a positive emotional state, and emotional states influence learning. Spacing out reading sessions to avoid cramming will help you; varying the places in which you read will help, too (Brown, Roediger III, McDaniel). Ellen Langer explains that "a familiar structure or rhythm helps lead to mental laziness" (21). Sometimes routines need to be broken to quicken the neurons.

2. When you set *personal* goals, you decide how you'll monitor yourself and your progress (taking notes, for example, or testing your knowledge), and how you'll reward yourself when you've done your reading. Monitoring is particularly important in those moments when you're tired and your eyes are passing over the words and you find

yourself rereading the same sentences over and over without getting anything. I know it's time for me to get up and stretch or take a walk when I start having funky nonsensical half-dreams unrelated to what I'm reading.

3. *Social* goals bring other people into your reading experience. Plan to talk to someone about what you're reading. Make a goal to explain what you've read to someone not taking the class. Form a reading or study group with people in the class, and review together the reading before going to class. (More on this in a moment.)

II. Practice

Reading, like writing, is a *process* involving prereading, reading, and reviewing. Here are a few things you'll want to practice as you read texts.

Preread

More often than not, you don't want to pick up a text and start reading cold, right from the top of the first page. You'll want to do some prereading; Kelly Gallagher calls it "first-draft reading" (*Deep Reading* 51). You want to know a little bit about who the writer is and what she's up to. You'll want to know the writer's background and rhetorical perspective (cultural context, history, potential biases); websites have sponsors and creators—who are they? You may want to do a little background research on the topic of the text (Wikipedia, baby!). Flip through the text itself, studying its genre and layout. Take a tour of the table of contents—or, if you're reading online, the navigation system of links and tabs and headings—and make some predictions about what you'll get from it. Before diving in, read the intro and conclusion (unless you don't want to spoil the reading experience; you wouldn't want to preread a novel like *Gone Girl*). Check out the chapter or section headings, and look at the way the pages are designed or data displayed. As mentioned earlier, ask yourself, "What does this writer want me to feel, think, or do? What kind of judgment am I being asked to make?"

Brake for the Unknown

If you stumble onto a term or concept you don't understand, slam on the brakes. Crack open a dictionary (apps work fine) or search for the term online. If the word, term, or concept is particularly important, you may want to write the definition in the margin and/or circle it or draw a box around it, like I did here in my copy of Reza Aslan's book *No god but God*, a history of Islam, when I stumbled onto the word *henotheism* (notice I boxed the abbreviation "def" in the margin):

> This remarkable proclamation, with its obvious resemblance to the Muslim profession of faith—"There is no god but God"—may reveal the earliest traces in pre-Islamic Arabia of what the German philologist Max Müller termed *henotheism:* the belief in a single High God, without necessarily rejecting the existence of other, subordinate gods. The earliest evidence of henotheism in Arabia can be traced back to a tribe called the Amir, who lived near modern-day Yemen in the second century B.C.E., and who worshipped a High God they called *dhu-Samawi*, "The Lord of the Heavens." While the details of the Amirs' religion have been lost to history, most scholars are convinced that by the sixth century C.E., henotheism had become the standard belief of the vast majority of sedentary Arabs, who not only accepted Allah as their High God, but insisted that he was the same god as Yahweh, the god of the Jews.

allah = yahweh

Make Marginal Notes

Taking notes in/on texts is popular. You can take notes right on the text—digital texts have all kinds of cool options for note-taking—or in a separate notebook if you plan to sell your texts. The tactile experience of writing while we read reinforces what we're reading, and it gives us an archive of our reading experience that we can review later.

John Bean says that some teachers forbid underlining or highlighting. It does seem too easy to underline or highlight a text to death, turning a once pristine page into what looks like a glowing nuclear accident. Bean suggests that when we feel the urge to highlight, we should instead write in the margin *why* we feel like highlighting that part. "Use the margins," he writes, "to summarize the text, ask questions, give assent, protest vehemently" (Bean 177). I really like this advice. Highlighting is useless if later we can't remember why we highlighted. So I try to use the margins of my texts to write questions, draw smiley faces when I find jokes and frowny faces when something depresses me, write exclamation marks when I'm shocked and awed, jot down or define key terms, or "star" key points and main arguments that summarize the text.

Skip

Yes, I'm giving you permission to skip stuff from time to time. You *have* to—and, hey, you *want* to. One of the most liberating moments of my life came when Professor Boswell, a rhetoric scholar in a graduate program, told my class that if we weren't understanding the texts we were reading, we were reading too *slowly*. The advice seemed contradictory, but it went into me like a javelin. I was so caught up in the minutiae of the scholarly articles I was reading that I couldn't see the Big Picture. Often, a text's Big Picture can be discovered in thirty seconds. Think about articles in academic journals. A scientist might read a 15-page scholarly article on particle physics by reading the abstract and conclusion and skipping the rest. When I'm working on a project, I'll go to the library and stack up a dozen books and search for the main argument in the introductions and then discard them. If you feel like a text you're reading is tedious, it might be that you've figured out what the writer is trying to say and now you're just forcing yourself to read stuff you already know. (But beware of illusions of knowledge! More on that in a moment.)

I find I can skip more readily if I'm reading mindfully enough to know what each section or paragraph is doing ("Okay, here's the author's set-up, and here is the main point—got it! And here the author is responding to critics—I don't care about that, so I'll skip ahead to here, where the author explains the whole research project, and now I'm bogged down in research methodology, so I'm skipping to the evidence, but now there are too many examples so skipping ahead…"). Sometimes topic sentences help me read more quickly. I'm all for deep and slow reading when the situation requires it, but there are reading moments when you'll save time and comprehend more if you skip mindfully. Varying your reading speed is another example of "varied practice," which is more "cognitively challenging" and therefore more likely to lead to retention (Brown, Roediger III, McDaniel 51).

Draw Pictures

Sometimes we retain what we read more deeply and carefully if we can make a visual representation of the text we're reading (Duke and Pearson 219). Consider drawing a text map or flow chart or timeline to capture what you've read. Use conceptual principles like contrast, development, or hierarchy in the visuals you draw. The rise of infographics has opened up incredible rhetorical possibilities for visualization. Such drawings are often called *concept maps*.

Summarize

Learning to summarize is essential. It's a survival skill; you can't read everything, and you can't remember everything about the texts you read. A summary captures the main point/argument/conclusion/message/

theme of a text in as few words as possible. It's an art of synthesis, focus, and also neglect.

It's tough to do, in part because earlier sponsors of literacy train students to read in preparation for quizzes, not for holistic comprehension. One Harvard study from the 1960s found that out of 1500 first-year students, only *fifteen* (that's 1% of the class) could summarize the main point of a thirty-page history chapter, even though they all scored well on a multiple-choice test (Harvard Report). Psychologist William Perry concluded that when students are assigned to read, they often slip into "obedient purposelessness" by reading without knowing why they're reading or what, in a macro-sense, they're reading. Another problem: Students often search texts for what Rebecca Moore Howard calls "killer quotes" instead of conclusions or overarching themes because they need to quote stuff in research papers. She and her colleagues discovered that only 6% of citations in student research papers showed summary; everything else was some form of quoting (Jamieson, Howard, and Serviss).

Summary breaks this habit. When you summarize, you search a text for the main point. Here it might be useful to draw from what you learned in chapter seven about arguments: find the claim, find the reasons to support the claim, and uncover the assumptions. When I ask students to write annotated bibliographies, I'll often ask them to write the main conclusion of a text, the methodology used to come to that conclusion (experiment? survey? interviews? observations? analysis? the Pensieve at Hogwarts?), and the implications (so what?). I also ask students to tell me what they want to use the text for (i.e., if they're working on writing with sources).

When I'm reading a book I own, I'll often try to "nutshell" the argument of a particular chapter on its first page, like I do here in Jane Mayer's book *The Dark Side*:

- Zubayda as test case for New Paradigm
- 8 or more host nations to ghost prisons
- 1984 Convention Against Torture (CAT)
✱ p.152 = The Torture 7 Memo   *CIA = not rendition to Egypt a Syria*

[SERE] INSIDE THE BLACK SITES

: CIA to experiment in torture post-Korea   *CIA had no experienced personnel in detention : interrogation @ time*

✱ p175-7 = false claims of what Zubayda revealed when tortured = KEY.

More than 3,000 suspected terrorists have been arrested in many countries. Many others have met a different fate. Let's put it this way: They are no longer a problem to the United States and our friends and allies.

—President George W. Bush,
State of the Union Address, January 28, 2003

You'll notice I put a star next to "p175-7 = false claims…" because I wanted to remind myself of *New Yorker* journalist Jane Mayer's startling claim that many post-9/11 terrorist suspects did not reveal anything of value to U.S. national security personnel during torture. I thought that point was the major "take home" of the chapter.

You can summarize either by writing or speaking. A particularly powerful method of summary is to look up from a text when completed, put away your notes, and talk through the main point of the text you're reading. This hard cognitive work is called *retrieval* or *self-quizzing*, and psychological research tells us it's far more effective than rereading the text (Brown, Roediger III, McDaniel).

Self-Monitor

We know from research that good readers are "*active* readers" who "constantly *evaluate*" their reading process and goals and "read *selectively*, continually making decisions about their reading—what to read carefully, what to read quickly, what not to read, what to reread" (Duke and Pearson 205). I don't know if this happens to you, but I often find myself rereading a paragraph because I've completely spaced out or, yes, dozed off. If you catch yourself dozing or spacing, stop reading. Stand up, take a walk, get a drink. Remind yourself why you're reading in the first place. Quiz yourself. Ask what the reading is preparing you to do (test? class discussion? living life more fully?).

Read Disciplinary Texts

Texts work in *contexts*, in rhetorical situations that meet the needs of discourse communities who use specific rhetorical practices to get work done in the world. If I am reading a text written by a disciplinary specialist (like a psychologist or botanist or art historian) to other disciplinary specialists (in a peer-reviewed academic journal, for example), I've found a specific reading strategy quite useful. The linguist John Swales has studied the academic article as a genre, and he's discovered that experts across disciplines use a common pattern to "create a research space" for themselves in an ongoing conversation. Here's how I would summarize the three rhetorical moves Swales sees in disciplinary texts:

> Move 1: *Why is this topic important?* In move 1, the scholar might explain, "Here's what we know about this topic AND/OR here's why it's important right now (*kairos*) AND/OR here's what previous research or texts have said about it."

> Move 2: *What's the problem?* In move 2, the writer justifies his/her text by showing, like a good storyteller, the trouble: "Here are the questions that remain AND/OR here's what hasn't yet been done AND/OR here's why or how previous texts have been wrong or mistaken AND/OR here's why we should keep talking about this topic."

> Move 3: *How do I intend to solve or explore this problem?* Move 3 is the gravy: "Here's the reason why I'm writing AND/OR here's my main point or argument AND/OR here's what I hope to add and what I hope it does for us AND/OR here's how I'm going to lay out the argument."

Often you can find these three moves in the first couple of pages of a text (often it's right there in the abstract). This model has been immensely important to me as a scholar because it helps me track the *conversation* we're having about a topic. When I write with sources, I enter these conversations myself, creating my own research space with these three moves. In short, you can read disciplinary texts more effectively if you think about how the writer uses these three moves to enter and contribute to a conversation. Conversations, in public life as well as disciplines, proceed when people make assertions or arguments and other people agree or disagree (in varying degrees), or change the subject (Graff). You should consider how to make these moves yourself when you write with sources.

Write Your Reading

We talked about taking notes in the text. It's also immensely helpful to take notes *about* the text—to write what you read, to put it in your own words (especially if you can do it "with your eyes closed," i.e., by not looking back at the text). You can summarize texts in writing. I like Kelly Gallagher's idea to use "sentence starters" when we write our reading. He suggests we begin a written response with the following phrases:

I don't understand…

I noticed…

I wonder…

I was reminded of…

I'm surprised that…

I'd like to know…

I realized…

If I were…

The central issue(s) is (are)…

One consequence of _____ could be…

If _____, then…

I'm not sure…

Although it seems…. (Gallagher *Deeper Reading* 70)

In graduate school, I used 4×6 notecards for every text I read, trying to capture the three Swalesian moves writers made. Other grad students mocked me because it seemed so old school, but it worked for me. You might want to try a "graphic organizer" or "T-chart" to organize your ideas as you write. A T-chart is a two- or three-column record of your reading experience (you draw the "T" on paper for the columns). As Gallagher points out, T-charts encourage deeper reading by inviting you to read once for comprehension (what a text says) and once for analysis (what a text does).

Here are a few T-charts and their uses:

for writing with sources

main point	how I'll use it in my paper

main point	research methods	*kairos* or credibility

for understanding and applying

what does it say?	what does it mean?	what does it matter?

(from Kelly Gallagher *Deeper Reading*)

main idea/point/argument	evidence/reasons/support

my summary	my uses	my questions

what do I expect the writer to say (before reading)?	what did the writer say (after reading)?	what does the writer want me to feel, think, or do?

what does it say?	how does it say it?	what are the consequences or implications?

rhetorical strategy	example from text	effect on audience

CLAIM:			
claim type:			
reasons	analysis	assumptions	analysis

Let me share an example of how this last one might work. My thirteen year-old son Ben plays an online video game called *League of Legends*. (I bet some of you are Leaguers. Ben likes playing with Draven.) On weekends, he goes with his friends to our university's library so they can use a local area network and play *League* together. My wife and I ask Ben to be home by 10:30 p.m. on the weekends, and Ben doesn't like this. He tells us we're the only parents in the neighborhood with such a strict curfew. So, if I wanted to analyze the strength or weakness of his argument, I might use the following graphic organizer:

CLAIM: I should *not* have a curfew

claim type: policy (could also be value, as in "curfew = bad!")

reasons	analysis	assumptions	analysis
Because none of my friends have a curfew.	Ben wants to use this reason as a fact—as extrinsic evidence. Turns out it ain't true. We checked. True, some of his *LOL* friends don't seem to have curfews, but others do. And he has non-*LOL* friends who have curfews.	What holds true for all of my friends should hold true for me.	It's easy to dismiss this assumption as a bandwagon plea: What's good for the herd is good for me. As parents, it shouldn't matter what the parents of our kids' friends do. If we think something's right, we should go for it. But sometimes bandwagon pleas are reasonable. What if it *is* true that *none* of his friends have curfews? What does that say about us as parents? Are we too controlling, too mistrusting? While we want to have our own policies, we don't want to be unreasonable.

12

PAUSE. Let's do some "retrieval practice." In *Make it Stick*, psychologists Henry Roediger and Mark McDaniel (and their collaborator, novelist Peter Brown) explain that retrieval, or "self-quizzing," is so much more effective than underlining, highlighting, or rereading (201–202). "Repeated recall," they argue, "appears to help memory consolidate into a cohesive representation in the brain and to strengthen and multiply the neural routes by which the knowledge can later be retrieved" (28–29). Retrieval practice takes *effort*, and effort aids memory.

So, remind yourself of the heading of this last section, and answer these questions (without looking back at the text): What new terms did you learn in this section? How did these concepts validate or challenge what you already knew? How does this section connect with what you've learned previously in this book and elsewhere? What will you do differently as a reader now that you've read this section? (This last question connects with what you thought about at the beginning of the chapter: what you want to "get out" of this chapter.)

III. Revise and Reflect

Okay, we've covered the *planning* and *practicing* stages of our self-directed model of reading. Now, a brief word on what it might look like to *revise* and *reflect* as a reader.

Revision, in a reading sense, means testing your knowledge to see whether your understanding of a text needs adjustment. Learning scientists call this practice *calibration:*

> the act of aligning your judgments of what you know and don't know with objective feedback so as to avoid being carried off by the illusions of mastery that catch many learners by surprise at test time. (Brown, Roediger, McDaniel 211)

Class discussions, for example, help us calibrate our reading. Even in situations where readings lead to different interpretations that could be equally valid (e.g., if you're reading a poem or novel), calibration helps you understand how a text works in context and how it yields various, often competing, readings. Sometimes a second, more thorough reading can act as a calibrating agent. I've read a text a second time and found myself talking back to my own notes.

Study groups do this, too. In graduate school, when I was reading Aristotle's *Rhetoric* for the first time, my friend Jason invited me into a small breakfast group that met before class, ate some bagels, and debated what the text meant. It helped me immeasurably to hear other people's interpretations.

Finally, any mindful reading practice includes some kind of reflection that helps you build a core narrative about yourself as a reader. Remember from chapter five that effective reflection involves projecting ahead to a looming task and reviewing back to a completed task. The questions from chapter five can be fruitfully applied to your reading process, specifically the questions you might ask yourself after you've done a few reading assignments for a class (what have I learned? how has my reading process helped or hurt me? what needs to change?).

PAUSE. Go back to chapter five and review the reflection questions, only this time think of the questions in the context of reading.

Reading Rhetorically, Writing Rhetorically

I hope what we've discussed in this chapter will help you read more effectively, especially when you need to read to prepare to write. Sometimes, as I've said in this chapter, you'll want to read quickly to get the gist and get out. Other times you'll want to savor what you read, like you'd savor a really good piece of chocolate. When you read like a rhetorical critic, you read not only for meaning (what does the writer say?) but for strategy and value (how does a writer say it? how *well* does a writer achieve her rhetorical purposes?). Writing a rhetorical analysis is one way to give a text your undivided attention. Rhetorical critics *classify*, *analyze*, and *evaluate* a text, and through their writing they teach readers how to do the same (Jasinski 125–144). You now have a toolbox for close rhetorical readings, with principles from rhetorical situation, argument, character, emotion, and style. Your instructor will work with you as you strengthen your ability to read critically, closely, thoroughly, rhetorically. I hope such reading will give you new equipment for living.

Works Cited

Ambrose, Susan A. et al. *How Learning Works: Seven Research-Based Principles for Smart Teaching*. San Francisco: Jossey-Bass, 2010.

Bean, John. *Engaging Ideas*. 2nd ed. San Francisco: Jossey-Bass, 2011. Print.

Brandt, Deborah. *Literacy and Learning*. San Francisco: Jossey-Bass, 2009. Print.

Brown, Peter C., Henry L. Roediger III, and Mark A. McDaniel. *Make it Stick: The Science of Successful Learning*. Cambridge: Belknap, 2014. Print.

Dehaene, Stanislas. *Reading in the Brain*. NY: Viking, 2009. Print.

Duke, Nell K. and David Pearson. "Effective Practices for Developing Reading Comprehension." *What Research Has to Say About Reading Instruction*. 3rd ed. Eds. Alan Fostrup and S. Jay Samuels. International Reading Association, 2002. 205–242. Print.

Gallagher, Kelly. *Deeper Reading*. Portland, ME: Stenhouse, 2004. Print.

— — —. *Readicide*. Portland, ME: Stenhouse, 2007. Print.

Gallagher, Winifred. *RAPT: Attention and the Focused Life*. NY: Penguin, 2010. Print.

Gee, James Paul. *Social Linguistics and Literacies*. 4th ed. London: Routledge, 2012. Print.

Graff, Gerald. *Clueless in Academe*. New Haven: Yale UP, 2003. Print.

Harvard Health Publications. "Blue Light Has a Dark Side." Harvard Medical School. 1 May 2012. Web. 8 April 2015.

Harvard Report on Reading. Cited in "Active Reading: Comprehension and Rate." Dartmouth Academic Study Skills Center. n.d. Web. 10 April 2015.

Hathaway, Bill. "Online Illusion: Unplugged, We Really Aren't That Smart." 31 March 2015. Web. 9 April 2015.

Jabr, Ferris. "The Reading Brain in the Digital Age." *Scientific American*. 11 April 2013. Web. 8 April 2015.

Jamieson, Sandra, Rebecca Moore Howard, and Tricia C. Serviss. The Citation Project. n.d. Web. 10 April 2015.

Jasinski, James. *Sourcebook on Rhetoric*. Thousand Oaks, CA: Sage, 2001. Print.

Keim, Brandon. "Why the Smart Reading Device of the Future May Be… Paper." *Wired*. 1 May 2014. Web. 9 April 2015.

Kim, Meeri. "Blue Light from Electronics Disturbs Sleep, Especially for Teenagers." *Washington Post*. 1 September 2014. Web. 8 April 2015.

Langer, Ellen. *Mindfulness*. Reading, MA: Merloyd Lawrence, 1989. Print.

Mangen, Anne, Bente R. Walgermo, and Kolbjorn Bronnick. "Reading Linear Text on Paper Versus Computer Screen." *International Journal of Education Research* 58 (2013): 61–68.

Posner, Michael I. *Attention in a Social World*. NY: Oxford, 2012. Print.

Robb, Alice. "92 Percent of College Students Prefer Reading Print Books to E-Readers." *New Republic*. 14 January 2015. Web. 8 April 2015.

Rockinson-Szapkiw, Amanda J. et al. "Electronic Versus Traditional Print Textbooks." *Computers and Education* 63 (Apr 2013): 259–266. Database. ScienceDirect.

Street, Brian. "The New Literacy Studies." *Literacy: A Critical Sourcebook*. Ed. Ellen Cushman et al. Boston: Bedford / St. Martin's, 2001. 430–442.

Subrahamanyam, Kaveri et al. "Learning from Paper, Learning from Screens." *International Journal of Cyber Behavior, Psychology, and Learning* 3.4 (2013): 1–27. Abstract accessed on Web. 8 April 2015.

Swales, John. *Genre Analysis: English in Academic and Research Settings*. Cambridge, 1990. Print.

Urist, Jacoba. "What the Marshmallow Test Really Teaches About Self Control." *Atlantic*. 24 Sept 2014. Web. 10 Apr 2015.

PART III

The Genres of Writing

In Part III, I've included student examples of some of the genres you might be asked to write in. These examples come from BYU students who won either first or second place in our annual writing contests. (Will next year's winner be you?) Each year, we'll publish the previous year's winners and the current year's winners in the back of *Mindful Writing*.

Remember what we learned from the *planning* stage of our learning model for writing tasks: You should study your targeted genre mindfully. Specifically, I encouraged you to follow a three-step process developed by scholars Amy Devitt, Mary Jo Reiff, and Anis Bawarshi in their fantastic book *Scenes of Writing:*

1. Collect as many *examples* of the genre as you can—both from professional writers and student writers. (Ask your instructor to show you successful and less successful examples.) You want to get a good sense of the full range of possible responses to the rhetorical situation from which the genre springs.

2. Study the *rhetorical situation* for which this genre is fitting. Who writes these things? Why? Who is the audience or discourse community? Why do they value this genre? What are the purposes of the genre? What topics or issues are covered? What makes an example of this genre effective or not for the situation?

3. Analyze the *rhetorical strategies* you see in the examples. How is the writing organized or designed? What rhetorical strategies are used (ACES, or others)? What kind of style or argument or document design or lexical field do you detect across the examples? What are the options (deviations), and what seems to be standard (conventions)?

You can make product goals more effectively after you've gone through this process.

In first-year writing, it is far more important to know *that* there are genres and *why* they are used than to get good at writing any particular genre you may not write again (like a rhetorical analysis). Genre awareness is one of those skills that can transfer with you to other writing tasks both in and out of school. I hope the following examples help you develop genre awareness as a critical thinking tool for writing tasks.

OPINION EDITORIAL

Example 1

"Stop the Brony Hate"
Marlene Schmidt
2015

Of all the smash hits in popular culture today, one of the most surprising is *My Little Pony*.

This 2010 reboot—titled "Friendship is Magic" to distinguish it from the 80's cartoon—swept geeks off their feet like a rainbow-colored tsunami. Good writing, superb characters, and high-quality art have all contributed to its fame—but what caught the public's attention was the presence of an unexpected fanbase. It was a shock to many when the show designed for young girls attracted adult admirers as well. Male admirers.

Going by the name of "Bronies"—a portmanteau of "brother" and "pony"—this fanbase sprang up almost as soon as the show started. It's spread all the way across the country, even to BYU—the "BYU Bronies" club (complete with its own facebook page and mascot) currently boasts 176 members and counting. I myself was caught off guard by this discovery. A crowd of grown men, celebrating a show that features effeminate equines? As I pondered the possibility, three questions ran through my mind:

Did it really exist? Yes; Bronies were undeniably a real thing.

Why did they like the show? That was a question to be answered later.

And finally—was there something wrong with this situation? This is the question I would like to discuss today. When I mention Bronies, I'm usually met with a disgusted look. Or at the very least, mild derision. Bronies may be unconventional, but there's no legitimate reason for the contempt they face. It is an all-too-common wrong which needs to be righted.

The main quarrel with Bronies is their gender. Men aren't supposed to watch "girl" shows like *My Little Pony*. It's just not done. Men should do men things and women should do women things. Isn't that how society works?

Anyone in the modern generation should see the problem with that statement. The last few decades have been a flurry of cultural revolution, mainly centered on women's rights. Girls are no longer expected to sit around and look pretty. They're allowed, even encouraged, to pursue interests outside their traditional gender roles. Sports, martial arts, video games—these aren't taboo to women anymore. Every day we hear messages that women are more than meat; that they are strong and unique and can do anything they want to, regardless of what society says. Why don't we tell this same message to boys? Why is it okay for a girl to like "boy" interests, but not for a boy to like "girl" interests? We can't keep touting freedom for women while forcing the men to stay in the confines of tradition. It's only fair—and reasonable—that men should get the same tolerant treatment as girls do as they explore interests outside of their stereotype.

Of course, not everyone agrees with the cultural revolution. Equal treatment is one thing, but homogenization is another. You can't just erase the differences between men and women; there's a point where it becomes not only impractical for societal functions, but morally wrong. I agree; there is a limit to how much we can healthily homogenize gender roles. Some differences need to stay, for the moral well-being of society. But I can't see how *My Little Pony* crosses that line. Yes, its main characters are ponies; yes, they're female. But that's not what the show's about. Watch even one episode, and you'll see that the show isn't about pretty ponies having tea parties. It's about *friendship*. It strives to identify the qualities of a good friend, and how those qualities help people to overcome adversity and solve problems. It's about finding common ground with those who don't share all your interests. It's about teamwork. It's about strength. It's about love. And these are things that men need to learn as well as women.

Artist Agnes Garbowska, who illustrates for the MLP franchise, recounted a story that she thought embodied the purpose of the show. A little boy came to her table at a convention once. His father, who accompanied him, was clearly not ecstatic about his son's interest. As Garbowska signed an autograph for the boy, he told her that "the other boys at school make fun of me for watching *My Little Pony*. I think they need to watch the show, because they don't know how to be very good friends and the show would teach them to be better friends." Hearing this, the father paused. With new understanding in his eyes, he gripped his boy's shoulder and muttered "You're all right, son; you're all right."

Most BYU students are familiar with the admonition to seek after "anything virtuous, lovely, or… praiseworthy." Doesn't a show about friendship and cooperation fit that bill? Whether it features ponies, talking bears, or giant transforming robots, an uplifting show should be embraced, not scorned. A person's interests say a lot about their character—if a boy would choose a G-rated show over a more popular crime series, or a first-person shooter game, that says a lot about his values. Frankly, I think it's a point in his favor—not something to be denigrated.

Of course, the Pony fandom isn't for everybody; like any other form of entertainment, it's subjective. Some people have a taste for it, some don't. And you know what? That's fine. Having differing opinions is good for society. After all, it was the phenomenon of different ideas, different interests coming together, that made American culture as rich as it is today.

But central to that culture is an idea, without which the union could never have happened: respect. Respect is something that has been instilled in our generation from birth. Respect for heritage; respect for religion; respect for humanity in general. I was always taught to be tolerant of differences, and my experiences as a teenager and now as an adult have reinforced the wisdom of that lesson. If there's one thing I've learned, it's that there are many good ideas in the world.

Just because someone isn't exactly like me doesn't make them *evil*. I may not agree with them; I may have very different tastes and beliefs than they do. But as long as our core values are similar, there's no reason we can't get along.

You might hate *My Little Pony*; you might think it's the stupidest thing in the world.

That's okay. Just don't look down on the people who *do* like it. Our generation has lived through an ever-increasing awareness of bigotry. The fight against racism, sexism, faithism, is a major issue in politics. I have to wonder, then: how can we hope to overcome these larger differences if we scorn people based on something as petty as their preference of TV show?

An internet saying comes to mind: "Being an atheist is okay; being an atheist and shaming religions and spirituality as silly and not real is not okay. Being a Christian is okay; being homophobic, misogynistic, racist, or an otherwise hateful person in the name of Christianity is not okay. Being a reindeer is okay; bullying and excluding another reindeer because he has a shiny red nose is not okay."

Disliking *My Little Pony* is okay. Having opinions on gender roles is ok. Hating on Bronies is not okay. Society needs to see Bronies as individuals, as people, before slapping labels and judgments on them. Their interest might seem weird at first—it might even make some people uncomfortable—but we're not confined by such petty and groundless mindsets. We can be better than that. We *are* better than that.

So if you ever meet a Brony—and if you're at BYU, you probably will—and start to feel the anti-Brony vibe, just shove it away. Get to know the guy as a person before drawing conclusions about his nature and lifestyle. Learning to accept those with different interests is a vital step in building an ideal society. Eliminating Brony hate may seem insignificant, but it can make a difference. By focusing on respect and compassion in our personal situations, we will invoke a magic that opens the doors to overcoming further barriers.

Because friendship is indeed magic.

Example 2

"Don't Judge an eBook By Its Cover"
Hailey Payne
2015

Like many poor, starving college students before me, when it came time to purchase my textbooks for this semester, I searched for and bought the dirt-cheapest options I could find. In one class, I had the choice between a paper copy of the assigned text for over 100 dollars, and an eBook for only 70. The obvious better deal was the online book, right?

At first, I was hesitant to buy a book that I could only access with a computer, but after studying for (and consequently doing quite well on) my first test, I was convinced that I'd made the right decision. eBooks are tragically misunderstood and often get a bad reputation for being "hard to study from" and straining peoples' eyes, but in my experience, the benefits of online textbooks far outweigh the drawbacks and certainly make them worth buying.

One of the main concerns students have with using online textbooks comes from the belief that people learn better from traditional hard-copy texts compared to eBooks. A study done at Indiana State University showed that when half of a class studied from an online book and the other half from a paper version, they actually performed equally well on a test over the material (Mann).

That same study mentioned the effect of computer screens on the eyes after prolonged periods of time. Factors like eye strain could, admittedly, deter students from learning as effectively online, but eye strain can be caused by any activity involving looking at a computer screen for too long and can be prevented simply by taking breaks, blinking more often, or looking away from the screen periodically. Everybody learns a little bit differently, but according to research, whether the book is electronic or not does not affect a student's ability to remember information for a test and eye strain doesn't make a big enough impact to change that (Mann).

Another doubt people have about online textbooks is whether they're reliable or not. We've all had that night where at 11:59 we're in a frantic time crunch to finish an online assignment and the internet crashes. Online books, like any other applications requiring the internet, are susceptible to such misfortunes. With more and more classes using online assignments, it is hardly fair to single out eBooks as being negatively affected by poor Wi-Fi.

A good way to avoid an internet emergency, which works for any online assignment or reading, is to not procrastinate. I've learned from experience that if you don't wait until the last minute, there's a better chance you'll have time to either find a place with a better connection or talk to your professor. So the answer to whether eBooks are reliable or not is that they're just as reliable as any other website you have to use for classes. On the bright side, some eBooks can be downloaded as PDFs which means you don't even need the internet when you do your reading.

Yet another worry people have concerning eBooks involves the tangibility of paper versus online books. Many people express their need to mark up and hold their textbooks in order to learn from them. I completely agree with that and have found that marking and making notes in my books helps me remember the information better. Fortunately, most eBooks I've encountered include features for doing exactly that. If you're willing to adapt a little, you will find, like I have, that online textbooks can be just as easy to learn from as paper versions.

One last misconception students may have is that using a laptop to access their book increases the risk of distraction by social media while trying to study. (If you don't even have a laptop, let me clarify that most eBooks can be accessed on a compatible tablet or smartphone. So don't fear, this paper still applies to you.) All online school assignments run the risk of distraction on the internet, but what it really comes down to is how hard you're trying to focus. If it's not too much of an inconvenience, you could try turning off your Facebook and Email notifications while you're studying online. If the temptation is still too great, then you could plan on giving yourself breaks to update your status or send a message.

With most of the misinformation surrounding eBooks clarified, you should now be more open to the idea of using an online text book. If not, here are a few more things that might convince you. Online textbooks offer several benefits that most hard copies do not. These include being generally cheaper, more portable, and having additional study resources. There are some exceptions of course, but the vast majority of eBooks are better priced, more convenient, and helpful to study from.

As much as I like being a pack mule, I'd rather not have to lug around my personal library of textbooks with me all day. With eBooks, I can keep all my required texts on my laptop which weighs only a fraction of the weight of one book. This also makes it less likely that I'll forget something I need at home because all my books are in one place.

Another thing not offered by heavy, hard-copy textbooks is the variety of online study resources. Many eBooks include access to study helps such as flashcards or quizzes to help you remember the material better. I found these to be especially helpful because they worked well with my learning style. It's also nice having several study methods to choose from.

With more and more professors offering the option of online books, it is important to be educated on the matter before deciding to buy one. "College students who study with digital textbooks perform just as well on tests as do their peers who use print textbooks"(Mann). Hopefully this fact, as well as the other evidence I've provided, has made you more knowledgeable about the subject and helps you realize that online text books are not as scary as they seem. When you have the option of a digital textbook on your booklist next semester, don't turn up your nose because of mistaken beliefs the way I nearly did. If you're as stingy as me and it's cheaper to buy an online book, don't be afraid to try it. Give eBooks a chance and you'll see for yourself how worth it they are.

Works Cited

Mann, Leslie. "Pros and Cons of Digital Textbooks." Chicago Tribune. N.p., 7 Aug. 2013. Web. 29 Sept. 2014.

Example 3

"Mom... I Think I'm a Socialist."
Claire Gillett
2016

A friend of mine recently recounted a conversation she had with her mom about the upcoming presidential election. After taking a survey from the popular online voting guide ISideWith, she found she aligned most with Bernie Sanders. Surprised, and somewhat alarmed, she called her mom for counsel. Upon answering her phone, my friend's mother heard the dreaded words: "Mom... I think I'm a socialist." The reaction that ensued consisted of nervous hand-wringing, a copious amount of sweat, and serious doubts regarding her success as a mother.

While her reaction may seem extreme, it represents fears Americans have had since the Cold War. For many today, the word "socialism" calls to mind images of well-groomed moustaches, starched military uniforms, long bread lines, and starving children. Recent polls suggest as many as 6 in 10 Americans have a negative reaction to the word ("Little Change"). As much as I hate to admit it, until recently, I was one of them. However, I approach you today fully recovered from my previous aversion, and I beg on behalf of a word with no voice of its own, to reevaluate your assumptions. Despite the historical connotations it carries, socialism, as an ideology, is neither inherently evil nor dictatorial. Quite the opposite, it firmly advocates equal opportunity for all. As the young voters of this generation, it is our responsibility to understand the real implications of modern socialism. If we rely on the Cold War stigmas for our understanding, we can't vote informatively, or keep up with America's ever shifting political scene.

To a large extent, the misconceptions surrounding socialism stem from its historical context. In the second half of the 20th century, with totalitarian regimes popping up throughout eastern Europe and Asia, mandated state economic control became increasingly more common. In the USSR, collectivized farming and a series of 5-year plans resulted in widespread industrial growth at the expense of the people's well-being. Executory purges and starvation claimed the lives of an estimated 15 million. Although the Soviet Union ultimately fell in 1991, the fear it induced in the baby-boomer generation lives on today. In the wake of the Red Scare, socialism, communism, and dictatorship were thought of as one and the same. This association, while understandable, is fundamentally inaccurate.

Communism and dictatorship are *political* ideologies, while socialism is an *economic* one. Oppressive dictators did indeed use socialist methods to forward economic growth, but socialism itself implies nothing of oppression. In contrast, socialism today, when combined with democracy, represents the essence of freedom and equality. While totalitarian regimes used oppression and government censorship, socialists today fight to reduce the income gap and protect wage equality. We shouldn't fear a mass uprising, class war, or tyrannical dictator because socialism is different than communism, different than dictatorship, and different than oppression. We must separate socialist theory from socialist history.

Apart from its connotations, many argue against socialism on grounds of impracticality. Many see extensive economic regulation as a violation of freedom. However, countries around the world currently operate under highly successful democratic socialist governments. We should pay particular attention to Scandinavian countries like Sweden, Finland, and Norway. These countries flourish economically, while maintaining not only their autonomy, but a high standard of living. The Nordic model, by which it is known, combines competitive capitalism with a large public sector (Andersen 2007). The government espouses roughly 30% of the workforce, while at the same time offering a generous welfare system, and a wide variety of social programs.

Parents get up to a year of paid leave following the birth of a child, and health care is universally provided at no charge to the patient. Contrasted to the often harsh effects of capitalism, democratic socialism in Nordic countries defines freedom and equality. This system is widely popular in the countries in which it has been implemented. Scandinavians welcome socialism with open arms. This is largely due to the fact that socialism in Scandinavia does not carry the emotional baggage it does in America. Young voters should be aware of this baggage and learn to rise above it. The demographics in Scandinavia and America are very different, and their policies would have to be implemented differently here, but the success of other nations should serve as a testament of socialism's viability in our society today.

In addition to guiding countries around the world, socialism permeates much of American policy today. This makes the socialist ideology not only applicable to us, but vital to our understanding of modern American politics. Public schools, national parks, highways, student loans, public landfills, and the FBI all contain elements of socialism. Funded by the public, they would not be possible without some degree of government regulation. These programs support millions of Americans every year, reinforcing the idea that socialism is not scary, but an everyday part of our identity. The United States Postal Service, a government run entity, employs over 600,000 Americans and brings an annual revenue of 67.8 billion dollars. 40% of the world's mail volume is handled by the Postal Service, with just over 155 billion pieces having been processed last year ("Size and Scope"). None of this would be possible without socialism. We must understand that socialism doesn't presume to take away the freedoms we enjoy; it simply advocates ways in which freedoms and conveniences can be available to everyone.

Although the Socialist Party itself remains on the margins in America, in recent years, socialist ideals have permeated liberal and conservative policy alike. The presidential campaign of self-proclaimed socialist, Senator Bernie Sanders is proof of that very fact. Running on the democratic ticket, he embraces the title "Socialist" rather than shying away from it like many a liberal before him. His increasingly large grassroots following suggests that times are gone when we can write socialists off as lunatics without doing serious inquiry into their policy. These ideas are a legitimate part of modern policy, and as such, young voters must understand the relative generality of socialist ideals.

Now, I'm not necessarily expecting everyone to "feel the Bern." I am not even trying to make people like the idea of socialism. I just want to give the word another chance. At the most basic level, socialism represents the desire to curtail wealth inequality, ensure equal pay for women, and provide cheaper college education. The youth of this generation need to understand that, rather than rely on its historically negative connotations. I challenge young voters to get involved in the furthering of our political understanding. It is our responsibility to improve upon the knowledge of past generations. Let's reject the obsolete connotations from long ago, and define socialism as it truly exists in America today. Doing so will allow us to make more educated decisions when approaching the polls. It's time to rescue Socialism from the trash bin labelled "scary" and bring it out to see the sun. At the very least, let's do it for the mothers who lose sleep worrying about the Stalinist dictators they fear they have raised.

13

Works Cited

"Little Change in Public's Response to 'Capitalism,' 'Socialism'" *Pew Research Center for the People and the Press RSS.* 28 Dec. 2011. Web. 28 Sept. 2015.

Andersen, Torben, and Bengt Holmstrom. "The Nordic Model: Embracing Globalization and Sharing Risks." *The Research Institute of the Finnish Economy.* Feb. 2007. Web. 22 Sept. 2015.

"Size and Scope: Postal Facts." United States Postal Service Information. Web. 20 Sept. 2015.

Example 4

"The Value of Speaking Carefully"
Lucia Johnston
2016

As a society, there are few topics we love to hate more than political correctness. In just the last month, it has taken the blame for ruining Halloween, increasing drug abuse, creating fragile children, and causing the San Bernardino shooting (Phillips; Quinlan; Goldberg; Duke). Leading republican presidential candidate, Donald Trump, said "I don't frankly have time for political correctness. And to be honest with you, this country doesn't have time either" (Samtani). Charlton Heston famously called political correctness "tyranny with manners" (Charles Heston). Today, most Americans agree with him (Is America Too PC?). Those who oppose political correctness generally believe that it's unnecessary, that it infringes on their freedom of speech, and that it stifles discussion. While these concerns are valid, much of the criticism is rooted in fear and defensiveness. As we step back and look at the true effects of political correctness, we see that its benefits far outweigh its potential harms.

The first criticism of political correctness is generally that it's unnecessary. You want me to replace one word with another? What's the point? The point is that words matter. Word choice affects how we think and how we act. As Maya Angelou wrote, "Words are things…They get on the walls. They get in your wallpaper. They get in your rugs, in your upholstery, and your clothes, and finally in to you" (LitNews).

Several studies have shown that word choice affects how people perceive reality. In one experiment, two groups were asked to read about rising crime rates in a fictional city. For the first group, the word "beast" was used to describe crime, connoting menace and danger. In this group, 71% of participants called for more police enforcement (Gorlick). In the second group, the word "virus" was used instead, bringing to mind medicine and prevention. In this group, only 54% of participants wanted more police enforcement (Gorlick). Changing only one word drastically influenced how participants viewed the problem. Imagine the power of changing more significant words like racial slurs and other "politically incorrect" phrases in our language.

Calling lame things "gay" and weak men "pussies" has a small but real influence on the way we think of gay people and women. Words subtly change our perception of reality. A movement that asks us to pay attention to how we use them should not be dismissed as frivolous.

People also criticize political correctness for infringing on our freedom of speech. I felt this way a year or two ago when I was talking to my friend, Marley. I asked her how I could get involved with an event that she was organizing to help the homeless. She politely requested that I refer to them as "people suffering from homelessness" instead of "homeless people." I nodded, but in my head I was complaining. *Ugh, political correctness is getting ridiculous! I'm so tired of people trying to control me with all these little rules! This is America! Where is my freedom of speech?* Marley had politely asked me to change a small thing, but I felt a strong defensive response. It seemed like my liberty was under attack, and I wanted to protect it.

At the event, I had a chance to some "people suffering from homelessness." Eager to justify my exasperation, I asked a group of women if they preferred one term over the other. Some didn't mind either way, but others said that it made a difference. One woman in particular said that "homeless" felt like a permanent label whereas "suffering from homelessness" felt like a temporary struggle that she could overcome. As I listened to her, my defensiveness evaporated.

I realized that Marley was not infringing on my freedom of speech by asking me to reconsider my words. The First Amendment protects our right to speak without fear of legal prosecution, not a right to speak without consequences. Is saying "people suffering from homelessness" inconvenient? Yes. But does it have real consequences on the way we think about their circumstances? Yes. I don't want to live in a world where saying "homeless people" is illegal; that would be a gross violation of freedom of speech. I do want to live in a world where we weigh the difficulty of saying a couple extra syllables against the possibility of giving a socially disadvantaged individual hope, and decide that the change is worth it.

People also denounce political correctness because they believe it stifles discussion. Free intellectual debate is essential for progress, and I am grateful to live in a country where it is so fiercely protected. Fears that debate will be inhibited by critically looking at the words we use are entirely understandable, as focusing on the details may keep larger issues from being discussed. However, research shows that political correctness may encourage debate. In a peer- reviewed study at Cornell University, diverse participants were put into groups and asked to come up with business ideas. Half the groups were instructed to be politically correct and half were not. The politically correct groups came up with more ideas, and those ideas were more creative (Demby). Significantly, women and minorities contributed more in the politically correct groups. This increase is undeniably important in a business climate where women and minorities combined make up less than 10% of Fortune 500 CEOs (Clark).

Political correctness takes effort, and effort is uncomfortable, especially when we are trying to devote our full attention to a discussion. However, this effort pays off as people feel more comfortable contributing to the discussion, especially those whose voices are traditionally less present.

Some people say that political correctness stifles discussion by suppressing unpopular ideas. But unpopular ideas will always receive backlash, no matter how "politically correct" the audience is. Currently, those who champion controversial opinions sometimes use "out of control political correctness" as a shield to discredit their critics. This response counterproductively halts the debate because it effectively communicates "I am not willing to listen to your criticism." As we strive to foster civil discussion in our society, we should be skeptical of those who say that people are "just too PC" to appreciate their ideas. Often the perceived overly politically correct comments are sincere criticisms, which may or may not be valid, but deserved to be discussed, rather than dismissed.

The issue of stifling debate has come to a head recently on college campuses. Many worry that political correctness and "word policing" will impede students' learning. I experienced a minor form of word policing in elementary school when I wrote a short story which involved a black couple whom I described as "Negro." My teacher carefully explained to me that the word Negro had connotations of which I was probably not aware. She taught me that "black" or "African American" would convey what I was trying to say and clarify my message by removing unintentional meanings.

Most college students understand the difference between "Negro" and "black," but many issues are more complex. As we study and use political correctness, we learn how and why certain words have power. College should not only teach us how to perform well in our field, but also how to communicate effectively with our coworkers. Part of communicating well is understanding how different words affect people of varied political and socioeconomic backgrounds. Political correctness is a essential part of a college education, not a distraction from it. Understanding the context and power of the words we use is an invaluable tool for life.

The political correctness movement is not without its flaws. Supporters can be rude and argumentative, especially over the anonymity of the Internet. I felt defensive when a close friend politely asked me to make a small change, so I understand why others feel attacked when strangers ask them to make big changes, sometimes impolitely. However, these issues stem from human nature, not political correctness. Whenever people feel passionately about any subject, some will become frustrated and rude. Discourteous politically correct "warriors" will almost always stop a productive debate. Recently, at the University of Missouri, racial justice activists physically and verbally harassed students who did not wish to join their protest. This only served to increase racial tensions at the university. However, rudeness is to blame for this break in communication, not political correctness. A movement cannot be condemned because some of its supporters are overzealous.

Throughout most of human history, the powerful have done their best to silence and oppress the weak. Political correctness goes against this trend by encouraging us to listen to those who are typically ignored and to use language which further invites them into the conversation. Everyone likes to do whatever they want, and no one likes to be told that what they're doing is wrong. Political correctness bumps against both of these instincts, making a lot of enemies in the process. If we are thinking only of ourselves, the movement seems ridiculous. Why would I purposely inconvenience myself for no personal gain? However, when we try to empathize with socially disadvantaged groups, we recognize that our words have power and foster a desire to use them carefully.

Works Cited

Charlton Heston - *Political Correctness Vs Common Sense*. Perf. Charlton Heston. YouTube. Google, 28 Jan. 2013. Web. 9 Dec. 2015.

Clark, Dorie. "Why So Few Women and Minorities at the Top?" *Forbes*. Forbes Magazine, 3 Sept. 2013. Web. 09 Dec. 2015.

Demby, Gene. "What Research Says About the Consequences of PC Culture." *NPR: National Public Radio*. 30 Jan. 2015. Web. 9 Dec. 2015.

Duke, Selwyn. "San Bernardino Shooting: Political Correctness Kills." *American Thinker*. N.p., 4 Dec. 2015. Web. 9 Dec. 2015.

Goldberg, Jonah. "Campus Commotions Show We're Raising Fragile Kids." *Townhall*. Townhall Media, 11 Nov. 2015. Web. 09 Dec. 2015.

Gorlick, Adam. "Is Crime a Virus or a Beast?" *Stanford News*. Stanford University, 23 Feb. 2011. Web. 09 Dec. 2015.

"Is America Too PC?" *Rasmussen Reports*. Rasmussen Reports, 28 Aug. 2015. Web. 09 Dec. 2015.

LitNews. ""Words Are Things"…by Maya Angelou." *"Words Are Things"… by Maya Angelou*. Yamina Today, 19 Jan. 2012. Web. 09 Dec. 2015.

Phillips, Judson. "Political Correctness Ruins Halloween and America." *Tea Party Nation*. Ning, 1 Nov. 2015. Web. 09 Dec. 2015.

Samtani, Hiten. "Top 7 Things Donald "Why is Obama playing basketball today" Trump Said During the GOP Debate." *The Real Deal*. Korangy Publishing, 07 Aug. 2015. Web. 09 Dec. 2015.

Quinlan, Casey. "Ben Carson Blames Drug Addiction On 'Political Correctness'" *ThinkProgress*. Center for American Progress Action Fund, 08 Nov. 2015. Web. 09 Dec. 2015.

14

PERSONAL NARRATIVE

Example 1

"Gloria and the Bear"
Mary Mortenson
2015

There's a certain feeling that comes with Thursday afternoons. It's the same feeling you get when you're mowing the lawn and only have two more back-and-forths to do. Or after you've already taken the very last repeat in Mussorgsky's "Night on Bald Mountain" and you know you'll be able to rest your arm soon. By Thursday, you have essentially made it through the week. And during the winter in Bozeman Montana, making it through the week without skipping class or getting the car stuck in the snow can feel like an accomplishment. Bozeman is beautiful, but for eight months of the year, the snowplows are in business and the sun sets before you get home from the school. By February, it physically hurts to get out of bed in the mornings. You find yourself constantly dragging and tired, challenging your own memory because there's no way that you were actually ever able to be barefooted on the permafrosted, cold tile of your kitchen…is there? You find yourself eating way too many of your high school cafeteria's cookies, because sugar tastes a lot like sunshine. You're counting the weeks until June and planning summer backpacking trips that you probably won't actually get around to doing. But by Thursdays, you've almost made it. Thursdays meant only one more day until you could catch up on sleep and homework and The Office. And Thursdays meant going to Aspen Grove.

Honestly, I don't really remember how I got started going to Aspen Grove. My mom knew Chris, the director, but I never really saw Chris when I was there. I took my orders from Bonnie, the activities coordinator. Sometimes Bonnie would text me on Thursday mornings saying : "Manicures today", and when I'd hurry over after school there would already be tables set up with bowls of warm water sitting on soft white towels. The old ladies would already be gathered into the big lobby, reading the Bible or outdated Women's Health magazines while they waited. There were only two of us: Bonnie and I, and sometimes up to sixteen of them, so getting everyone a manicure usually took a couple hours. Plus, they always took a while to decide which color they wanted. Most ladies chose colors like

"Ballet Slipper Pink" or "Soft Mocha Nude". But occasionally one wanted "Pimpin' Purple" or "Batman Black". Bonnie would cringe and I would laugh. I instantly fell in love with the whole thing. The ladies were so wonderful and sweet. They would tell me about their new diabetic socks and their grandchildren's birthday cards and how girls these days color their hair too much. I'd massage their thin hands with Bonnie's lotion that smelled like hospitals and paint their nails Champagne Pink. I loved it.

One Thursday in early October, Bonnie had to run an errand. I'd been volunteering at Aspen Grove for over a year already, so I knew all the ladies and how things worked. Bonnie pulled on her coat as she punched in the security code on the double doors, telling me she'd be back in half an hour or so. The old ladies read or knitted as I sat at the lobby's piano playing "Only Hope" for the eight millionth time because Charlotte loved it. It was a pretty uneventful evening actually, until Leslie, who was sitting by the big window, yelled: "THERE'S A BEAR!"

Leslie was the youngest patient at Aspen Grove, probably around age 60. I once overheard some staff talking about the bad stroke she had had when she was younger that left her with severe mental disabilities. Even with her stained Tigger pullovers, clunky velcro sneakers, and often incoherent comments, she seemed pretty functional and healthy. And Leslie was *exceptionally* thoughtful. She always helped the older ladies with their wheelchairs and walkers, and was quick to hold doors and help clean up. She really loved those cheap foam visors from The Oriental Trading Company—the kind your mom forces you to wear during family reunions—and probably had 20 of them in her room, decorated with glitter, paint and stickers. She was one of the women who liked to get her nails done in the more unconventional colors, like "Grinch Green", or every finger a different color of Skittles. So when she screamed about a bear, no one even flinched. Outbursts like these weren't that uncommon.

Leslie stood at the huge bay window, pointing across the street and continued yelling "Oh! Gloria! A bear! Ooohh!"

Being the terrible overseer that I was, I stayed at the piano and ignored Leslie, until Grace, who had wheeled herself over to the window too, said: "Holy toledo! There's a bear!"

At this point I hurried to the window, amid ten other old women who were trying to maneuver their bulky wheelchairs and walkers to get a better look. There it was, a big black bear, sniffing at the grass that had grown in between the sidewalk squares on the opposite side of the empty street. In the spring, the more active old couples loved to walk The Loop, which followed that patchy sidewalk and a trail around the entire assisted living senior neighborhood. Yep. It was a black bear, and a pretty good-sized black bear.

BUT GLORIA.

Gloria, a tiny, 300-year-old Russian woman, was getting her mail on the same far side of the street, just closing the mailbox. The distance between her and the bear was probably around 20 feet. I almost peed.

We watched helplessly from the window as Gloria quickly noticed the bear. We could see panic on her face, but she stayed miraculously cool as she positioned her walker to begin crossing the street to come back to us. The bear looked up for a moment after hearing her movement, but went back to investigating the grass, which was apparently more interesting than a completely vulnerable elderly woman who reeked of Johnson and Johnson's baby lotion and stale quilts. Slowly, Gloria shuffled across the road in her spotlessly white old-lady Keds. She would push her walker out in front of her, step her right foot in, then her left foot in. She was moving slower than the rate the earth rotates around the sun, and each walker-push only moved her about one foot forward. I felt sick. BUT I WAS SUPPOSED TO BE IN CHARGE. GLORIA WAS GOING TO BE TORN APART BY A BEAR, AND I WAS IN CHARGE. WE WOULD ALL WATCH IT FROM THIS WINDOW. CHARLOTTE WOULD FAINT. WANDA'S HEART WOULD PROBABLY STOP ALTOGETHER. AND I WAS IN CHARGE. What would Bonnie say when she got home, with Gloria's chewed-up and bloody Keds in the road, Charlotte unconscious and Wanda keeled over dead? I don't think I was even on Aspen Grove's insurance policy. I was as unofficial as my little sister and her freshman boyfriend.

Gloria was about halfway across the street by now. She was surprisingly calm, but I could see the determination on her tiny wrinkled face as she continued to slowly come towards us. Leslie kept quietly repeating "Gloria, Gloria come on, keep coming Gloria…" And just like a bad movie about high school sports, before I knew it, all the other old ladies were chanting with her. "Glor-ee-uh! Glor-ee-uh!" She had crossed the road now, and only had to cross the brown lawn to get to the lobby doors. The chanting got stronger.

The bear suddenly stopped being interested in the grass and looked up, watching Gloria inch her way to safety. His ears perked up and he sniffed the air. He was a big bear. He watched the little Russian snack, dressed in a gray velvet sweatsuit, as she made it to the double doors. By now we had collected quite the crowd in the lobby, as patients and kitchen staff drifted out after hearing the commotion. I came to myself and ran to the double doors and punched the button to let her in. Gloria shuffled in, her eyes huge and glossy. It felt like the end of Rudy; everyone was cheering triumphantly. They made their way to Gloria to squeeze her hand and pat her back, everyone talking at once, telling bear stories from when they grew up in Idaho and Canada and how that was a big bear but their first husband had shot bigger. Someone pulled up a big leather chair for Gloria to collapse into. The on-duty nurses showed up too, trying to calm everyone down before Aspen Grove experienced a mass heart attack.

Soon Bonnie got home, and Leslie told her the story six times in a row. Gloria went to bed, as the excitement had worn her right out. The kitchen staff started to set up for dinner, and I knew I needed to go home.

When I came again the next Thursday, the ladies were still talking about it. I guess soon after I had left, Bonnie called Montana Fish Wildlife and Parks to report the bear sighting. Apparently the week held a record number of in-city-limit bear encounters. I poked my head into Gloria's room to see her sitting in her overstuffed lazyboy as she listened to a Russian opera on cassette tape, just like usual. Leslie got her nails painted "Pumpkin Orange" for Halloween. Grace told me the rather specific and almost graphic details of the arrival of her 14th grandbaby, a girl, named Grace. I played the same songs for Charlotte that I played every time she asked me to play.

My remaining Thursdays spent at Aspen Grove were all about as exciting as finding remnants of medicine hidden in your applesauce. Patients came and went, the snow fell and melted and fell again.

But Thursdays have always had a special place in my heart, right next to tennis balls on the sharp ends of walkers and aqua-blue bottles of nail polish.

Example 2

"Intentionally Bare"
Jenny Wilson
2015

I have hit a wall and I don't know why. They call it writer's block but it's more like a squishy wall, the kind you do handstands against in gym class in high school. It's steady and big and blue and it doesn't hurt when you hit it, but you can't move it unless you ask the boys to help you. Are there boys to help you move a squishy writer wall block?

*

When I was nine, I went to Sweden. All by myself. I sat in first class when we took off and when we landed. The Qantas stewardess asked me if I wanted water with lemon and ice and smiled at me kindly. Her lips were strawberry red, and she made me feel safe. I was a child traveling alone.

I stayed with Inga and Affe on a street called Solrosvägen. Sunflower way. Inga was my Morfar's sister and looked a little like a garden gnome. The cute kind that protect your daisies from hungry horses. She felt stressed when the dishes weren't done and sometimes German would come out when she tried to speak to me in English. Affe was Inga's husband. He was tall and gave me great big bear hugs. He could speak English but spoke to me in Swedish anyway, so that I could learn. They gave me pear ice cream and carbonated water and hugged me lots and lots. I would tell them how it made me feel to be half Swedish, living in Australia. They would laugh and say that I wasn't Swedish, I was Australian. I ate the chocolate from the bowl in the downstairs room until it was gone. The bowl would be magically refilled the next day. I stayed for six weeks.

*

I was nine, turning ten. I was standing in the shower, letting the steam fog up the mirror. Looking down at my left hip, (as one does while in the shower), I noticed a giant purple bruise. It was the size of a squished banana, and much the same color.

Did you know that not all bruises hurt? They don't when you don't have enough platelets. My parents—who both had Bachelor's degrees in Science—told me that platelets were the cells in your body that rushed to help when you got hurt. They held hands and formed a net and made the blood thicker. I didn't have enough. We went to the doctor.

*

The Children's Hospital at Westmead in Sydney pretends to be a happy place. The rooms are big and clean and bright. The curtains are white with tiny pictures of koalas in sky blue and rose pink and sunflower yellow. The gift shop sells lots of balloons and the Italian women in the sandwich shop make delicious chicken avocado almond sandwiches. I don't eat. I'm not hungry.

The drip next to my bed bips…bip…pause…bip…pause…bip… As if bipping is somehow more polite than beeping. I am sitting in one of the big, clean rooms on a big, clean bed. Space Jam is playing for the millionth time. I look out the window and have a thought that not many nine year olds have. I wish I could go back to school.

*

I stand in the middle of a grass square, no bigger than a backyard sand-pit. My feet are intentionally bare. I want to feel the blades of grass poking into me. My mum is standing nearby and I try to explain to her how amazing it is to feel the grass beneath your feet. Just grass.

Normal, boring, green grass. How I'm sure that I have never felt this way about grass before. How I've never wanted so badly to stand in it. Even if it's only for a few minutes. They'll want me back inside soon, so they can make sure the grass hasn't killed me. I cock my head backwards to look at the sky and love how it goes on forever. There is no ceiling, and no floor. Only grass and sky.

*

When I was 11, my uncle found a Mother's Day competition in the local newspaper. The competition was being run by a jewelery store. They wanted a fifty words (or less) explanation of "Why your mother is the best". If your mother did indeed turn out to be "the best", she would win a diamond and sapphire ring. My uncle figured I could win it for mum, me having had cancer and all. It's true that most people have a special place in their heart for kids with cancer. I felt manipulative writing about how my mum looked after me in hospital. It was true. And she deserved more than a diamond and sapphire ring for it. But unless there was some other cancer kid entering the Mother's Day competition, I knew I would win.

I did.

*

When I was fifteen I went to the hospital for a checkup. It still pretended to be a happy place. I had to meet the endocrinologist. I assumed that I would not like such a person.

I didn't.

*

My dad loves to garden. He grows raspberries for my mum and feijoas for himself. Feijoas are to Kiwis as mangoes are to Aussies. They are green and round and look like they might bounce if you tried, but they don't. The middle is like a jelly and the outside is like a pear. To my dad, they taste like New Zealand. To me, they taste like family.

He grows flowers too. Only sunflowers. Ten giant sunflowers along the paddock fence, with heads that grow heavy and hang down when the sun doesn't pay them attention. The sunflowers are tall and strong. One day the horses come and eat the sunflowers. My dad is sad.

*

Her name was Doctor Donaldson. She probably went to university for ten years or more. Maybe that's worth it when you can charge $70 for a 15 minute appointment. Maybe it's not. Dr. Donaldson told me lots of things. I didn't understand all of them. I did understand that she was telling me that I could not have children. My mum started crying. I never wanted to talk to her again. She was the only person I could be mad at. Then Dr. Donaldson was talking about Jamie Lee Curtis and people who adopt and people with fertility problems. And I didn't want to be one of those people, even if some of those people were famous. I had already been one of those weird cancer kids with no hair. And now I was one of those people with fertility problems. I didn't want to be with the weird people. I wanted to be with the normal people. It sounds dramatic and lame and not even possible but I think a piece of my heart died that day. How else do you describe it when you see a little girl in your head with brown hair and hazel eyes and she's three years old and she looks just like you. And you think you'll never have her. And you cry.

*

I am standing in the front paddock, surrounded by thousands of sun-flowers. They make a giant circle and I am the center. We are far from the fences and the hungry horses and the grass is making friends with my knees. Dad meant to plant hundreds of sunflowers, but accidentally planted thousands. Some shyly greet the sun as it moves slowly across a sky that seems bigger than the world itself. Others do not have the cour-age to do so. Yet.

*

I stand in the middle of the sunflower circle, bigger than a backyard sandpit but smaller than a playground. My feet are intentionally bare and I hope the snakes are feeling timid today. The little girl with brown hair and hazel eyes is standing next to me, and she tells me to greet the sun. I'm sure that I have never felt this way about sunflowers before. I cock my head backwards to look at the sky and love how it goes on forever. There is no ceiling, and no floor. Only sunflowers.

Example 3

"Numbers"
Maddy Sharp
2016

I am nineteen years. I am two eyes, two ears, two arms, two legs. I am seventy-three credit hours. I am five feet and seven (maybe eight) inches. I am eighteen hours a week at work. I am a 3.5 GPA. I am nine hours of sleep every night.

I've always measured myself in numbers—lacrosse goals, class rank, calories, weight. It's a perfectionism thing.

I used to think Perfectionism was my best friend. Even when she kept me up all night recopying notes or redoing assignments I'd finished hours before. Even when she punished me for an A- on a quiz, telling me I'd never get into college. Even when she stood next to me in the mirror and murmured "not good enough" until I could count my ribs through my shirt. Perfectionism was a slave driver, but she kept me at the top of my class and at the top of my game. I wasn't happy—she never lets you feel content because content leads to complacency and complacency leads to catastrophic inadequacy—but I was flourishing. Sure, she never let me relax or eat or sleep, but she rewarded me with A's in calculus, history, English, and anatomy, or a record low weight.

But she wasn't my friend.

We first got acquainted after I didn't make the varsity lacrosse team in tenth grade. My coach said I wasn't "athletic" enough. She convinced me that my coach was really trying to say I was "not skinny enough." Standing in front of the mirror while I pinched at fat, she whispered in my ear that I had to get rid of the weight and together we decided that I would spend every day at the gym that summer. And that's exactly what I did

With junior year and its chorus rehearsals, lacrosse conditioning, honor society meetings, tests and tests and more tests, I didn't have time for the gym. I didn't have time to sleep. My anxiety was like constant electricity without a destination, pulsating and constantly searching for an outlet. I was up all night studying optic nerves and Custer's last stand and Latin roots. I was at school from seven until five almost every day. I didn't have a second to spare at my shrine. What was I going to do? I had to keep losing, *needed* to keep losing, if I wanted that varsity spot. That's when

Perfectionism introduced me to Anorexia. I couldn't cut anything from my busy schedule, but I could cut calories. And if I weren't eating, I'd have more time to study.

They say that when you stop eating you stop functioning. Your focus is shot. You can't sleep, even though it's all you ever want to do. You're always dizzy. Your skin turns pale and blue, but it's not the pretty kind of pale like Nicole Kidman's skin. It's this marbled, sickly, cancer patient hue. You're hair falls out, and you're always cold, even on the hottest days of Florida's sweltering summers.

That's a lie.

I mean, my hair did fall out and I could barely keep my eyes open, but I thrived under the stress. I didn't need to eat, I didn't need to sleep. I could do it all, and I could do it well. I had the best grades I'd ever had since starting high school, a varsity spot looked promising, and I was strong. Strong enough to do the weightlifting team for lacrosse conditioning. Strong enough to skip two, sometimes even three, meals a day. Strong enough to make myself throw up when I'd eaten too much. And strong enough to fight the human body's most basic instinct to survive.

I thought I was in control. I had a new friend who was bringing out the best in me. I didn't realize what a toxic relationship it was. She became needy and clingy. Soon, I couldn't go anywhere or do anything without consulting her first. She took my autonomy, and in return she gave me anxiety to govern all my decisions. "Which way should I walk to class?" *Whichever burns the most calories.* "What should I have for breakfast?" *Nothing.* "What should I wear?" *Whatever hides your fat.* She took my food, my sleep, my focus, my happiness. It wasn't a very fair friendship. Anorexia was a boa constrictor, wrapping around me like a hug at first, but then squeezing and strangling me. She was killing me and I loved her for it.

Whispers followed me everywhere. *She's so skinny. Do you think she ever eats? What is wrong with her? She looks sick.*

I didn't care. I stared at myself in my mirror and admired a body that was so thin it was starting to resemble the skeletons we used in Ms. Weaver's anatomy class. The satisfaction never lasted. Anorexia would soon call attention to my flabby arms or my squishy stomach. I would quickly be reminded that I hated myself, and resolve to cut my allotted calories by another 100. Eventually I stopped needing her to put me down to galvanize my iron-will to skip meals. I didn't need her to hiss at how ugly I was because I did it myself.

Winter semester, junior year: wake up, weigh myself, throw away my breakfast, weigh myself again, go to seminary, go to class, skip lunch, go to lacrosse practice, come home, weigh myself, study all night, sleep for two hours, and wake up to do it all again the next day. Weighing, measuring, counting. It became a religious practice that was consuming my whole life.

I remember standing in front of the mirror crying because I hated what I looked like. I remember standing on the scale hyperventilating because I hadn't lost that half a pound—or worse, I'd gained it. I remember feeling empty. It was more than an empty stomach; my whole life was desolate. I had cut out everything that once made me happy for fear of gaining weight. I didn't go out with friends—I couldn't eat in front of them I didn't go to school dances—every dress I tried on made me look fat.

My lacrosse coach pulled me aside at conditioning the month before tryouts. We didn't talk about calories or weight or eating, but I knew that he knew. "Stop worrying. You are good enough."

It'd be nice if the story ended here. *After a heart to heart with my coach, I started eating and loving myself again, and I championed self-esteem and healthy living.* It's not so simple. Eating disorders are like a rip current. You can see the shore of recovery, but as you get closer, the current drags you back in. Anorexia didn't just disappear—you can't just unknow someone who used to be the biggest part of your life. Though it didn't go away, things started to change—including my parents' approach.

"Eat your dinner." I'm not hungry. "You're not leaving this table until you eat everything." Doors slamming, screaming, crying. Even though I didn't want to be sick, I still didn't want to eat 2,500 calories a day and a well-balanced diet. I was in limbo, wanting to be healthy but wanting to be skinny. They seemed to be mutually exclusive.

We saw therapists, nutritionists, family friends "who know what you're going through, honey." There were tears and prayers and long talks and hugs. And finally there were cleared plates and uncounted calories and desert. Anorexia still comes back to visit every once in a while, when I'm shopping for swimsuits, or on prom night. I'm always wary when she appears to point out how much weight I've gained since I started eating again. But she doesn't own me anymore. I've stopped compulsively checking food labels (mostly). I got rid of the journal where I used to record every calorie as red on my ledger and replaced it with one where I can memorialize experiences instead of tally up my mistakes. When I'm disheartened by what I see in the mirror, I pray to see myself the way Heavenly Father does. I finally threw out the scale, and with it, the association between my weight and my value.

In some ways, numbers still define me. I am nineteen years. I am two eyes, two ears, two arms, two legs. I am seventy-three credit hours. I am five feet and seven (maybe eight) inches.

But I am also numberless, breathtaking Florida sunrises over the Atlantic Ocean. I am sand and surf and sea breezes. I am a busy morning and an afternoon nap. I am art history and limitless daydreams of Europe. I am vintage dresses. I am *Breakfast at Tiffany's* and *The Princess Bride*, a thousand times over. I am a spinning record player with U2 and James Taylor on vinyl. I am Mickey Mouse and countless days at Disney World. I am lazy Sundays spent in bed. I am Cheesecake Factory birthday dinners and endless "what would Dave Ramsey do?" lectures. I am unfinished Pinterest projects. I am late night drives with the windows down and the music loud. I am late night conversations that go on forever. I no longer measure myself in calories, in pounds, in minutes at the gym. Instead, I measure myself in smiles, in laughter, in moments.

What counts the most cannot be counted.

Example 4

"A Real Mormon"
Ryan Poch
2016

"But you're not a *real* Mormon."

The unfamiliar steamy blanket of humidity seemed to throttle my throat, baste my white tee with its salty juices. The unbearable heat pounded my forehead like an enthusiastic mariachi band and my heartbeat pulsed rhythmically in my head: "Yeah! *Anybody* can be Mormon in Utah." The words cut into me like knives: I'm not a real Mormon? Just because I was born and raised in Mormontown, America? What does it even mean to be a "real" Mormon?

Convenient to the village of Manchester, Ontario County, New York, stands a hill of considerable size, and the most elevated of any in the neighborhood In Rochester County, New York. Every year on this hill there is a spectacle that would make anybody's head turn—people dress up in elaborate costumes, giant fireballs erupt on stage—even Jesus makes a showing. I guess you could call it a really big "Mormon party." Tens of thousands of people from all across the world stream into the little town of about 8,000 people to gawk and gape, and take pictures. These enthusiastic visitors flow as the lifeblood of the town—for about two weeks in the year the hotel staff bustles, the local "Chill and Grill" spits oil, and the church historical sights flood with "Spirit- junkies." The sleepy town of Palmyra is loudly awakened from its 50-week slumber for the "Hill Cumorah Pageant."

The first time I visited Palmyra, my family had gone up to "Joseph-stalk." That is what we youngsters affectionately called the holy Mormon pilgrimages that had become increasingly common during those precious summer weeks away from school. Instead of snoozing and relaxing like normal people, the parents decided that we needed to "appreciate the sacrifices" of those early saints and fly back east. "It's important to do," said Mom. So we did do. We joined the throng of chittering saints; we elbowed each other for hours in the compact Avis rental. We sat through a performance at the hill and got drenched to the bone in the torrential rain. We flew home and I dialogued with the Smith boy: "Joseph, it was a good time, but I think we are pretty much even now." I thought he agreed…

"Oh look, we can sign up to participate in the Pageant ourselves!"

One year later and I stood back in Palmyra, sweat-soaked in a group of gangly teenagers with my standing as a "real" Mormon in jeopardy. "How hard can it be, growing up Mormon in Utah? I mean, everybody has the same standards! You never have to stand up for your beliefs, much less get ridiculed for them." All of the real Mormons nodded their heads. "You know, there are only two members in my school, me and my brother?"

"Umm, that must be hard…"

"What time do you have to wake up for seminary?" "I once did take early-morning…"

"How often do you have to give a talk in church? I give one every month. I really just don't think that there are *real* Mormons in Utah."

Those Utah Mormons: The spoiled ones. Because in Utah there are no temptations. There are members and non-members, two distinctly separate groups. The members have standards, and the non-members do not. As long as you hang around the members, there are no problems.

The shrill ringing of the Utah bell unleashes the tide of Mormon high school students and with them their raging hormones. The hallways bristle with chattering girls and brawny boys, and the social scene is once more at hand. The shrewd senior girl walks by, her carefully adjusted shirt flapping open and her tight leggings accentuating her

well-shaped posterior. She pauses, accidentally brushing up against the unsuspecting guy at his locker, and then innocently struts by, feeling his eyes follow her and warmth of accomplishment at the degradation of his thoughts.

In Utah there are no temptations.

In that same Utah high school, those same Mormon students rush from one class to the other, like well-programmed robots or a little colony of ants. The bell rings, and a giant game of "musical chairs" ensues. The homework assignment is due at the end of the class, and some of those ants didn't work as diligently as the others: "Hey, can I see your assignment?" the harsh whisper comes from behind. "Come on, seriously, man.

Don't be a tool—I was going to do it but I just didn't have time… Hey, quit acting like you're better than that—as if you've never copied!"

The members have standards, and the nonmembers do not.

The Utah sun had begun to set on the party. Sticky roasted marshmallow strings clung to fingertips like sugary icicles and the hot coals had already been flung around from person to person. The Mormon teenagers laid themselves in a circle on the soft grass and the conversation began to darken just as quickly as the sun. "Ok, we are all cool here, right? We can talk." The general murmur was positive. "How much have you guys done? I mean, sexually. You all have played around, right?" The rumble increased in volume and enthusiasm: that boys smile froze on his face, but his belly froze to the ground. "Well, let's hear about it!"

As long as you hang around the members, there are no problems.

The moment passes, and the group laughs it off—so the Utah boy has got it good. How hard could it be to sift between the wheat and the tares when you're surrounded by wheat? Maybe they'll never know the moral dilemma that presents itself when the enemy you've sworn to fight is the very people who swore to fight with you. Life isn't a seminary video. Perhaps it is hard to imagine a world where "Mormonism" is not a belief, but an unavoidable description—like gender, or age.

But then how often do I see myself, the Utah Mormon, in times of temptation succumbing to the very moral crimes I publicly denounce in others: one moment I am the judge, the other, the accused. Maybe the jeerers are right: we Utah Mormons *are* just all hypocrites: *true* Mormons live a constant uphill battle whereas *we* just look down, fall down.

In the Pageant I play a Nephite warrior, one like many who, at the end of the show, has committed the sins my people once swore to fight against. We leap and stretch, we fight and we die. Nine thousand people cooly perceive my dead corpse hanging upside-down off the edge of the stage. Then a war-weary Moroni cries out to the audience:

"Behold, I speak unto you as if ye were present, and yet ye are not. But behold, Jesus Christ hath shown you unto me, and I know your doing… I know that ye do walk in the pride of your hearts; and there are none save a few only who do not lift themselves up in the pride of their hearts… and your churches, yea, even every one, have become polluted because of the pride of your hearts…Why are ye ashamed to take upon you the name of Christ?"

Honestly? Maybe we just prefer the name of Mormon. *Anybody* can be a Mormon in Utah.

15

RHETORICAL ANALYSIS

Example 1

"Who are *You?*"
Bronte Thurgood
2015

What began as a whimsical story to entertain the Liddell girls on a summer's day in 1862 has become one of the most beloved, well-worn tales of all time. In *Alice's Adventures in Wonderland*, Charles Dodgson—under the pen name Lewis Carroll—tells the story of Alice, a young girl based off of Alice Liddell. In Wonderland, Alice undergoes physical, mental, and emotional growth as she struggles with her fluctuating height, sanity, and identity crisis as she attempts to achieve her normal height and get into the flower garden. Although Carroll insisted that the book was written purely for entertainment, there is a prevalent theme of growing up and finding identity. Through this theme, Carroll argues that identity is not discovered through physical growth or other external influences, but is rather found emotionally through internal growth and experiencing unfamiliarity.

Alice's identity crisis begins even as early as the first chapter after she drinks a bottle that makes her shrink, and eats cake that makes her grow unnaturally tall. "How queer everything is to-day! And yesterday things went on as usual. I wonder if I've been changed in the night? Let me think: *was* I the same when I got up this morning?...But if I'm not the same, the next question is 'Who in the world am I?'" (8). It is clear that because Alice was out of her daily routine and familiar life, she felt unsettled and began to question her intrinsic self, believing that what she is experiencing must be part of the bizarre life of someone else. This implies that Carroll is arguing that finding our identities will not work by being dependent on daily routine and normalcy.

However, Alice further mulls over this notion by weighing the possibilities of whom she might have become, listing the names of other girls she knows. She determines that she must be a simpleminded acquaintance named Mabel, after reciting clumsy multiplication and geography, and incorrectly repeating the nursery rhyme "How Doth the Busy Bee." While the intention of this passage may not have been written for more than sheer humor, twisting the familiar nursery rhyme and distorting it into "How Doth the Little Crocodile," as well as the faulty performance of Alice's math and geography skills demonstrate how Alice incorrectly bases her identity off of a test of intelligence. As she frets over her fate of assuming the identity of Mabel because of her incorrect demonstration of her multiplication, geography, and lesson rhymes, she has not actually turned into someone else. Nevertheless, Alice still feels as if she is someone different because of the unfamiliar circumstances happening to her that are beyond her control.

This idea of an unfamiliar, different Alice is continued when she is mistaken for a housemaid by the white rabbit, who calls her Mary Ann. Although Alice has long since moved on from thinking she may be Mabel, the fact that she is called by another name by someone else and how she reflexively responds to obey the orders meant for Mary Ann suggests that Alice is still uncertain of who she is, even though she recognizes that the rabbit is mistaken. "He took me for his housemaid…How surprised he'll be when he finds out who I am! But I better take him his fan and gloves—that is, if I can find them" (19). This implies that Alice may be beginning her process of self-realization, but is not strong enough to define or defend it quite yet to herself or even a white rabbit.

As Alice progresses through the story, Carroll argues that identity does not correlate with physical size, appearance, or any other type of physical changes. Alice experiences more dramatic height fluctuation where she fills up a house, then shrinks to a size where she fears for her life in the face of a seemingly enormous puppy. It is in this short state where Alice stumbles upon an unsympathetic caterpillar, who immediately and intermittently asks her the simple question "Who are *you?*" (27). At this point Alice is really unsure how to answer the question: "I—I hardly know, Sir, just at present—at least I know who I *was* when I got up this morning, but I think I must have been changed several times since then" (27). The irony of this is that Alice is attempting to convey to the caterpillar her struggle of losing her sense of identity through physical changes—imminent fate for this creature who has yet to make a chrysalis and become a butterfly. "…(W)hen you have to turn into a chrysalis…and then after that into a butterfly, I should think you'll feel it a little queer, won't you?" (28). When asking this, Alice is looking for reassuring feedback and understanding. To her disappointment, the caterpillar tersely replies to Alice that he will not. One could argue that the caterpillar will not feel strange when he undergoes metamorphosis because this series of changes will be purely physical; his intrinsic self and sense of identity will remain untouched and unchanged. While the caterpillar will only undergo one session of dramatic physical change, Alice has the opportunity to experience many, and has the potential to recognize her internal growth through these strange, fanciful experiences and find her identity.

However, *Alice's Adventures in Wonderland* never explicitly states when or even if Alice finds her identity. Rather, it is implied after she finds herself in the garden face-to-face with the Queen of Hearts: "'My name is Alice, so please your Majesty,' said Alice very politely" before she denounces the threat of the cards. "Why, they're only a pack of cards, after all. I needn't be afraid of them!" (53). This is an implied example of how Alice is beginning to find who she is; she is not afraid because she knows that she is more powerful than the cards. Alice also becomes more assertive and frank. When asked how she felt about the Queen and her game of croquet, Alice gave an unreserved, "Not at all" and that "I don't think they play at all fairly" (56). She finally begins to definitively speak her mind, and she also begins to grow physically; a metaphor that may be representative of her internal growth. When she finally awakes on her sister's lap to find herself back in the real world from her adventures, Alice's waking up from Wonderland can also be seen as an internal waking after exploring her more unfamiliar inner-self.

Regardless of intentional meaning or not, it is clear by Alice's progression from an uncertain little girl to a confident, capable young woman throughout the book that Carroll cared for Alice Liddell. One of the messages to her from the story is that he wanted her to be able to find herself in the midst of growth and maturity in an unfamiliar, changing world to show her that that is what she has the potential to become. *Alice's Adventures in Wonderland* demonstrates that finding internal identity is a personal adventure—perhaps the realm Wonderland was modeled after. Lewis Carroll is able to convey to the reader by means of strange bottles and cakes, name confusion, disagreeable caterpillars, and an outlandish game of croquet that identity is not found through physical growth or external influences, but through internal growth and adaptation and change through experiencing unfamiliarity.

Works Cited

Carroll, Lewis. Alice's Adventures in Wonderland. New York: Dover Publications, 1993. Print.

Example 2

"Fundamental Pain"
Gabriel Lee
2015

Imagine that you are in an infinite space, a place without walls or ceiling and no floor to press against. There is no temperature, no gravity, no smells, no colors or shadows, no coffee tables to bruise your shins against. You do not move; why would you? There is nothing to see towards which you could walk. No place from which you have come to tell where you are. In fact, there is nothing anywhere against which you could judge that you exist at all. What is the impact of structure on one's identity? Regardless of a person's ultimate freedom to choose their own way, what part do their circumstances play in the use of this critical liberty? In his exploration, *Man's Search for Meaning*, Viktor E. Frankl reveals that the structure of a person's life requires suffering as the crucial impetus to discover purpose and meaning to their existence, that without suffering meaning for one's life cannot be ascertained.

Let us consider the impact of structure on one's identity. The fifteen hundred persons traveling by train to Auschwitz had luggage, a few personal possessions, their own clothes, and faces familiar to them. Though densely packed they were on a train, a locomotion not unfamiliar to them, and therefore it is without surprise that Frankl refers to these, as no doubt the others on the train did themselves, as *passengers* with names and occupations, families and aspirations; not yet "prisoners." They journeyed, but to where they knew not. The first sight of "Auschwitz" on a sign marked a moment of change, and with it the first changes in their personal perception. They were no longer merely *passengers*; their minds began to gingerly finger the identity of *prisoner*. The familiar clothes and possessions allowed them to cling to their former selves as merely "fellow travelers" (33) for a time, but these too were stripped away, and with them the last shred of material structure was gone. The sign, the loss of luggage and familiar clothing were external changes in circumstances resulting in an alteration of the mind and heart. Back in the comfort of home or good society, modesty and civility are a social staple. In the terror-baked camps the prisoners "tore off their clothes" [with] "unspeakable haste" (33), revealing their nakedness on command. Frightening questions began to slither carelessly in their terrified minds. Who were they now, without their briefcases and weddings rings and hair? The outward manifestations of inner alterations grew yet more severe. The prisoners became afraid to make decisions (77). Forthright lawyers and proactive doctors preferred to leave choice to hateful fate in the form of the S.S. men and Capos. When "herded" (70) from place to place the prisoners responded like "sheep" (70) before "bad dogs" (70), and within weeks most men were reduced to a state of base necessity, fighting without scruple to survive.

The inner transformations manifested themselves in moral behavior; the structure created a framework wherein the prisoner acquired moral identity. For example, compassion for the suffering of other men would dull with time. Frankl recounts, "At first the prisoner looked away... he could not bear to see fellow prisoners [suffer]. Days or weeks later things changed... [he] did not avert his eyes anymore" (40), no longer moved by the pain of another. Frankl describes even staring into the eyes of the dead without emotional response (42), and even the sorry suffering of the typhus patients became an irritation to Frankl trying to maintain a clean infirmary hut for S.S. inspections (85).

Frankl observes that under such structural pressure the value of human life and human dignity is reduced to nothing; a crust of bread worth more than a breathing man. The prisoners were no longer men; they were numbers, unlucky numbers worth a kick or blow. The culture of violent treatment increased the impulse within the prisoners to do violence to others (84), where under other circumstances violence was viewed as a deplorable response to external irritants. Again, the structure of camp life altered moral behavior. Opportunities to do kindness or act bravely were forsaken in the scramble to remain alive.

This loss of identity became the cause of great suffering amongst the inmates. But, Frankl contends that, "without suffering and death human life cannot be complete" (88). We must ask ourselves, then, what is "human life," and what is the accomplishment of it? Frankl says that a complete human life is a life that has imbued meaning, a definite purpose, and that this meaning is acquired by active choice. Where does suffering play a part in the discovery of meaning, or the choice to live with purpose? Let us return, for a moment, to our infinite space in the opening paragraph. In such a space a meaning to one's existence, or even an awareness of oneself is impossible to achieve; there is nothing from which one can gain self-perspective. Now, insert a table upon which is placed a hot aromatic food into the space. Suddenly there is something that you see against which you can reference distance. The smell of the food enters your nostrils and your stomach pangs. You are hungry and uncomfortable. Suddenly you walk towards it; you are something with legs. The movement requires exertion; an unfamiliar sensation. You're looking down at the table; you now become aware that you are something of definite dimensions, taller than the low table. You reach for the food, and taste for the first time. You are a person, capable of so much feeling. The bite of hunger, the yearning for satisfaction that prompted your motion was essential to your understanding, the discovery of self and meaning.

Any person, unprompted by external influence (i.e. camp life, athletic strain, expectations from others [professors, parents, friends, Capos, etc]), will certainly never change, develop or seek a greater purpose for living. The structure of the death camps, or any experience of difficulty can afford in Frankl's words, "an opportunity and a challenge" (93) to make one's experiences an inner victory, and that true "human greatness" (93) depends on a person's choice to respond to challenges. If Frankl had never been called to suffer at death's doormat would anyone know his name? Had he never been reduced to a state which "compelled [him]… to think of only trivial things (relief from discomfort, bread to survive, worldly advantage in the camp)" (90) would he have been motivated to give meaning to his sufferings? His "disgust" (90) at the spiritually insubstantial fight to stay alive led him to develop his revolutionary logotherapy: a balm to millions of searching souls.

Suffering, or even the easy life of the safe and well-fed, can afford every person a chance to choose a life with purpose, but those who rob their present struggle of its opportunity for growth run the risk of never joining the ranks in the fundamental human struggle, never begin their own search for meaning.

Work Cited

Frankl, Viktor E., *Man's Search for Meaning*. New York: Washington Square, 1984. Print.

Example 3

"Rhetorical Experiment Gone Wrong: Argumental Corruption in 'Why I am Not a Vegetarian'"
Emily Grant
2016

You are what you eat. This catchy phrase is traditionally meant to imply that physical health is strongly associated with the diet of one's choice. Now imagine this argument on steroids: you are dangerous if you are a food extremist. In the article, *Why I am Not a Vegetarian*, author William T. Jarvis aggressively argues that vegetarian extremism causes harm to the individual and society. However, this article failed to be efficacious; the methods he employed in his rhetorical "experiment" were corrupted with fallacies, misleading evidence, and judgmental diction.

In this article Jarvis' rhetorical persona is a fallacious scarecrow, not one meant to protect the vegetables, but rather to deter people away from them. An example of this strawperson fallacy is when he portrays vegetarians as a religion divided into two different sects: pragmatic and ideologic. As a member of the Seventh Day Adventist church himself, Jarvis then takes the time to make his opinions concerning the beliefs of said "religions" quite clear. In other words, he plays preacher. During an emotional tirade Jarvis proclaims, "for the ideologic, vegetarianism is a hygienic religion", even going so far as to say that, "it attracts masochists because it gives guilt a boost" (106). He then goes on to bash the belief system of this religion as being misguided, wrong, and outright devilish. For instance, under the subheading about the bible condemning vegetarianism, Jarvis exclaims that people will become "followers of teachers with devil inspired ideas…", teachers that say it is "wrong to eat meat" (107). This is the epitome of the strawperson fallacy; Jarvis strung up the ideologic vegetarian religion like a piñata and then proceeded to hack away at its beliefs with his bat of personal opinions. By making no effort to soften his malicious doctrine against ideologic vegetarians, the congregation— his audience—is forced to take the brunt of this verbal abuse. They begin to feel wounded, like they went to church seeking peace and instead were lectured about hellfire and damnation. What he essentially did was make the exit sign look incredibly desirable; no one wants to listen to—or in this case read— something that makes them feel uncomfortable.

Jarvis also uses the slippery slope fallacy, a desperate move designed to scare the fence sitters into staying out of the vegetable garden. His argument went like this: first a vegetarian will eliminate unhealthy foods from his or her diet, then food safety concerns will grow to neurotic proportions, and finally the health foodist will turn to veganism (104). But that's not all, the cherry on this fallacy sundae is this statement, "it is at this point that vegetarianism becomes hazardous" (104). Here is the real issue; Jarvis has it out against ideologic vegetarian extremists, not the average vegetarian. So what does he do? He makes it seem like all average vegetarians will become extremist, that all forms of this diet will snowball into a food paranoia of "neurotic proportions." To the careless reader this slick argument causes them to slide down a slippery slope; they are brainwashed into quickly swallowing the questionable logic of this fallacy before they realize they ate a lie. Although the fallacy sundae looks appealing at first glance, the aftereffect leaves the audience with a funny taste in their mouths. It leaves them confused, wondering why a supposedly pro health argument is catered with sweet treats of logical deception. It's a bad sign for the article if Jarvis is starting off his rhetorical experiment with faulty procedures. If fallacies are the method he is using to prove his argument, it means that by default, any evidence he has gathered must be riddled with fraudulent claims.

The life force of rhetorical experimentation is unadulterated evidence, a detail that Jarvis conveniently threw out the window when he used misleading stories and facts as a means of persuasion. Examples of this argumental perversion include his story of the vegetarian extremist parents and his anecdote about the vegetarian runners. When coupled together, these two pieces of "evidence" expose a gaping hole in the articles' logos. In the case of the parents: vegetarian extremists consulted with a self-styled herbalist that convinced them to give their child "a vegetarian diet of raw, organic foods" and "dissuaded them from having the infant immunized and from continuing to see a pediatrician" (105). As time passed, the baby's health failed and the child "died of bronchial pneumonia complicated by severe malnutrition" (105). According to Jarvis, the cause of death is ideologic vegetarian extremism, but something is fundamentally wrong with this assumption. For one, there is more than one variable in this case—the vegetarian diet *and* the lack of sufficient medical care— yet Jarvis disregards the factor that detract from his argument. Secondly, this is not an accurate depiction of the average vegetarian. According to the rules of logical and rhetorical experimentation, in order to reach true conclusions it is customary to exclude outliers (unusual cases that misrepresent the average data.) Here, Jarvis is purposely including this extreme case *because* it is misrepresentative. If Jarvis wanted to present an applicable example of the harmful effects of a vegetarian diet, he would have picked an average case and acknowledged the influence of extraneous factors.

Now compare this to the story of the vegetarian runners aspiring to break a 24-hour distance record. An undergraduate seeks out Jarvis' advice in order to increase the team's chance of breaking the record and thereby "[demonstrate] the superiority of a vegetarian diet" (109).

When presented with this situation Jarvis relates how distance running ability is not only affected by one's diet, but is rather a skill attributed to a conglomerate of factors such as genetics and capacity for oxygen uptake (109). Sound advice, but his counsel is contradictory to his analysis of the parent extremism case. In his first piece of evidence he asserts that a vegetarian diet had everything to do with a child's death, while in the running story he recognizes the effect of outside factors. What he disregarded in one he acknowledged in the other. When the audience discovers the hypocrisy laced within his argument, their trust catches on the snagged evidence and unravels the fabric of this article. The readers feel betrayed by the misleading evidence, here they were walking down this road only to find out the signs dictating which path to take was switched. Since corrupt methods spoiled the validity of his evidence, Jarvis' analysis was deduced from expired information. The ramifications of him basing his experiment on logically "inedible" data means that his analysis in this rhetorical experiment is unsafe to believe.

Because Jarvis' argument is seasoned with sharp, almost indigestible verbiage, one must have an acquired taste in order to swallow his conclusion on vegetarianism. Readers find themselves picking out the judgmental diction and shoving it to the side of their plate, unable to bring themselves to eat the tainted meal. He first starts off with a simmer when he uses phrases such as "health neurotics" and "vegetarian zealots" (106, 107). Then the heat gets turned up and his words reach a boiling point when he vents how, "because they consider themselves morally superior, many vegetarians exhibit no reservations against using mind-control techniques or terrorism to actualize their agenda" (112). The example he gives of vegetarians committing this behavior is their use of the slaughterhouse tactic, where a field trip to a slaughterhouse turns into a form of psychological terrorism against animal foods (112). What Jarvis fails to realize is that he is just as guilty when it comes to using this tactic. His extremist examples and harsh word choice are meant to scare his audience into believing him. Why else would he choose stories centered on sickness and death? In fact, most of his stories include fear-triggering phrases—examples include mental and growth retardation, nutritional rickets, scurvy, malnutrition, and death (105). Emotionally charged words are just as dangerous as a loaded gun, and Jarvis wields his words in the same way that he claims vegetarians wield theirs. The audience finds themselves caught in the crosshairs of this situational irony, but luckily the hypocritical nature of his judgmental diction has a strong enough kickback to make this article ineffective, thereby letting the audience escape its dangerous war of words. Regardless of the judgmental diction piercing holes in his article, Jarvis' analysis couldn't be considered safe from the get go; drawing conclusions from manipulated evidence automatically undermined its validity.

Jarvis' rhetorical experiment was a failure because he based his argument off a poor experimental design. In doing so, he allowed faulty methods lead to biased evidence, which in turn led to corrupted conclusions. This essentially allowed him to justify his claim that all vegetarians will turn into vegetarian extremists. Or in other words, a potato will become a tomato simply because they sound the same. If this article becomes a precedent for rhetorical experiments, then all genres of persuasive writing will become tainted with personal bias and argumental corruption. Consequently, a responsibility is placed on the readers. In order for rhetoric to be held to a high standard and remain pure, the audience needs to be critical of writing by being watchful for fallacies, misleading evidence, and judgmental diction.

Works Cited

Jarvis, William T. "Why I am Not a Vegetarian." *Perspectives on the Environment*. Provo, UT: BYU Academic Publishing, 2011. 100–115. Print

15

Example 4

"Liberty or Death—a No-Brainer"
Ashley Holmes
2016

The year is 1775. On a crisp March day in Richmond, Virginia, the Second Virginia Convention convenes in what is now called St. John's Church. The American colonies are on the verge of war with Britain, with whom relations have been strained for decades. The tension is palpable for everyone involved. This group of esteemed men gathers for one purpose: to once again determine the proper course of action for Virginia and the other colonies after suffering so much at the hands of the British. Thus far, peaceful petitions to King George have gone unanswered and all but unnoticed. Despite this, the delegates suggest only further patience, endurance, and petitioning. After several such addresses, Patrick Henry, a respected lawyer and famed patriot, stands and says what nobody else is willing to. He implores his fellow delegates to realize that "the war is actually begun!" and to fight for their freedom (Henry par. 5). His famous concluding words, "Give me liberty or give me death!" echo through the centuries as the pivotal moment of this Convention (par. 5). In his famous speech, Patrick Henry uses tools such as rhetorical questions, allusions, and anaphora to create an urgent tone that will convince the Virginia Convention to vote in favor of revolution.

Rhetorical questions serve as one of several ways in which Patrick Henry argues the urgency of declaring war on Britain. These questions slowly build from asking, "Is this the part of wise men?" (par. 2) to demanding, "Is…peace so sweet, as to be purchased at the price of chains and slavery?" (par. 3). He uses such questions throughout his speech to increase the intensity of his words and the urgency of what he is saying. Each rhetorical question leaves a clear impression on the minds of each audience member, who is automatically inclined to agree with Henry's passionate rage. This contagious, barely-contained intensity spreads through the room like a wildfire, and even the most unbiased listener could not help but empathize with Henry's cause. By asking questions instead of merely stating his argument, Henry effectively reduces the "extremist" persona that could easily follow him after delivering such an impassioned speech. Rhetorical questions posed by Henry, in the minds of the delegates, enhance the logic behind supporting revolution.

Patrick Henry also employs allusions in his attempts to sway his audience at the Virginia Convention of 1775. Right from the onset of the argumentative portion of his speech, Henry alludes to Greek mythology when he compares the colonists' hope to the song of a siren (par. 2). Sirens were known for luring sailors to their deaths; they sang songs to attract the seamen, who were so preoccupied that they failed to notice the dangers of the sea that surrounded them. Sirens were notoriously distant, deadly, and unattainable. Such was the hope of the colonists—a peaceful resolution with the British government followed by life as it had been. By alluding to this well-known myth, Henry illustrates to the delegates that by holding on to their *illusion of hope*, they are being blinded by the dangerous environment set up all around them by the English (par. 2). In addition, because the British and the "false hope" that they have given the colonists are being portrayed as the siren or the "villain" in this situation, Henry's allusion also compares the colonists to the hero of their story. Orpheus, arguably the most famous hero to face the sirens, successfully brought himself and his companions past the demons by playing music to drown out the sirens' song (Sirens par. 3). This comparison suggests to the colonists that they, too, should consciously ignore the vain promises of the British, and promises success in their "quest" for freedom if they do so.

Later, Henry alludes to the Bible and, in doing so, suggests a correlation between the colonists and Christ. He makes this statement: "Suffer not yourselves to be betrayed by a kiss" (par. 3). Christ was betrayed by Judas, one of his supposed friends. By making this allusion, Henry also draws a parallel between the colonists and the Savior. He suggests that, like Christ, the colonists are innocent and pure, good in every sense of the word. Judas traded Jesus for sixteen pieces of silver, demonstrating that he valued this person the same way he valued money, no more than that. The parallels drawn by Henry between Christ and the colonists continue, because he suggests that the British value the Americans as tax income, and nothing more. By comparing these two entities, Jesus and the American colonies, Henry can more easily convince the delegates that they have been wronged by the British and that war will only bring justice. Furthermore, by comparing his countrymen to Christ, Henry makes the bold statement that God is on the side of the Americans. Christian doctrine, which was the predominant belief system in Henry's day, centers on the fact that Jesus is God's Son, described by God Himself as "Well-Beloved," and of whom God often said, "I am well pleased." This knowledge further emphasizes how effective this allusion is in swaying the members of the Virginia Convention.

Henry suggests that American is "well-beloved," and that God is well pleased with the efforts of the colonists who live there. The belief that God was on their side in the upcoming war gave great confidence and an overall assurance of victory to the delegates as they listened to Henry speak in support of the revolution.

Patrick Henry also employs anaphora in several areas of his speech in order to convince the other delegates to move in favor of revolution. He lists ways in which the colonists have attempted to peacefully resolve the conflict at hand: "We have petitioned; we have remonstrated; we have supplicated; we have prostrated ourselves before the throne, and have implored its interposition." (par. 3). The repetition of the phrase "we have" in this instance emphasizes not only each individual action taken, but also the great overall effort made by the colonists while striving to keep the peace. With this anaphora, Henry acknowledges everything that the colonists have endured, which further isolates revolution as the only course of action that they have not yet attempted.

Additionally, Henry uses anaphora to grant the delegates hope for victory if they choose to fight. He says, "If we wish to be free, if we mean to preserve…privileges…if we mean not to abandon the noble struggle… we must fight." (par. 3). This example of anaphora repeats two resounding concepts: *if* and *we*. As previously discussed, Henry pointed out to his comrades that they were holding to a vain hope of a peaceful resolution. Now, acting in the role of Orpheus, Henry, in a sense, drowns out the song of the siren with his own music. Here, he gives them something new for which to hope through the use of the word *if*. *If* is a powerful word when used to administer hope. By repeating it as many times as he does, and then connecting it with the phrase "we must fight," Henry very efficiently—and very boldly—declares that the colonists' *only* hope is to declare war and fight against Britain.

Henry's anaphora involving *we* in this same example emphasizes the necessity of unity in decision. Henry starts his speech talking about his own opinion, but by this point in his remarks, he has changed to the inclusive *we*. This change in subject essentially brings his own strong feelings upon everyone involved, and prematurely unites the delegation against Britain. Because he so directly involves the peace-driven delegates, quite possibly without their notice, Henry has created accomplices and allies who now feel obligated to join the fight that he has begun for them. The anaphora present throughout the speech accentuates minor details that serve as major support for Patrick Henry's argument and increases the overall feeling of urgency required in declaring war on Britain.

By interweaving rhetorical questions, allusions, and anaphora with his already impassioned rhetoric, Patrick Henry is able to reiterate just how essential an immediate war with and divide from Great Britain will be for the safety and liberty of the American colonists. Henry knew that his exclamatory sentences alone, while powerful and filled with emotion, would not be nearly enough to convince a group of highly educated, extremely stubborn individuals of the gravity of their situation. But by appealing to their logical sides as well as their emotional sides, he was able to sway the convention before him. Henry's endeavors were ultimately successful, and the delegation voted to establish and train a militia in the colony of Virginia with the purpose to defend the colonists against the British. The vote was close, but Henry's address to the delegates was undoubtedly the turning point of the convention. He left everybody in the room momentarily speechless because of the power of his simple, profound words. Thomas Jefferson, author of the Declaration of Independence, attributed much of the success of the revolution to Henry when he said, "It is not now easy to say what we should have done without Patrick Henry. He was before us all in maintaining the spirit of the Revolution" (Andrews, par. 14). Henry's final words echoed through St. John's church and through history: "Give me liberty or give me death!" (Henry, par. 5).

Works Cited

Andrews, Evan. "Patrick Henry's "Liberty or Death" Speech, 240 Years Ago." *History.com*. A&E Television Networks, 22 Mar. 2015. Web. 9 Oct. 2015.

Henry, Patrick. "History.org: The Colonial Williamsburg Foundation's Official History and Citizenship Website." Patrick Henry's "Give Me Liberty Or Give Me Death" Speech : The Colonial Williamsburg Official History & Citizenship Site. Colonial Williamsburg. Web. 7 Oct. 2015. <http://www.history.org/almanack/life/politics/giveme.cfm>.

"Sirens." *Sirens*. GreekMythology.Com, 2015. Web. 15 Oct. 2015. <http://www.greekmythology.com/Myths/Creatures/Sirens/sirens.html>.

SOURCE-BASED ARGUMENT

Example 1

"A Wolf in Sheep's Clothing: The Danger of the e-Cigarette"
Lily Oda
2015

You walk into an elegant restaurant, readying yourself for a make-or-break meeting with a potential business partner. As the tuxedoed host leads you to your $150 a plate table, you almost lose him in the dense, foggy air. All around you, men and women dressed to the nines are wining and dining, all whilst delicately holding thin, smoking tubes between their manicured fingers. Their faces reflect the orange glow emanating from the tips of the cigarettes. This vignette of the high class engulfed in swirling smoke makes you wonder whether you have been transported to a 1950's movie. You glance around for signs of Gene Kelly or James Dean. A closer examination of the scene, though, will reveal that some of these smoking, glowing cylinders are not actually cigarettes. Dispersed among their ash-producing counterparts, electronic cigarettes blend almost incongruously. These new age adaptations of the traditional tobacco cigarette have stealthily brought the practice of smoking back into the twenty-first century.

Invented in 2004 by the Golden Dragon Group of Hong Kong, electronic cigarettes, more commonly known as e-cigarettes, have made waves in the ever-controversial tobacco industry. The big hook of these new gadgets is that they deliver nicotine, the substance held primarily responsible for cigarette addiction, without tobacco and other harmful additives. e-Cigarettes work as follows: a cartridge, designed to look like a regular cigarette filter, is screwed into the main body of the e-cigarette. The cartridge contains nicotine dissolved in propylene glycol and the main body houses an electric circuit powered by a rechargeable battery. When the user inhales, this circuit is activated, causing the vaporization of the nicotine-propylene glycol mixture which is then sucked into the lungs. The activated circuit also causes a red light at the end of the device to light up, lending to the representation of the electronic device as a traditional cigarette (Goniewicz, Lingas, Hajek).

The marketers of e-cigarettes are very selective in what information they choose to present to consumers. e-Cigarettes present a myriad of unexplored risks, the least of which being their potential to make lighting up once again a regular public occurrence. Should the advertisers of such a product, carefully avoiding the mention of these risks, be allowed free reign in the public marketplace? The current marketing of e-cigarettes suggests that they are a better alternative to cigarette use when, in reality, this innovation in nicotine delivery may cause the renormalization of the harmful practice of smoking (Fairchild, Bayer, Colgrove). e-Cigarettes should therefore be subject to the same marketing regulations applied to traditional tobacco products.

The Façade of the Electronic Cigarette

If one was looking for ingenious use of persuasive communication, there would be no need to look beyond the marketing of e-cigarettes. Deliberately avoiding any specific health claims, advertisers are attempting to overcome the prejudice the public has against traditional tobacco products. They carefully present electronic cigarettes as a safe, cost-effective alternative without the social stigma associated with the appearance and odor of regular cigarettes.

A main argument of e-cigarette manufacturers is that e-cigarettes are safer than their traditional counterparts. One would be hard-pressed to find an e-cigarette package that doesn't feature the phrase "tobacco-free." Advertisers are working hard to combat the image of tar-encrusted lungs associated with traditional cigarettes. Unfortunately, the lack of tobacco in e-cigarettes does not equate to their being a salutatory product. Nonetheless, the advertisers strive to defend against a widespread wariness to "smoker's lung."

Advertisements also frequently point out how e-cigarettes are much more cost efficient than traditional tobacco products. According to New York Magazine, switching to e-cigarettes could save a customer nearly $4,000 a year (de Koff). Who isn't fearful that they're paying more than they need to? Buy an e-cig, coax the advertisements, and you'll save more than your lungs' rosy hue.

To bypass the social stigma associated with cigarettes, some e-cigarette companies are craftily choosing to market their products under different names. Produced in bright colors and candy or fruity flavors, these "hookah pens" or "vape pipes" don't look overwhelmingly similar to e-cigarettes, and are therefore often perceived as completely different products. Teenagers unwilling to experiment with cigarettes or anything closely related will often concede to try a colorful, fruit-flavored "e-hookah."

16

Much to the chagrin of anti-tobacco advocates and public health officials, these alternate devices are virtually identical to e-cigarettes. They are just as packed with unregulated chemicals and, more importantly, many contain highly-addictive nicotine (Richtel). With the colorful makeover and rechristening of electronic vaping devices, producers are successfully sidestepping the reproach associated with cigarettes.

In another tactic to evade the social stigma of traditional tobacco products, advertisers are presenting e-cigarettes as a clean, odor-free alternative. Listed first on one manufacturer's "Five Leading Benefits Electronic Smoking has over Traditional Cigarettes" is "e-cigarettes do NOT have that distinctive odor". They describe the clinging odor vividly, painting an almost palpable and *very* unpleasant picture of the musty aura that hangs about cigarette smokers. The article specifically mentions how many people, especially former smokers, avoid close contact with anyone carrying this distinctly unpleasant odor ("5 Leading Benefits"). Here the manufacturers play on the consumers' fear of social reproach.

Digging Deeper: A Critical Look into e-Cigarette Marketing
These advertising campaigns cannot be pegged as outright lies, but that doesn't mean they aren't deceptive. Nonetheless, when confronted by activists who aim to regulate the marketing of electronic cigarettes, producers adamantly resist. Miguel Martin, president of LOGIC Technology, an independent electronic cigarette brand, said, "...inherently, it's a different product. The only commonality between the two is the presence of nicotine. What we would say is, don't take the easy path out and just apply cigarette regulations to this product, because it's not a cigarette" (Belasco). Despite this and comparable claims, the similarities between the products and their marketing are decidedly worth looking into. All the focus on the social stigma, safety hazards, and relative expense avoided when using e-cigarettes distracts from the fact that this new invention is still a *cigarette* in the most important senses of the word.

Firstly, the electronic cigarette, like its traditional predecessor, is a highly dangerous and addictive product. Most e-cigarettes contain nicotine; in fact, nicotine delivery was the driving purpose of the e-cigarette's invention (Fairchild, Bayer, Colgrove). This stems from the fact that nicotine is a highly addictive substance—those dependent on it would be willing to get it in ways in distinction from the traditional cigarette. A study in a cancer-oriented clinical journal argued the harmful nature of nicotine. According to their research, nicotine presents, among other dangers, the risk of accelerated coronary artery disease (Benowitz). A *Clinical Pharmacy and Therapeutics* study revealed that, though maximum nicotine levels in users were about the same between regular cigarettes and nicotine gum, there was roughly twice as much overall nicotine exposure with the gum (Benowitz et al.). Without the "speed bump" nature of tobacco smoke, receiving nicotine through tobacco-free devices like electronic cigarettes can lead to prolonged exposure to this dangerous chemical.

Beyond this, like traditional cigarettes, the electronic variation contains a myriad of questionable chemicals. What's more disquieting, though, is that due to the relatively recent invention of e-cigarettes there has not been sufficient time to conduct studies on their contained chemicals (Abrams). There is simply not enough information on the risks and effects of e-cigarettes for them to be considered safe.

One study, examining the effects of e-cigarettes on air quality, recognized this fact. "…[W]ith regard to a health-related evaluation of e-cigarette consumption, the impact of vapor inhalation into the human lung should be of primary concern" (Schripp). Yes, e-cigarettes may be pleasant-smelling and attractively-colored, but that does not change their nature: devices delivering harmful chemicals directly to the user's lungs.

Despite these compelling physical risks, the real danger of the *e-cigarette* lies in its visual, and consequently social, perception. When an individual sees a billboard of a posh twenty-something enjoying a brand name e-cigarette, for all intents and purposes, the individual is seeing someone *smoking*. "…[T]he wild west marketing of e-cigarettes is not only encouraging youth to smoke them, but also it is promoting regular cigarette smoking among youth," says Stanton A. Glantz, PhD, director of the USCF Center for Tobacco Control Research and Education (Fernandez). According to the *Morbidity and Mortality Weekly Report*, the use of both e-cigarettes and traditional cigarettes nearly doubled among middle and high school students during the 2011–2012 school year. About 160,000 of the children who experimented with e-cigarettes had never tried a conventional cigarette ("Notes from the Field"). Unwilling to dapple with stigmatized traditional tobacco products, children are nonetheless drawn to the newer, "cooler," electronic version. The danger of e-cigarettes lies in their ability to renormalize a practice that, through much campaigning and regulation, has been on a downward trend for several decades.

Comparable Calamity: The Parallel Between Conventional Cigarettes and e-Cigarettes

A provocative comparison can be made when one juxtaposes electronic cigarettes with traditional cigarettes. As to their marketing, both products are presented to appeal to the desire to be "cool" and, even more noteworthy, to appeal to youth. Another parallel between the two products is their widespread opposition. Here, though, the two stories diverge—while the popular sentiment condemning the conventional cigarette brought about widely effective anti-smoking laws and regulations, the same disapproval has not led to federal marketing restrictions concerning the e-cigarette. By examining the traditional marketing of conventional cigarettes, as well as the public opposition they generated, the parallel between conventional cigarettes and e-cigarettes cannot be missed.

Early on, advertisers presented cigarettes as unmistakably cool. A 1958 L&M advertisement features "Gunsmoke" actor James Arness smoking the brand's cigarette. The television star wears a cowboy hat and a smug grin. The advertisers carefully linked their cigarettes with an aura of rugged masculinity (Feloni). Today, marketers of electronic cigarettes are chasing the same image. In a 2013 ad, a man who looks remarkably like a modern-day James Arness enjoys a Blu e-cigarette. Wearing a denim button-up shirt and a scruffy beard, he is truly a "man's man." Though the 2013 version lacks a cowboy hat, the message remains the same as 55 years earlier: smoke our product, and you too can be "cool."

Another potent similarity between the marketing tactics of traditional and electronic cigarettes is the targeting of youth. In a 1933 advertisement for Camel cigarettes, a starlet of New York's social elite says, "when my two younger children grow up and start to smoke, Camels will probably be their cigarette" (Davidson). What 1930's child wouldn't be dazzled by this glamorous woman's lifestyle? If smoking Camel cigarettes is what her children would do, smoking Camel cigarettes is what any child who wanted to amount to anything must do. As discussed earlier, today's advertisers are appealing to youth by presenting e-cigarettes under different names in colorful, flavored packages. No matter whether it is tobacco-containing or electronic, it is an insidious, lasting pattern among cigarette advertisers to get consumers hooked, and hook them young. 70% of adults who have ever smoked started the habit at or below the age of 18 ("Smoking: Health Effects"). The only thing better than a loyal customer is a lifelong customer.

In an inevitable response to the pervasive 20th century advertising of cigarettes, public outcry against tobacco products was heard throughout the nation. A fundamental event in the anti-tobacco movement was the 1964 first report of the Surgeon General's Advisory Committee on Smoking and Health. Based on over 7,000 biomedical articles, its conclusions included the heretofore little-known information that smoking is a cause of laryngeal cancer as well as the leading cause of chronic bronchitis ("History of Surgeon General's Reports"). Cigarette smoking was no longer an innocuous and acceptable habit and the American public demanded regulations that reflected this.

Today, the general public is likewise troubled by the rising prevalence of e-cigarettes. Reflecting the concerns of their constituents, twelve U.S. congressman sent letters of inquiry to electronic cigarette manufacturers in 2013. They were concerned about the labeling, distribution, and marketing efforts the manufacturers were employing (Mitka). Due to the high level of public interest, newspapers, medical journals, and online health forums churn out dozens of articles concerning e-cigarettes daily. The precedent is there, but will opponents of the new-age cigarette be able to bring about the same level of regulation as was achieved by earlier anti-cigarette campaigners?

Regulatory Considerations
The public outcry sparked by the cigarette's exposure as a harmful and potentially deadly product spurred federal regulatory action almost immediately. In 1965, only one year after the Surgeon General's report, Congress enacted the Federal Cigarette Labeling and Advertising Act of 1965, soon followed by the Public Health Cigarette Smoking Act of 1969. These laws required cigarette packages to carry a health warning, appropriated an annual report on the effects of smoking on health, and, arguably the most significant provision, banned cigarette advertising in broadcast media ("History of Surgeon General's Reports"). The Federal Trade Commission, which regulates the marketing and advertising of tobacco products, plays an increasingly significant role on today's anti-smoking battleground (Davidson). In an age where Americans watch 250 billion hours of television annually, the effect that tobacco ads would have on youth would be unprecedented (Herr). Fortunately, daytime television programming jingles, as well as their cigarette-promoting cartoon characters, have become a thing of the past. Today's generation is one that has never seen a cigarette commercial on television, nor even heard a tobacco-promoting blurb while scanning radio stations.

The regulation of tobacco products, specifically their marketing, has paid off emphatically. In 1964, 42.7% of America's adult population smoked. Today, the smoking rate is at 18.1% (Schroeder). This statistic is simply too significant to be overlooked. It's not as if nicotine has become less addictive—the dive in the smoking rate is due to governmental regulations increasing public awareness. This is a model to which society should look to control the rising popularity of electronic cigarettes.

The Big Picture

The introduction of electronic cigarettes has changed the smoking marketplace in a big way. Boasting cost efficiency, a lack of tobacco, and the avoidance of social stigma, e-cigarette marketers are working hard to disguise the true nature of their product. Advertisements fail to mention the hazardous nature of nicotine as well as the other harmful, unregulated chemicals swirling within an e-cigarette cartridge. The most dangerous aspect, though, of these new "vaping" devices is their potential to bring smoking back as an acceptable habit. Those who wish to combat this must look to the parallel between e-cigarettes and their conventional predecessors for a solution. Tobacco cigarettes were initially marketed in the same ways that are now being utilized to promote the electronic variety. The popularity and prevalence of cigarettes was brought down with public-catalyzed regulations. If there is any hope of achieving the same with e-cigarettes, similar regulations must be enacted as soon as possible.

In a 2014 e-cigarette ad, Steven Dorff declares, "I'm tired of feeling guilty every time I want to light up. We're all adults here. It's time to take our freedom back. Come on guys, rise from the ashes" (Fairchild, Bayer, Colgrove). Two can play at that game. If the object is to regain the anti-smoking ground gained over decades of advocacy, those working for the health of Americans must rise from the ashes and demand timely and effective regulation of the wolf in sheep's clothing: the e-cigarette.

Works Cited

"5 Leading Benefits Electronic Smoking Has Over Traditional Cigarettes." *eversmoke.com*. Web.

Abrams, David B., PhD. "Promise and Peril of e-Cigarettes: Can Disruptive Technology make Cigarettes Obsolete?" *JAMA* 311.2 (2014): 135–6. Print.

Belasco, Jessica. "E-cigarettes on rise, but questioned." 2014. Web.

Benowitz, N. L., et al. "Nicotine Absorption and Cardiovascular Effects with Smokeless Tobacco use: Comparison with Cigarettes and Nicotine Gum." *Clinical Pharmacology and Therapeutics* 44 (1988): 23–28. Print.

Benowitz, Niel. "Nicotine and Smokeless Tobacco." *CA: A Cancer Journal for Clinicians* 38.4 (1988): 244–7. Print.

Davidson, D. K. *Selling Sin : The Marketing of Socially Unacceptable Products*. Westport, Conn: Praeger, 2003. Print.

de Koff, Derek. "Smokeless Smokes; with Cigarette Taxes Up and Smoking in Bars, Restaurants, and Parks Now Banned, a Subculture has Grown Up Around e-Cigarette Nicotine Delivery Devices." *New York Magazine* October 31 2011. Print.

Fairchild, Amy L,PhD, MPH, Ronald Bayer PhD, and Colgrove, James,PhD, MPH. "The Renormalization of Smoking? E-Cigarettes and the Tobacco "Endgame"." *The New England Journal of Medicine* 370.4 (2014): 293–5. Print.

Feloni, Richard. "The New E-Cigarette Ads Look Exactly Like Old-School Cigarette Promos." 2014. Web.

Fernandez, Elizabeth. "E-Cigarettes: Gateway to Nicotine Addiction for U.S. Teens, Says UCSF Study." 2014. Web.

Goniewicz, Maciej L., Elena O. Lingas, and Peter Hajek. "Patterns of Electronic Cigarette use and User Beliefs about their Safety and Benefits: An Internet Survey." *Drug & Alcohol Review* 32.2 (2013): 133–40. Print.

Herr, Norman. "Television & Health." 2014.Web.

"History of the Surgeon General's Reports on Smoking and Health." 2014. Web.

Mitka, Mike. "Marketing Tactics of e-Cigarette Manufacturers Questioned." *Journal of the American Medical Association* 310.18 (2013)Print.

"Notes from the Field: Electronic Cigarette use among Middle and High School Students—United States, 2011–2012." *Morbidity and Mortality Weekly Report (MMWR)* 62.35 (2013): 729–30. Print.

Richtel, Matt. "E-Cigarettes, by Other Names, Lure Young and Worry Experts." *The New York Times*, sec. Business Day:March 4, 2014. Print.

Schripp, T., et al. "Does e-Cigarette Consumption Cause Passive Vaping?" *Indoor Air* 23.1(2012). Print.

Schroeder, Steven A. "Tobacco Control 50 Years After the 1964 Surgeon General's Report." *Journal of the American Medical Association* 311.2 (2014)Print.

"Smoking: Health Effects." 2014. Web.

Example 2

"The Future of Nuclear Power in the United States"
Trevor Casper
2015

Ever since its unfortunate public debut in 1945 with the dropping of the first atomic weapons on Hiroshima and Nagasaki, the public eye has generally taken a wary, if not disapproving, view of the use of nuclear fission as a power production source in the United States. On the other hand, generally the federal government continues to support the expansion of the United States' share of electricity produced by nuclear power.

But how safe is it really? Certainly Hollywood and media have painted a dismal picture in the public mind of the potential of nuclear power plants. What could be more dramatic than a threatened nuclear attack? Or more terrifying than the catastrophic meltdown of a neighborhood nuclear reactor, releasing a flood of radioactive green fluid into the surrounding city? These kinds of images may come to mind when one thinks of nuclear power. But are they accurate?

How well is the technology and safety of nuclear power truly understood by the public at large? Despite inherent risks in the technology, its use has continued to grow worldwide since WWII. The US Energy Information Administration, or EIA, reported that in 2011, nuclear power plants accounted for 19% of the electricity produced in the United States, and 13% Worldwide ("What Is the Status"). Even after the recent nuclear accident in Japan following their 2011 earthquake and subsequent tsunami, M. V. Ramana, a member of the International Panel on Fissile Materials, pointed out that major world powers including the United States, China, India, Russia, and the United Kingdom have all recommitted their support to expanding their nuclear programs (Ramana 69).

With so many conflicting views of the nuclear industry assaulting the public, it's no surprise that nuclear power can be so controversial. However, when modern nuclear technology and need for nuclear power are understood, the advantages of nuclear energy over other forms of energy are so significant that that the United States should continue to develop nuclear power and expand its use throughout the country in the coming decades.

Nuclear Power
In order to really understand the viability of nuclear power, it's critical to know what nuclear power is. Nuclear power derives its name from

the splitting of the cores, or nuclei, of atoms inside a specially-designed reactor. This process, called nuclear fission, releases intense heat, which is then used to boil water, generating pressurized steam that is funneled through turbines to produce electricity, similar to the way water rushing through a hydroelectric dam turns turbines to generate electricity.

The fuel generally used in these reactions is the variety of the element uranium called uranium-235, which is found in rock across the world. The EIA estimates that uranium is about 100 times more common in nature than silver, but the needed uranium-235 isotope is relatively rare ("Where Our Uranium Comes From"). Uranium ore must be mined and go through several refining and enrichment processes to increase the concentration of uranium 235 before it can be processed into nuclear reactor fuel. Unlike more traditional fossil fuel-burning power plants, nuclear plants can operate for a long time on a single batch of fuel, and most only need to be refueled every three to five years.

Advantages of Nuclear Power
Nuclear power has many advantages that make it an attractive option and alternative to the burning of fossil fuels that currently dominates the world's and United States' power production. While burning fossil fuels is a cheap and readily available source of energy, it also produces pollution and greenhouse gases that contribute to acid rain and may affect global warming. In 2011, the EIA reported that only 19% of the 4,100 billion kilowatt-hours of electricity produced in the United States was generated by nuclear power, while 68% was generated by the burning of coal and natural gas ("What Is the Status"). According to the US Environmental Protection Agency, that 68% released the majority of 2.2 *billion metric tons* of CO_2 equivalent gases into the atmosphere, in 2011 alone ("Sources of Greenhouse Gas Emissions"). Comparatively, according to EIA statistics only 13% of US power was generated by renewable energy sources, like wind, solar, hydroelectric, geothermal, and biomass ("What Is the Status").

Renewable energy sources sound like the ideal alternative to fossil fuels because they are considered to be very safe and they produce no greenhouse gases. Unfortunately, their limitations reveal the need for a more stable source of power. The US power grid requires "base load" power sources, or those that can be relied on for consistent, dependable power any time of the night and day. Because the sun does not always shine and the wind does not always blow, neither solar nor wind can form the foundation of our power supply. Hydroelectric does qualify as base load, but unfortunately dams can only be built in certain locations, and building too many has negative environmental consequences. Geothermal power has similar drawbacks. After these sources, nuclear power remains the only other major power source that can be built anywhere, and operates with zero emissions.

Some opponents of nuclear power are quick to point out that the mining and processing of nuclear fuel is a process that requires large amounts of energy, including the burning of fossil fuels to power the equipment. Because of that, they say that nuclear energy is not truly a "clean" power source. However, is this not the case with all other sources of energy? Don't coal and natural gas take significant energy to mine and extract? Solar panels and windmills also undergo expensive industrial processes to be built. When all these processes are taken into account, the results are surprising: The World Nuclear Association compared studies done by nuclear agencies, government agencies, and universities, and found that, over the entire life cycle of these power plants, the emissions of coal and natural gas are, respectively, thirty and fifteen times that of nuclear, while the emissions of solar power are actually three times *greater* than nuclear, biomass emissions are one and a half times that of nuclear, and hydroelectric and wind power produce emissions roughly equivalent to nuclear (*Comparison of Lifecycle Greenhouse Gas Emissions* 8). Clearly, Charles Forsberg, a nuclear engineer at MIT in Cambridge, is justified in saying, as quoted by editor Michael Waldrop in the journal *Nature*, "If you're going to get off fossil fuel, you have to have a serious nuclear pro-gramme" (qtd. in Waldrop 28).

Nuclear fuel has an extremely high power density, allowing nuclear plants to be relatively small in comparison to other types of power plants. Nuclear fuel is composed of small pellets that are roughly the size of half of a AA-size battery. These are stacked into fuel rods, and then grouped into assemblies. According to the Idaho National Laboratory, each of these pellets, "Contains the same amount of energy as 17,000 cubic feet of natural gas, 1,780 pounds of coal or 149 gallons of oil" ("Benefits of Nuclear Energy"). This power density allows for a small, confined plant to be built, as opposed to the dozens of square miles of wind turbines or solar panels that it would take to produce the same amount of power. On the smaller scale here is also potential for small, modular reactors to be built that would produce enough power to power a single industrial complex. The US Navy currently utilizes such technology to power its fleet of aircraft carriers worldwide.

This flexibility of nuclear means it can even be employed in other capacities. Gioietta Kuo, a research physicist specializing in energy and a senior fellow at the American Center for International Policy Studies, names two such applications. One is utilizing the plants to produce hydrogen to fuel the new fuel-cell cars that are now beginning to hit the market (such as the new Toyota FCV). Another potential application includes desalinating seawater to produce fresh drinking water to areas with a limited clean water supply (Kuo 37). According to Waldrop, small versions of a newer technology called high-temperature nuclear reactors:

> …Could slash carbon emissions by supplying heat for industrial processes. In the United States, roughly 23% of all energy is used in industrial applications such as petroleum cracking and plastics manufacture, many of which need temperatures of at least 700 °C. Currently, those temperatures tend to be generated by burning natural gas; high-temperature reactors could provide a zero-carbon alternative. (Waldrop 28)

As the market grows for smaller reactors, perhaps even for reactors small enough to be portable, the possibilities are nearly endless for how many ways this energy source can be harnessed.

Safety

The foremost concerns that critics of nuclear energy have usually relate to issues of safety. And these concerns are well founded. When working with an energy source as potent as nuclear energy, extreme caution must be taken. Many people fear that a nuclear power plant being built in their community would be the equivalent of building a large cold-war era nuclear bomb. However, there is a very significant difference between the two. As mentioned previously, most uranium found in nature is not the uranium-235, or U-235, variety which is needed for nuclear fission, but it is instead the uranium-238 isotope. In fact, less than 1% of natural uranium is U-235. Uranium most go through an enrichment process before it becomes suitable for nuclear fuel. However, as explained by Geoff Brumfiel in the science journal *Nature*, the concentration required for reactors is only about 3.5–5%. Nuclear weapons, on the other hand, require a much higher grade of uranium in order to react with explosive force—over 90% U-235 (Brumfiel 282). The difference between nuclear fuel and weapons-grade uranium is directly comparable to the difference between whole milk and solid butter. Even in the worst possible scenario, it would be impossible for a nuclear power plant to "go nuclear."

Unfortunately, though a nuclear bomb is out of the picture, the worst disaster a nuclear reactor can experience is that of a meltdown, which can be a serious accident. In the sixty years of nuclear power plant history, there have only been three significant accidents, and each was well publicized. The first accident took place at a place in Pennsylvania known as 3-Mile Island. Gioietta Kuo, a senior fellow at the American Center for International Policy Studies, explains that due to mechanical and operator failures in 1979 this reactor experienced a partial meltdown. Although no deaths or cancer cases were ever reported as a result of this accident, Kuo specifies, it received significant media hype and triggered a wave of anti-nuclear sentiments (Kuo 35).

The second accident occurred in 1986 at Chernobyl in the former Soviet Union. There, a poor reactor design, according to Kuo, "That would not even be considered for a permit in the West" was utilized, and an unexpected power surge caused the reactor to rupture, catch fire, and spew out highly radioactive smoke across the surrounding area. The official death toll for this accident was thirty-one, but the effect this disaster had on the health of the people and the environment in the surrounding area is much greater (Kuo 35). These effects still linger and are felt today.

The third incident was much more recent. On March 11, 2011, a strong earthquake greater than magnitude nine struck off the coast of Japan, causing damage but also triggering a tsunami, which pounded the coast of Japan soon afterward. The massive Fukushima-Daiichi nuclear power complex was located on the coast, and lost power as a result of the accident. Kuo notes that unfortunately, these reactors did not cool down as they were supposed to in the loss of power, but instead, three of the six reactors overheated and experienced a meltdown (Kuo 35).

Looking back over these three incidents, it's important to recognize some key elements that link each of the accidents. First, each of the accidents involved some degree of human error. As Kuo notes, 3-Mile Island was made worse by the insufficient training the operators had to deal with the mechanical failures. Chernobyl was caused largely by a poor reactor design. And Fukushima was partly due to the safety company TEPCO failing to properly check all the backup and safety features that they were under contract to maintain (Kuo 35–36). In other words, in each of these accidents, people failed to follow established safety procedures.

It is also important to note that in each of these situations, the reactors affected were each over 30 years old. 3-Mile Island took place thirty-five years ago, Chernobyl was nearly thirty years ago itself, and the recent Fukushima event happened with reactors that, as Kuo explained, "… Had all been built in the 1970's and were near the end of their useful lives" (Kuo 35). Since the accident in Chernobyl nearly thirty years ago, the US government and governments worldwide have greatly increased the standards for safety for newer plants, and there has never been an accident involving newer plants with these improved safety features. Any nuclear plants built in the United States prior to these improved safety features are nearing the end of their lifespans today and will soon need to be replaced with these upgraded models. Since 2001, Kuo also points out that many newer reactors built in China are designed to not only be able to endure any natural disasters, but also to withstand the force of a direct impact from a passenger jet (Kuo 36). The safety features that are standard today on new reactors probably would not have allowed these kinds of accidents in the past to occur at all.

Apart from newer reactors being build today with state-of-the-art safety features, new technologies are being developed and built that promise to be even safer. Most reactors worldwide today are of a type called "light-water" reactors, meaning that water is used to directly cool the nuclear reactor and transfer heat to the boilers. However, Kuo also describes a different variety of reactor beginning to be utilized in China called a Pebble-bed Reactor. With this type, a steel tower is filled with billiard-sized balls of uranium coated in heat-resistant graphite. Helium, which is an inert, non-reactive gas, is then blown through the tower in a continuous loop, and used to convey heat to a separate boiler and turbine system. In the case of overheating, the helium would not be subject to pressurized explosions like a light-water reactor, but would simply dissipate into the atmosphere without conveying any radiation contamination. The billiard-ball sized fuel "pebbles" themselves would not be able to get hot enough to experience a meltdown (Kuo 36).

Other types of reactors that would be virtually immune to meltdown are still in the developmental state. One such technology is the high-temperature reactor mentioned earlier. This variety of reactor also uses helium gas as its coolant instead of water. It is designed to operate at temperatures up to 1000 C, according to Waldrop, but the fuel itself is stable up to about 1,600 C. This is hotter than the core would become even if all safety features failed and all the helium coolant was lost. Another elegant safety feature comes in molten-salt reactor design. Such a reactor has liquefied uranium hexafluoride mixed into a pot of coolant. Such a design is much more stable with uranium kept in the liquid phase, and overheating would be difficult. But as an additional safeyy feature, in the event of all backup power systems failing, a plug at the bottom of the tank that is normally kept cool by a refrigeration system would be melted by the liquid metal which would drain all the reactor's contents safely into an underground holding area until the crisis can be resolved (Waldrop 28–29). These new reactor designs that are impervious to meltdown promise to significantly decrease the danger of even the worst nuclear disasters.

In addition to concerns over nuclear accidents, another major concern is that of what to do with the spent fuel removed from the reactors. Along with the heat released, there are also byproducts left behind after nuclear fission takes place. These byproducts, collectively called nuclear waste, are eventually removed from the reactor and are put into storage canisters. Due to the high radioactivity of nuclear waste, these canisters require careful cooling and storage until they break down into less harmful elements. Depending on the type of waste, this could take anywhere from several thousand to several hundred thousand years. Currently the United States has no central depository for nuclear waste storage, so most nuclear plants have temporary storage sites located near the reactor.

An interesting feature of nuclear waste from light-water reactors is that it actually still contains a considerable amount of usable uranium fuel in it. The original plan when light-water reactors were first becoming widespread was that the spent fuel would be sent to a reprocessing plant to have the usable fuel extracted. This has the double benefit of one, recycling fuel and reducing the cost of processing new fuel, and two, significantly reducing the amount of actual nuclear waste that remains afterwards. Incredibly, this leftover waste is also significantly easier to deal with. Instead of taking hundreds of thousands of years to break down, Waldrop explains, it breaks down over several hundred and is much easier to store and transport (Waldrop 27).

Unfortunately, part of the reprocessing process involves highly concentrated uranium, even potentially weapons-grade uranium or plutonium, and there has been some concern about this concentrated uranium falling into the wrong hands. This led to President Carter in 1977 banning commercial reprocessing, even though most other nations still utilize it. As a result, the US has been collecting spent fuel for decades, but has not yet come up with a long term solution for how to handle it.

Remarkably, newer reactor designs operate in a way that they could potentially burn through the leftover uranium contained in nuclear waste, meaning that they could actually be fueled by the nuclear waste that currently hampers the nuclear industry. According to Waldrop, the high temperature and molten salt reactors mentioned earlier, as well as another technology known as fast reactors, could recycle our current and future spent fuel, greatly reducing our need to find long term nuclear waste storage (Waldrop 27).

Conclusion
All in all, the advantages of utilizing nuclear power are significant. It is a clean source of energy that offers the only truly viable zero-emission alternative to fossil fuels. The flexibility of the technology allows for many potential future applications, both in the energy sector and the industrial sector. Despite accidents that have occurred in the past, new safety designs and new technologies promise to make nuclear meltdowns a thing of the past. In addition, these new technologies promise to actually *reduce* the current problem we have with spent nuclear fuel instead of adding to it.

But even with all these promising signs, nuclear energy still has a long way to go. With the exception of the Pebble-bed Reactors, these new reactor designs are still in the developmental stage, and some are only just barely having prototypes built. At the current rate of research, it may be years, or potentially a decade or two, before these technologies fully emerge into the energy market. In the meantime, problems with pollution and greenhouse gases only accelerate. Though the United States and the Obama Administration have reaffirmed their support of nuclear power, the United States needs to allocate more resources towards the development of this important technology to ensure that we have a safe, clean, and energy-secure future.

Works Cited

"Benefits of Nuclear Energy." *Benefits of Nuclear Energy*. Ed. Ehresman, Teri. Idaho National Laboratory, n.d. Web. 04 Apr. 2014.

Brumfiel, Geoff. "Iran's Nuclear Plan Revealed." Nature 479.7373 (2011): 282. Academic Search Premier. Print.

Comparison of Lifecycle Greenhouse Gas Emissions of Various Electricity Generation Sources. Rep. London, UK: World Nuclear Association, 2011. Print.

Kuo, Gioietta. "Nuclear Energy After Fukushima." World Future Review (World Future Society) 3.4 (2011): 35–37. Academic Search Premier. Print.

Ramana, M. V. "Nuclear Policy Responses To Fukushima: Exit, Voice, And Loyalty." Bulletin Of The Atomic Scientists 69.2 (2013): 66–76. Academic Search Premier. Print.

"Sources of Greenhouse Gas Emissions." *Sources: Climate Change: US EPA*. United States Environmental Protection Agency, 09 Sept. 2013. Web. 04 Apr. 2014.

Waldrop, M. Mitchell. "Nuclear Energy: Radical Reactors." Nature 492.7427 (2012): 26–29. Academic Search Premier. Print.

"What Is the Status of the U.S. Nuclear Industry?" *Energy in Brief*. U.S. Energy Information Administration, 14 Dec. 2012. Web. 12 Apr. 2014.

"Where Our Uranium Comes From." *Energy Explained, Your Guide To Understanding Energy*. U.S. Energy Information Administration, 28 Aug. 2013. Web. 04 Apr. 2014.

Example 3

"The Fizzy Alternative"
Ryan Poch
2016

America is under attack—from the inside out. The assailant is silent, yet seductively sweet. With the most glamorous of commercials he lures the unsuspecting with lurid promises of smiling friends and bikinied beach parties. We swallow his poison willingly, and die a slow death. I speak of sugary soda beverages. Time magazine asserts that sodas are "a short cut to heart disease, obesity and diabetes" and that in the United States, soda is our "most consumed beverage" in comparison to European countries where sugary sodas aren't gulped "like water at every meal" (Sacharow). Europe looks on, laughing at obese America: what are they doing that we aren't, and what habits do we need to adopt from our cousins across the sea to dodge the deadly danger?

Upon returning to America after two years living in Germany and doing as the Germans do, I had a hunch. I began to ask around—why don't we as Americans drink plain carbonated water like our Germanic cousins? Surely plain carbonated water would be healthier than sugary sodas? The responses I received from friends and family members were varied (and sometimes passionate): sparkling water is more acidic than normal water and thus causes tooth decay; carbonic acid leaches calcium from the bones, causing osteoporosis while at the same time somehow increasing the concentration of other minerals leading to kidney stones; there is simply no demand for unsugared carbonated water—nobody likes it. The Germans as a whole are unimpressed by these reasons, drinking seltzer water with great relish—do they know something that we don't? Considering the obesity and diabetes epidemics that are sweeping our nation and if these claims against sparkling water were wrong, could the addition of sparkling water in American schools and the American workplace combat those epidemics while still providing the fizz we have grown accustomed to in our beverages? Carbonated (sparkling) water as a refreshment beverage has been given an undeserved bad reputation in America, and if these negative ideas would be actively combated and sparkling water made more economical and accessible in the school and workplace, it would improve the overall health of Americans as they make the switch from sugary sodas and colas to a healthier alternative.

It is a common belief (in America at least) that carbonated water some-how leaches calcium from the bones. I examined this claim. It turns out that much of the culture of calcium leaching comes from a study done by two researchers in 1994, aimed at "[exploring] the association between carbonated beverage consumption, as well as other nutritional intake, and the occurrence of bone fractures in girls" (Wyshak 210). They looked at different children's ages, genders, diets, medical history and activity level, among other factors, to determine if there was a correlation between soda drinking and health challenges. Their conclusion? "The high con-sumption of carbonated beverages and the declining consumption of milk are of great public health significance for girls and women because of their proneness to osteoporosis in later life" (210). Case closed? Not even close. The media took these findings and ran with them, exaggerat-ing their meaning and implications. A closer reading of the study reveals that the published conclusion was poorly worded; the actual study reads otherwise:

> The consumption of cola beverages is associated with bone frac-tures... [but] No association between non-cola drinks—Fresca®, diet 7-UP®, diet ginger ale, or ginger ale with sugar, or 7-UP® with sugar—and bone fractures was found...[suggesting] that the effect is due to the cola (phosphoric acid containing) drinks. (213–214)

An unfortunate misuse of vernacular in the published conclusion ("car-bonated beverages" instead of "cola") led to confusion in the masses. In attempt to rectify this mistake, other studies have cropped up in recent years, such as the aptly named study: "Colas, but not other carbonated beverages, are associated with low bone mineral density in older women: the Framingham Osteoporosis Study," a name so explanatory that its findings are described in the title alone (Tucker et al. 936). The calcium-leaching theory has been proven valid in regard to colas, but we lack sufficient evidence to incriminate plain carbonated water.

Acidity is another aspect of carbonated water that must be assessed in regards to health. It cannot be denied that the carbonic acid has an effect on the pH of water; the only question remaining is whether the effect is great enough that it can adversely affect the enamel of human teeth. A team of scientists at the University of Birmingham performed a very thorough study examining exactly that: the acidity of carbonated water (among other substances) on the rate of dental erosion. The actual experiment is quite intense, submerging actual extracted human teeth "in six consecutive 5-min exposures to the test solutions" (Parry et al. 768). Because mineral waters contain a varying amount of dissolved minerals, fourteen different types of water (carbonated and otherwise) were tested alongside sugary sodas and several control solutions. The amount of dissolved solids (mineral dissolution) was then assessed and expressed as mean phosphorous dissolution per five minutes of exposure (see figure 1). While the slightly more acidic nature of sparkling water dissolved minerals in the teeth slightly more than noncarbonated water, the dissolution was nowhere near that of the sugary sodas. Even orange juice was acidic enough to have a more recognizable effect in comparison to sparkling mineral water.

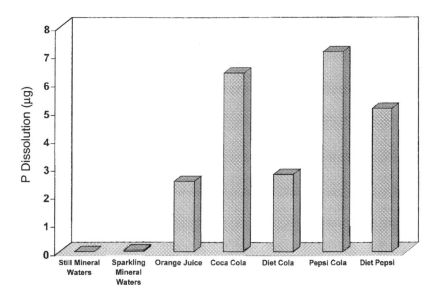

Fig. 1. Phosphorus dissolution (µg) from human dental enamel after in vitro incubation with mineral waters (mean values) and comparator soft drinks (Parry et al.)

The results of the experiment were summarized as follows:

Whilst sparkling mineral waters showed slightly greater dissolution than still mineral waters, these levels of dissolution were nevertheless very low. This provides important quantitative evidence that these mineral waters represent alternatives to more erosive acidic beverages. Thus, the increasing consumption of these sparkling mineral waters can be advocated even in patients with a high frequency of drink consumption. (771)

Those are pretty shocking numbers. Not only did the University of Birmingham's study contradict the claim that sparkling water is bad for your teeth, it actually advocates the drinking of it in place of sugary sodas (a clear conclusion, considering the decay shown when the teeth were submerged in the colas). Our nation's dental situation would be much better if we were to replace our love of cola with a love of sparkling water.

Another team tackled the kidney stone claim. It is widely-believed (at least in my unofficial polling pool) that mineral water fails to flush out the toxins like normal water and that the increased mineral content in the mineral water actually contributes to kidney stone build-up. A large team of researchers from many different educational backgrounds performed a study in 1992 that was created to investigate if there is a causal relationship between soda drinking and kidney stone recurrence among males. This study, actually published two years before the 1994 study on soda and calcium (and equally persistent in its use of unspecified and confusion-causing terms in its title) was called "Soft Drink Consumption and Urinary Stone Recurrence: A Randomized Prevention Trial" and concluded that sodas acidified with phosphoric acid (colas) were indeed linked to increased production of kidney stones, whereas citric-acid acidified sodas (non-colas) did not have a statistically significant influence on kidney stone production (Schuster et al. 911). Once again, because of the wording of the study, many assumed that the blanket term "soft drink" meant all carbonated beverages, when in reality that is not the case. In fact, further follow-up studies done by German researchers actually discovered that drinking magnesium- and bicarbonate-rich mineral water could actually *decrease* the number of kidney stones in subjects (Karagülle et al. 322). Poorly written titles of studies and word of mouth pseudo-science has led society to believe many conclusions about carbonated mineral water that are short-sided and untrue. The same conclusions about cola, however, have been thus far justified by the data.

With these initial myths disproved, are there any reasons to not switch over to the European way? Nutrition and health specialist Marie Dannie asserts that some could have adverse reactions to carbonated water including "bloating and discomfort in [the] abdomen [of those with irritable bowel syndrome]," increased chance of acid reflux (heartburn), and increased irritation of an existing ulcer (Dannie). While these reactions are potentially irritating, it is also important to note that all of them are dependent on a preexisting condition (irritable bowel syndrome, acid reflux disease, and ulcers) and are not caused by an inherent property of carbonated water. When compared, especially, with the adverse affects of traditional colas (as discussed in the various research articles cited throughout this work) it becomes clear that plain mineral water is a much better alternative to colas and sugary sodas. Colas and sodas have these carbon dioxide-linked adverse reactions as well, but they also have the increased detriments of calories and sugar and the obesity and diabetes that come from so much sugar consumption.

For those who have overcome their initial fear to actually try the stuff, the most common complaint had with plain carbonated water is the taste. To the unaccustomed tongue, sparkling mineral water is unpalatable, bitter, and, well, nasty. I'll be the first to admit my initial aversion to the bubbly stuff during my time in Germany. One's initial response, however, can be overcome. It took a few tries, but pretty soon I didn't mind the taste. I actually grew to really like it! And I'm not the only one: Further data from Beverage Digest and marketing research firm Mintel indicates that there has been a "33 percent surge in the sparkling water category in [the U.S. in 2013]" (Aristotle). As more people are exposed to sparkling water and acquire a taste for it, more people would be willing to drink it regularly if it was only more affordable and available! And if that exposure were to happen from a young age, many children would grow up with an ingrained love of the bubbly, a preference that would pay health dividends throughout their lives- just like it does in Europe.

The intent of this paper is not to outline a plan how to introduce sparkling water into American schools and businesses, rather to raise awareness of how beneficial that could be. A big change like this would have many stumbling blocks that would need to be addressed. According to an American Journal of Public Health article published in 2011, a major stumbling block in attempts to integrate alternative forms of hydration in America's schools is the advertising funding the schools get from soda-producing corporations—more specifically the fear of the financial repercussions that would come if that funding were diverted away, explaining that "many US schools rely on revenue from beverage sales and advertising as a discretionary funding source for school activities" and that "schools may fear revenue loss if they remove sugar-sweetened beverages... and ban junk food marketing" (Patel 1373).

Unfortunately, by monopolizing the school and workplace beverage industry with sugary beverages, big soda corporations are affecting the potential health of students and citizens. In order to overcome these stumbling blocks, there would have to be a fundamental change to how we as Americans look at sparkling water as a refreshment beverage, and demand for it would have to increase.

So, do the Germans have it all figured out? The Germans, at any rate, have had a greater chance to fall in love with this beverage alternative. Sparkling water is a staple of their society, and I too grew to love it while I was there. If we can provide the opportunity and the right information, Americans, too, will choose to consume ice-cold sparkling water. Sparkling water has been given an undeserved bad reputation, and if it were adopted in American schools and the American workplace, it would significantly improve the health of Americans as they make the switch from sugary sodas to healthy water: There would be less dental problems, less kidney stones, even less osteoporosis! Maybe it won't solve the obesity crisis all at once, but it will at least be a step in the right direction: people will still get that soda burn in the back of their throats, that fizzy alternative.

Works Cited

Aristotle Munarriz, Rick. "SodaStream Switches Focus From Soda to Sparkling Water." DailyFinance.com. AOL Inc., 6 Nov. 2014. Web. 19 Mar. 2015.

Beck, Leslie. "To Quench Your Thirst, Plain Old Water Is Best." The Globe and Mail. Ed.

Phillip Crawley, 9 June 2010. Web. 12 Mar. 2015.

Dannie, Marie. "Are There Health Risks of Carbonated Water?" Livestrong. com, 2 Aug. 2014. Web. 19 Mar. 2015.

Karagülle, O., U. Smorag, F. Candir, G. Gundermann, U. Jonas, A.J. Becker, A. Gehrke, and C. Gutenbrunner. "Effect of Mineral Water Containing Calcium and Magnesium on Calcium Oxalate Urolithiasis Risk Factors." World Journal Of Urology 25.3 (2007): 315–23. Print.

Sacharow, Anya. "Can We Drink Soda Responsibly?" Time Inc., 5 Feb. 2013. Web. 6 Apr. 2015.

Schuster, J., A. Jenkins, C. Logan, T. Barnett, R. Riehle, D. Zackson, H. Wolfe, R. Dale, M. Daley, I. Malik, and S. Schnarck. "Soft Drink Consumption and Urinary Stone Recurrence: A Randomized Prevention Trial." *Journal of Clinical Epidemiology* 45.8 (1992): 911–16. Print.

Tucker, Katherine L, Kyoko Morita, Ning Qiao, Marian T Hannan, L Adrienne Cupples, and Douglas P Kiel. "Colas, but Not Other Carbonated Beverages, Are Associated with Low Bone Mineral Density in Older Women: The Framingham Osteoporosis Study." *The American Journal of Clinical Nutrition* 84.4 (2006): 936–42. Print.

Parry, J., L. Shaw, M. J. Arnaud, and A. J. Smith. "Investigation of Mineral Waters and Soft Drinks in Relation to Dental Erosion." *Journal of Oral Rehabilitation* 28.8 (2001): 766–72. Print.

Patel, Anisha I., and Karla E. Hampton. "Encouraging Consumption of Water in School and Child Care Settings: Access, Challenges, and Strategies for Improvement." *American Journal of Public Health* 101.8 (2011): 370–79. Print.

Wyshak, Grace, and Rose E. Frisch. "Carbonated Beverages, Dietary Calcium, the Dietary Calcium/phosphorus Ratio, and Bone Fractures in Girls and Boys." *Journal of Adolescent Health* (1994): 210–15. Print.

Example 4

"The Dirty Underbelly of Farm Subsidizing: The Harm It Does
and What Can Be Done About It"
Aliah Eberting
2016

I shot out of bed with all the elegance of a caffeinated baby hippo. With equal grace and restraint I scrambled into my overalls and flew out the door. It was finally morning, and I was here! On a *farm*!

I had just turned seven, and, in honor of that momentous step to adulthood, my aunt had taken me on a trip to Idaho to visit family—to Idaho to visit *farmers*. I had never seen a farmer before and regarded them in the same light as elephants, pirates, or other creatures purely of adult fiction. But I had seen farmers in movies, and some things I knew were, 1. All farmers have a cow, a pig, some chickens, and a horse. 2. Farmers plant crops. 3. I had seen a plow once.

Farming was *awesome*. I couldn't wait to get started.

But when I told my aunt my plans, she got a funny look on her face and kindly said, "Dear, my father doesn't really do that kind of farming. We don't have animals, and he doesn't work the fields." My aunt went on to explain that her father hadn't farmed for decades. In fact, her father was paid to not farm. The blow was quite painful to my seven-year-old psyche. It felt as if I'd just been told, "Dear, we are not standing on the ground, we are hanging off the sky."

It would take me many years to learn that my distant relative's farm, is, due to farm subsidizing, somewhat typical of modern agriculture. And the quintessential farm of the storybooks is incredibly scarce. Over almost a century, the Farm Bill has utterly reshaped how we, as a nation, view farming. Though farm subsidies met the country's great needs at their inception, our needs have changed drastically since then, and subsidies as they stand do not meet these new needs. Now, instead of promoting public health, economic well-being, and environmentally responsible farming, subsidies encourage unhealthy eating, economic problems, and poor treatment of the environment. But this doesn't need to be the case. If subsidies became focused on nutritional quality then subsidies could be used to meet our current day needs.

Historical Background

Since the 1930's Farm Board first pushed agricultural help, government has been juggling subsidies (which can be received for either farming or not farming) in an attempt to keep market prices steady for such staples of life as wheat and corn—both high calorie and high yield crops. As the nation headed into the Great Depression, this subsidizing was meant to provide some stability for farmers and, since they knew that they were guaranteed pay for their crops regardless of how the market was doing, encourage them to continue providing much needed food for the starving masses. These subsidies helped poor farmers to stay afloat and kept food flowing into the economy. Times were desperate, and food, whether healthy or not, was a blessing and not to be turned away. However, we emerged from the Depression and standards of living rose across the board. Nowadays, most Americans can afford to look beyond the basics of simply as many calories as possible for as cheaply as possible in their food. For the first time in Earth's history on so wide-spread a scale, we have the leisure-time and resources to explore healthy food and nutrition.

Subsidies Effect on Health

What has come as an unwelcome surprise to many, however, is that eating healthy is often the more expensive choice. But this is the unfortunate truth. The fact of the matter is that foods with higher calorie counts (processed foods) are far cheaper than those with low calorie counts—things like fresh vegetables—making the most-sensible option for consumers shopping on a budget an unhealthy one, low on lean meats, fresh vegetables, and fresh fruits (Drewnowski, Specter 1).

Oddly enough, higher calorie-count foods such as refined grains and oils used to be trade- marks of the wealthy while the poor where consigned to subsist on the simple foods of the earth. What brought about this surprising change of pricing? As bestselling health author Michael Pollan put the question, "Compared with a bunch of carrots, a package of Twinkies, to take one iconic processed foodlike substance as an example, is a highly complicated, high-tech piece of manufacture, involving no fewer than 39 ingredients, many themselves elaborately manufactured, as well as the packaging and a hefty marketing budget. So how can the supermarket possibly sell a pair of these synthetic cream-filled pseudocakes for less than a bunch of roots?" (1).

To understand this conundrum, we need only look to the heart of the farm bill. Because the government sought to ensure the production of as many calories as possible when it was created, the vast majority of subsidies were, and are, in support of only five main crops: corn, wheat, soy, rice, and cotton (USDA). Subsidies are offered in an attempt to keep the price of these crops stable. However, because government monetary backing eliminates a farmer's risk in growing subsidized crops in comparison to growing unsubsidized crops, more farmers flock to these crops than any others. Subsidies are handed out per bushel of crop grown, and so the more farmers grows, the more they get paid in the end. This creates a vast interest in farming these crops above all others and a vast surplus flooding the market, lowering prices on these ingredients and making them desirable to food manufacturers. In addition, because relatively few farmers cultivate other crops, the prices of fruits, vegetables, and unsubsidized grains rise in turn.

Now, corn, wheat, soy, and rice are not, by nature, unhealthy. But because they are cheaper than other ingredients, food manufacturers include these far more often than any other ingredients. Corn and soy derivatives in particular are in practically every manufactured food.

Based on a 2000 calorie per day consumption, the average American gets 554 of these calories from corn, 768 from wheat, 257 from soy, and 91 from rice (Pollan 124), leaving just 330 calories to get from other sources. Consuming these foods in such large quantities, especially as refined grains or byproducts (corn syrup and soy oil, to name two) is very unhealthy. Stephanie Bernell's study, "The Twisted Path From Farm Subsidies to Health Care Expenditures" marks the definite affect subsidies have on national health, finding that agriculture studies lead to a 0.062 to 0.105 percent increase in BMI—a measure of body fat (3). In a country where the surgeon general has declared obesity an epidemic, we can no longer afford to give promotion to the foods that brought us there (Caromona 1).

Farm subsidies have also had another unforeseen effect on our country's health in moving the focus of crop breeding from quality to rest blindingly on quantity. The amount of crop grown and not the nutritional content determine the amount of subsidy farmers receive. Since they are naturally interested in receiving as much subsidy as they can, they are also interested in producing as much as they can. The nutritional content of the food produced, whether good or bad, doesn't effect their payout and isn't considered when selecting which strains will be planted. Though slight from year to year, this focus has had drastic effects on the nutritional content of today's crops. When compared with that of the 1920's, the nutritional content of today's produce is remarkably lower (Pollan 125).

To live healthy lives, we also need to gather our nutrients from many sources, but the goliaths of corn and soy have swept away the wide variety of plants that used to ensure our diet contained all the micronutrients it needed. Pollan points out that whereas farmers used to grow all manner of fruits and vegetables in addition to grain, the overwhelming majority of farmers now grow only corn, wheat, soy, or rice (123). This has resulted directly in the populations' lack of access to all the nutrition it needs and increased access to high-calorie foods. Because subsidies have caused lower nutrition and inexpensive high-calorie foods to be normal, for the first time in history we have "the human being who manages to be both overfed and undernourished," (Pollan 126).

Subsidies Effect on the Environment

But health is not the only thing farm subsidies' push of quantity hurts. The environment also takes a blow. More corn, more soy, more wheat—farming nowdays is about making money. And because of subsidies, farmers can now afford to farm on marginal land. Marginal land is ground that does not produce enough to support farmers on its own, because it lacks the nutrients to produce a crop load that can make a profit. But, thanks to subsidies, it can now be profitably farmed. This land requires more work, more energy, more fuel to farm and is sometimes very important to the surrounding ecosystem left undisturbed, as it is meant to be. Marginal land also requires more water to farm.

In an attempt to fix this problem, additional subsidies were offered to farmers across the nation to be used in upgrading watering equipment to be more environmentally friendly. What researchers found, however, is that these subsidies actually led to more water use as farmers used the money they saved, by using more efficient equipment, to begin farming more land. In some cases, the water table has fallen 150 feet, as subsidies provide incentive to irrigate more land (Nixon).

Though it may seem hard to believe, subsidies have also affected air quality. With the rise of corn, ethanol production is at an all-time high. And with that increased ethanol production comes an increase of ethanol production plants. These plants are notoriously high polluters. For example, in 2004 a single ethanol plant in Clinton, Iowa created 20,000 tons of pollutants (Lilley)—for comparison, a garbage incinerator outputs only 4799 tons of pollution per year (Goldstein 40). When 20,000 is multiplied by the 216 ethanol plants currently producing, the amount of pollution they create and spread over the earth is nearly unimaginable (Ethanol Producer Magazine).

Subsidies Hurting Poor Farmers

And, just like the pollution from ethanol plants, the economic side of farm subsidies in America ends up impacting more than just Americans. In fact, American subsidies are having a big effect on corn farming in Mexico The world has shrunk considerably with a tangled network of communication and transportation encompassing the globe. The world's economies are equally tangled up. When crops are subsidized in America it allows them to be sold on the world market for far less than it costs to grow them. Farmers in other countries, particularly Mexico, do not have such luxurious subsidies in place and must sell their crops for much more. And so, in a battle between Mexican corn exports and American corn exports, the United States wins every time. The effect of U. S. subsidies on Mexico have been so marked, in fact, that Mexico has lost approximately 1.5 million agricultural jobs and the U. S. Department of Agriculture estimates that the total portion of U. S. corn in Mexican consumption will double from its current position at one fifth of all corn within the decade (Greene). Once these Mexican farmers have lost their livelihoods to U. S. subsidies, they begin to look to immigration to America as the solution, becoming yet another casualty of farm subsidies.

Not only do subsidies hurt the poor of other countries, but they also hurt the poor and struggling farmers of our own country. Again, subsidies are based on quantity, meaning the large producers—mainly large corporate farms—get the helping hand, leaving average and small farms to struggle in the competition. The Environmental Working group found that in 2010, "$394 million in farm subsidy payments [went] to residents of U.S. cities with populations of 100,000 or more," (Sclammacco). Miami, Florida rode the peak with 203 investors or absentee landowners "earning" $2,472,071 in subsidies (Sclammacco). Farm subsidies were created to help the struggling farmer, to give him or her security to keep producing, even though the year might be rough. No longer. Subsidies are not the poor farmer's friend. Subsidies encourage production of a few specific crops, and as farmers flock to grow these, the market is flooded with surplus, dropping the prices further which has the greatest effect on family-owned farms. To compensate, the government then pays many farmers to hold their lands in reserve (to not farm their land) to decrease supply and encourage prices to rise again. As prices rise, more farmers flock to grow specific crops. This cycle continues indefinitely. Far from creating the stability they were intended too, subsidies cause a tipping market that is ideal for wealthy farms, which have enough growing space to make a pretty profit through subsidies, and harmful to struggling farms for whom every rattle of the market is an economic earthquake (El-Osta).

Subsidies as Motivation to Grow Healthy Foods
Subsidies are a powerful motivator, a persuasive tool capable of creating great change across the face of farming. While we have mostly seen signs of their ill-effects upon a country, if applied properly they can be used to create good change. Instead of encouraging unhealthiness, disregard for the environment, and economic problems, they could be used to encourage health on all levels of the income distribution, good environmental stewardship, and they could be changed to prevent this beating on the poor farmers of our country and other countries.

If applied to a whole spectrum of grains, fruits, and vegetables, instead of largely to corn, wheat, soy, and rice, the affect subsidies have of promoting food to manufacturers would be very beneficial. Funds for subsidies to these major crops could be gradually, experimentally cut down and the used to back popular fruits, vegetables, and other grains. Instead of corn, soy, wheat, and rice being by far the cheaper option for ingredients, fruits and vegetables would again be competitively priced. If we want to turn the tide of obesity in America it's time to stop giving the Twinkie more help than the carrot.

Some may be worried that if subsidies to corn, soy, wheat, and rice are trimmed down to allow subsidizing of other crops, food prices will rise as fewer farmers grow these crops and supply decreases. This will be the case—foods containing largely corn, soy, wheat, and rice products will become slightly more expensive. However, this will be very evenly balanced out as more farmers begin to farm other subsidized crops, increasing supply, and making these alternatives less expensive. Prices of food based on these products will decrease. And so food prices will remain stable over all. Because healthier alternatives will be cheaper, those with tight budgets will also be able to afford health. And the higher costs of unhealthy food will act as a natural discouragement to consuming them in large quantities (Powell).

Additionally, though perhaps slightly harder to enact, subsidies should also be given to farmers with crops of the highest 10% of nutritional content, as determined by testing. With farmers then competing to grow the healthiest crops instead of competing to grow the most of unhealthy crops, and breeding their crops accordingly, over the ensuing decades our food's nutritional content would again begin to rise until it reached 1920's levels and perhaps beyond.

Subsidies as Motivation to Care for the Environment

The transition of focus on quantity back to quality will also have environmental benefits. Once emphasis is removed from quantity and placed on quality, environmentally sound practices will follow. The best environment produces the best food. If the environment is happy, the plants it grows will be too. In pursuit of highest nutritional content, farmers will have incentive to enrich their soil beyond dowsing it in pesticides and bulk fertilizers. Because competition will be based around nutrition, it will foster growth in the alternative plant care industry, assisting society's quest for more natural alternatives to NPK fertilizer and more sustainable farming methods. Subsidies can also be used to reward more environmentally friendly efforts directly, with bonuses for farmers who use less water, energy, and fuel per bushel of crop grown than their competitors.

Subsidies as a Help to Poor Farmers

And with subsidies less concentrated on one set of crops, competition with other countries will decrease, and international relations with the countries we have continually hounded out of the market will improve. For our own struggling farmers the competition will be less fierce as well. The market will widen for all, production will increase, and market prices will finally stabilize.

Conclusion

Farm subsidies have changed our idea of farming and come with unfortunate side-effects. But, with a few adjustments, these very subsidies can just as easily change farming again to match our current day needs. Money is an incredibly powerful incentive, so when applied the right way it can be used to encourage many good practices. We no longer have to grub in the dirt, simply scrambling for any food, whatever the cost to the environment or others. We are Americans, and we have progressed so far since those days. We can do better.

Works Cited

Bernell, Stephanie. "The Twisted Path From Farm Subsidies to Health Care Expenditures." *Health* 4.12A (2012): 1509. Web. 10 November 2015.

Caromona, Richard H. "The Obesity Crisis in America." *Surgeon General*, Government Publications, 16 July 2003. Web. 2 November 2015.

Drewnowski, Adam and Specter, S. E. "Poverty and Obesity: The Role of Energy Density and Energy Costs." *The American Journal of Clinical Nutrition* 79.1 (2004):6–16. Web. 10 November 2015.

El-Osta, Hisham. "Dimensions of Wealth Dispersion Among Farm Operator Households: An Assessment of the Impact of Farm Subsidies." *Journal of Agricultural and Applied Economics* 37.1 (2005): 187. Web. 10 November 2015.

"The Farm Bill." *USDA*. Government Publications, 13 July 2015. Web. 2 November 2015.

Goldstein, Eric, and Mark Izeman. *The New York Environment*. New York: Island, 2009. 39–40. Print.

Greene, Julie. "Corn and Country." *Dissent* 57.4 (2010): 48–51. Web. 10 November 2015.

Lilley, Sasha. "Debunking False Solutions: Ethanol Subsidies Harm Environment, Benefit Corporate Agriculture." *Race, Poverty & the Environment* 13.1 (2006): 77–79. Web. 10 November 2015.

Nixon, Ron. "Farm Subsidies Leading to More Water use." *The New York Times* (2013): A17. Web. 10 November 2015.

Pollan, Michael. "You Are What You Grow." *New York Times*. New York Times Company, 22 April 2007. Web. 2 November 2015.

Pollan, Michael. "The Industrialization of Eating: What We Do Know." *Perspectives on the Environment*. Provo: BYU Academic Publishing, 2011. 116–134. Print.

Powell, Lisa M., Zhenxiang Zhao, and Youfa Wang. "Food Prices and Fruit and Vegetable Consumption among Young American Adults." *Health & place* 15.4 (2009): 1064–1070. Web. 19 November 2015.

Sclammacco, Sara. "City Slickers Continue to Rake In Farm Payments." *EWG*. Environmental Working Group, 23 June 2011. Web. 2 November 2015.

"U. S. Ethanol Plant." *Ethanol Producer Magazine*. BBI International, 21 October 2015. Web. 12 November 2015.